Social Work Practice with Adults

Sara Miller McCune founded SAGE Publishing in 1965 to support the dissemination of usable knowledge and educate a global community. SAGE publishes more than 1000 journals and over 800 new books each year, spanning a wide range of subject areas. Our growing selection of library products includes archives, data, case studies and video. SAGE remains majority owned by our founder and after her lifetime will become owned by a charitable trust that secures the company's continued independence.

Los Angeles | London | New Delhi | Singapore | Washington DC | Melbourne

Social Work Practice with Adults

Learning from Lived Experience

Sally Lee
Louise Oliver

Learning Matters,
A SAGE Publishing Company
1 Oliver's Yard
55 City Road
London EC1Y 1SP

SAGE Publications Inc.
2455 Teller Road
Thousand Oaks, California 91320

SAGE Publications India Pvt Ltd
B 1/I 1 Mohan Cooperative Industrial Area
Mathura Road
New Delhi 110 044

SAGE Publications Asia-Pacific Pte Ltd
3 Church Street
#10-04 Samsung Hub
Singapore 049483

Editor: Kate Keers
Development editor: Sarah Turpie
Senior project editor: Chris Marke
Marketing manager: Camille Richmond
Project management: TNQ Technologies
Cover design: Sheila Tong
Typeset by: TNQ Technologies
Printed in the UK

Library of Congress Control Number: 2023930700

British Library Cataloguing in Publication Data

A catalogue record for this book is available from the
British Library

ISBN 978-1-5297-8126-7
ISBN 978-1-5297-8125-0 (pbk)

Contents

Series editor's preface   ix
Introduction   xi

Part I   Key concepts and ideas   1

1   Key themes in social work practice with adults   3
    Sally Lee and Karen Maher

2   Assessment in social work practice with adults   16
    Penny Riggs, Charlotte, Liz, Pam and Sally Lee

3   Trauma informed social work practice with adults   27
    Jenny Bigmore, Amy Trim, Stefan Kleipoedszus, Sally Lee and Louise Oliver

4   Decision-making in social work practice with adults   37
    Stefan Kleipoedszus

Part II   Working with adults in practice   47

5   Working with mental health issues   49
    Sarah Lake, Hazel Mayall and Rosslyn Dray

6   Working with the Mental Capacity Act 2005   62
    Michael Lyne

7   Working with substance use   73
    Orlanda Harvey, Cathi and Seb

8   Working with marginalised adults   85
    Chris Kidd with Jo, Keith and Marie

9   Working with domestic abuse and supporting adults with care and support needs 95
    Karen Maher, Serena and Michael

10 Working with children (under the age of 18 years) who are abusive
    towards their parents   106
    Louise Oliver with Katie Bielec and Gael

Contents

11 Working with disabled adults   117
    Josh Hepple and Sally Lee

12 Working with adults with learning disabilities   129
    Robert Murray, Toby, Sue and Pam

13 Working with older adults   140
    Louise Downes and Jonathan Parker

14 Working with adults living with dementia   151
    Jemma Goddard

15 Working with adults at the end of life   161
    Jo Jury, Sally Lee and Louise Oliver

16 Working with unpaid carers   173
    Loren, George, Louise Oliver and Sally Lee

Conclusion   186
Sally Lee and Louise Oliver

Appendix 1: Professional capabilities framework   191
Appendix 2: Subject benchmark for social work   193
References   201
Index   223

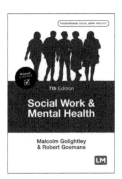
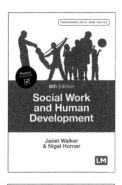
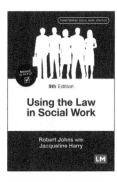

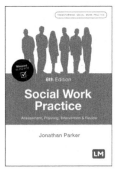
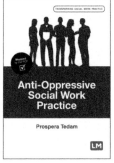
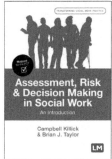
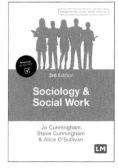

Series editor's preface

Over the past few years, the world has changed significantly as a result of many disparate factors. The United Kingdom has left the European Union with the economic, political and social ramifications of the act affecting us all and creating greater vulnerability for many. The world has experienced the deadly COVID-19 pandemic leaving strains on our helping professions, social work included, and the continuing issues arising from health concerns, economic and work difficulties among many others. The prosecution of an unjust and brutal war in Ukraine by Putin's Russian forces has led to many seeking refuge in the United Kingdom, while at the same time right-wing ideologues protest against those fleeing into Britain from other conflict and oppressive situations. The intensification of the climate crisis is having deeper and impacts on people made vulnerable by poverty, political alienation and general marginalisation from society. These factors have also highlighted the need for adult social care and within that a now sometimes marginalised, but essential element of it, adult social work.

This book is, therefore, timely and important. It is crucial that we reflect on what is happening around us as social workers, what the experiences of the wider world mean for us. We can then use our reflections to challenge and adapt our practice to meet the needs of people who come to us for a compassionate, skilful and knowledgeable service – the head, heart and hand social work promoted in this book.

During my teaching sessions for student social workers and others, I have been struck keenly by the impact that changes permeating our contemporary world have on the perceptions, behaviours and mental health of participants. The need for quiet as well as active reflection starting from the time of learning onwards is central to the social work mentality. This needs to be underpinned by robust knowledge, understanding of theory and how it apples to the messy world which we navigate. Values and ethics lie at the heart of social work and social work education, and these intertwine throughout the separate discussions of adult need.

The positions that we take in terms of values and ethics are, to an extent, determined by context, time and experience, and these are expressed in different ways by students coming into social work education today. Since the turn of this century, we have witnessed shifts and challenges as the marketised neoliberal landscape of politics, economy and social life may attract little comment or contest from some. We have observed the political machinery directing much of statutory social work towards a focus on individuals apart from their environment. However, we have also seen a recent turn to the social in the #MeToo campaign where unquestioned entitlement to women's bodies and psychology is exposed and resisted. We have seen defiance of those perpetuating social injustices that see long-term migrants alongside today's migrants abused and shunned by society, institutions as well as individuals. It is likely that, as a student of social work, you will lay bare and face many previously unquestioned assumptions, which can be very perplexing and uncover needs for learning, support and understanding. This series of books acts as an aid as you make these steps. Each book stands in a long and international tradition of social work that promotes social justice and human rights, introducing you to the importance of sometimes new and difficult concepts, and inculcating the importance of close questioning of yourself as you make your journey towards becoming part of that tradition. The books also act as a beginning step in your preparation to dig deeper, to learn, to reflect and by doing so to protect yourself while serving others.

There are numerous contemporary challenges for the wider world, and for all four countries of the United Kingdom. These include political shifts to the 'popular' Right, a growing antipathy to care and support, and dealing with lies and 'alternative truths' in our daily lives. Alongside this is the need to address the impact of an increasingly ageing population with its attendant social care needs and working with the financial implications that such a changing demography and, at the time of writing, a brutal cost-of-living crisis brings. As demand rises so do the costs and the unquestioned assumption that new austerity measures are necessary after the disastrous consequences of the imposition of earlier measures continues to create tensions and restrictions in services, policies and expectations. The costs of adult social work and, more broadly, adult social care continue to be debate and recommendations made continue to be laid dormant. These issues permeate the contexts of each of the 16 chapters in the book.

It is likely that as a social worker you will work with a diverse range of people throughout your career, many of whom have experienced significant, even traumatic, events that require a professional and caring response. As well as working with individuals, however, you may be required to respond to the needs of a particular community disadvantaged by local, national or world events or groups excluded within their local communities because of assumptions made about them.

The importance of high-quality social work education remains if we are adequately to address the complexities of modern life. We should continually strive for excellence in education as this allows us to focus clearly on what knowledge it is useful to engage with when learning to be a social worker. Questioning everything, especially from a position of knowledge, is central to being a social worker.

The books in this series respond to the agendas driven by changes brought about by professional bodies, governments and disciplinary reviews. They aim to build on and offer introductory texts based on up-to-date knowledge and to help communicate this in an accessible way, so preparing the ground for future study and for encouraging good practice as you develop your social work career. Each book is written by educators and practitioners who are passionate about social work and social services and who aim to instil that passion in others.

This book introduces you to core concepts practice areas and issues involved in social work practice with adults. This will help you to set the scene for exploring more specialised areas of social work and providing you with a grounding from which to enhance your learning in practice.

Professor Jonathan Parker

December 2022

Introduction
Sally Lee and Louise Oliver

The International Definition of Social Work (IFSW, 2014) states:

Social work is a practice-based profession and an academic discipline that promotes social change and development, social cohesion, and the empowerment and liberation of people. Principles of social justice, human rights, collective responsibility and respect for diversities are central to social work. Underpinned by theories of social work, social sciences, humanities and indigenous knowledge, social work engages people and structures to address life challenges and enhance wellbeing.

The premise of this book is very closely linked to the last part of this definition that 'social work engages people and structures to address life challenges and enhance wellbeing'. It is clear that a key part of the social work role is to proactively engage with individuals to recognise the impact of adversities in their life and to work towards wellbeing. Similarly, the British Association of Social Workers (BASW) Code of ethics states:

Upholding and promoting human dignity and well-being social workers should respect, uphold and defend each person's physical, psychological, emotional and spiritual integrity and wellbeing. They should work towards promoting the best interests of individuals and groups in society and the avoidance of harm.

(BASW, 2021, Principle 1, p6)

This again places a duty on social workers to not just look at the symptoms or behaviours being displayed and medicalise or blame the individual, but to look holistically at the whole person and work in partnership with them to understand how past experiences have impacted throughout their life. This book seeks to learn from the lived experienced and recognise the importance of how to work in partnership with others, including offering practice advice and guidance.

Aims of the book

When considering the value of learning from the lived experience, Hughes (2019) notes that engaging with the voice of service users not only deepens knowledge and understanding but also supports a change in perceptions and thinking regarding practice and also their world view. This book, therefore, aims to enable readers to develop a critical understanding of professional social work through the lens of those who access services and those who provide services. The book is part of a growing body of work that prioritises voices of experts by experience (Hughes, 2019).

The book comes at a time of change in adult social work which is facing significant challenges due to long-term financial constraints as well as growing demand due to the impact of poverty, inequality and demographic changes to the UK population. The authors hope to enable you to critically engage with the current context of practice in order to understand how wider social conditions and strategic responses to social problems impact on everyone, but most especially on often marginalised communities and people with whom social workers work. Throughout the book reference is made to law and social policy. The citations are primarily from English legislation such as the Care Act 2014 along with the statutory guidance. The authors acknowledge that each of the UK nations have equivalent legislation and policy although with specific details related to location. Links to specific legislation for each of the nations can be found at:

https://www.legislation.gov.uk/

Approaches and structure of the book

A particular focus of this book is on experts by experience, and each chapter offers insight from contributors from a diverse range of backgrounds and experiences. This means that chapters vary in their presentation, voice and style. For example, Chapter 4 discusses decision making in professional practice and features case studies drawn from social work practice to explore the lived experience, while Chapter 7, which addresses substance use, is co-authored with experts by experience. As such, each chapter has a different way of bringing the voice of people engaging with services to the forefront of social work with adults.

While chapters promote diverse voices, there are strong themes emerging and running throughout the book. The necessity of good communication in social work practice is one such theme, and chapter authors argue that effectiveness in practice relies on each practitioner's communication skills. Good communication underpins ethical social work as without it social work is something done **to** individuals and families rather than done **with** them.

The chapters in this book are ordered to create a narrative approach that takes readers through introductory chapters introducing the context of contemporary practice and establishing key knowledge, skills and activities involved in social work with adults. This leads into chapters discussing social work practice with specific groups, for example, people with learning disabilities. These chapters reflect the way in which contemporary social work is structured in terms of teams and client groups.

The book acknowledges, but does not explore in depth, that the history of social work with adults is long, complex and convoluted. It asks you to critically engage with how and why social work is done in the way it is now and to understand that this is based on its historical development from the days of Poor Laws and the 'impotent' yet 'deserving' poor through to the implementation of the Welfare State in 1948 when practices we associate with contemporary social work became formalised (Burt, 2020; Parker, forthcoming). The current focus in social work on the ideals of inclusive and empowering approaches of personalisation remain unattainable in full as they are constrained within budgets and resources; however, this book will encourage you to develop your practice skills and knowledge to work in ways to positively enhance wellbeing while also being honest to ourselves and to those with whom we work as to what can be achieved.

Key features within the book

This book is written to support you to gain learning that is transferable across the diverse range of settings in which social work with adults takes place. It will do this by employing a range of pedagogical features based upon the experiences of adults who access services/carer/practitioner, such as, case studies, and stories and reflective exercises. Using this range of pedagogical features grounded in the lived experiences of those who access services, layered with theory, research and legislation, will engage you and encourage critical reflection to develop your understanding, judgements and values. As Hughes (2019) surmised, there is growing evidence that learning from the lived experience and considering the complexities and dilemmas of real-life can further develop social work practice.

Each chapter within this book is therefore different; however, key features are found within every chapter to help guide you through the book as a whole.

These are:

- A Learning from Lived Experience statement (so that the reader knows who has authored the chapter and why they contributed their expertise)
- Activities (these are to help promote critical thinking and critical reflections and provide opportunities to make vital links to practice)
- Annotated further reading recommendations (to help guide the reader on what they might like to read next, as recommended by the authors of the chapters).

Chapter summaries

To further help the reader navigate the book, the chapters in the book are ordered in two parts. Chapters 1–4 discuss the fundamental aspects of social work with adults that underpin practice with all client groups. The book then moves into the second part which focuses on working with specific populations.

Chapter 1 explores key themes within the current context of social work with adults in the United Kingdom. It informs readers about the legislation and policy widely used in practice and discusses what the authors call 'core concerns' for social workers by taking an analytical perspective to consider what social work with adults is for and why it is part of the UK state response to social need.

Chapter 2 discusses assessment from the perspective of people engaging with adult social work and practitioners. The chapter focuses on Care Act 2014 (section 9) care and support assessments which are the 'bread and butter' of social work with adults. It discusses how assessment is the pathway to understanding an individual's circumstances, their strengths and their needs and leads into finding ways to support that person in ways that enhance their wellbeing. The issue of professional power is woven throughout this chapter as it discusses anti-oppressive and ant-discriminatory practice.

Chapter 3 discusses trauma informed approaches to social work with adults by considering the impact of trauma on health and wellbeing and exploring adult attachment styles and the implications for social work practice.

Chapter 4 investigates social workers' decision making and explores different decision-making styles. Decision making is a core element of social work practice, with some decisions being life altering; therefore, it is crucial that we understand how we make decisions and expand upon our understanding of the decision-making process.

Chapter 5 focuses upon understanding mental health and social work. Core principles within key legislation are addressed regarding wellbeing and understanding peoples' rights and social workers duties and powers. The authors of this chapter also share ideas for practice to ENGAGE with the person you are working with.

Chapter 6 provides an overview of the Mental Capacity Act 2005 and how this can be applied within practice. The Mental Capacity Act 2005 is core legislation when working with individuals when their decision-making capacity is impaired. This chapter examines the complexity of working in potentially complex situations while keeping the person at the centre of decision making.

Chapter 7 discusses social work and substance use, and it enables your understanding about the motivations leading to substance use. The chapter explores the stigma associated with illicit drug use and considers how personal judgement can influence practice especially in risk management.

Chapter 8 explores social work with marginalised communities and offers insight into nomadic communities to give you an understanding of Gypsy, Traveller and Roma culture. The authors address legislation that supports nomadic individuals in receiving health care and support, as well as guidance for practitioners to work alongside nomadic individuals and families.

Chapter 9 discusses social work and domestic abuse and includes definitions of key terms to aid your knowledge and understanding. The value of trauma informed practice when working with people experiencing domestic abuse is discussed to help in your understanding as to why people remain in abusive relationships, but also how practitioners can work with people who are experiencing this complex form of familial violence and abuse.

Chapter 10 discusses child-to-parent violence and abuse (children under the age of 18 years). This area of practice is often located within children and families social work; however, it is important to contextualise this within a whole family approach, and therefore it is essential knowledge for social work with adults. The authors draw upon research and practice experience to explore what child-to-parent violence and abuse is and how to work with parents experiencing it.

Chapter 11 focuses on social work with disabled adults and provides an understanding of the diversity and complexity of disability. The authors discuss how society and discourse can impact people who are disabled and how to uphold anti-oppressive and anti-discriminatory practice. This chapter draws on models of disability to show how different approaches to disability may impact upon the person.

Chapter 12 discusses social work with people with learning disabilities. It supports ways in which practitioners can work with and promote the rights of adults with learning disabilities.

Chapter 13 concerns social work with older people and identifies how older people are often viewed through an ageist lens which can impact services and practice. It brings in key theories which focus upon ageing and how this can be challenged and overcome in practice to promote wellbeing in older people.

Chapter 14 focuses upon dementia and applying methods of humanisation including person-centred and strengths-based approaches to decision making, care planning and positive risk taking, therefore promoting dignity and choice. The authors suggest different approaches to practice in order to generate positive outcomes for people living with dementia.

Chapter 15 discusses social work with people at the end of life. The authors of this chapter address palliative care and social work, a complex area to work within, especially as this is often set within a medical setting. This chapter reinforces the strengths-based approach to assist people to make decisions and be in control of what happens to them.

Chapter 16 The final chapter focuses on social work and unpaid carers who at the heart of adult social care. The chapter explores the experience of being a carer and includes key insights for practice which supports carers in ways which enhance their wellbeing. This chapter completes the book and is deliberately placed at the end because the contents is relevant to every client group and form of practice discussed within the book and it, therefore, needs to be read with an appreciation of its overarching applicability.

Achieving a social work degree

This book will help you to develop social work capabilities from the Professional Capabilities Framework (PCF) (BASW, 2018), which sets out the values, knowledge and skills that social workers should command at different levels of experience including student social workers and those who are newly qualified. There are nine professional domains included in the PCF and these are addressed and supported throughout the chapters contained in this book:

1. Professionalism
2. Values and ethics
3. Diversity and equality
4. Rights, justice and economic wellbeing
5. Knowledge
6. Critical reflection and analysis
7. Skills and interventions
8. Context and organisations
9. Professional leadership

See Appendix 1 for the Professional Capabilities Framework Fan and a description of the nine domains:

This book will also introduce you to the academic standards in the 2019 social work benchmark statement (see Appendix 2).

Concluding thoughts

The key message of this book is that listening to and learning from experts by experience is fundamental to good practice. This message underpins the diverse approaches to individual chapters and creates a unifying narrative which makes links to professional ethics and values including anti-oppressive and anti-discriminatory practice.

Part I

Key concepts and ideas

1

Key themes in social work practice with adults

Sally Lee and Karen Maher

Learning from experts by experience

This first chapter is written by Sally and Karen. Sally worked with adults as a social worker for many years and is now an academic at Bournemouth University and Karen Maher who is a social worker of many years and who has held a range of senior roles in adult services. The themes discussed in this chapter have emerged from the authors' reflections on, and analysis of, their own experience as social workers, researchers and teachers of a diverse range of practitioners and learners at different stages of their professional development.

Chapter objectives

By the end of this chapter you will be able to:

- Identify key concerns for social work practice with adults
- Understand how the historical development of social work informs current practice
- Recognise how an individual's social context impacts their life
- Critically consider how societal organisation impacts on peoples' lives
- Start thinking about the ways in which social work with adults can challenge social structures and address the key concerns

Introduction

This chapter introduces readers to social work with adults, by providing contextual information, about the profession to illustrate that it is a dynamic activity responsive to social change. The chapter also introduces six key concerns of practice. The authors use the term 'concern' to mean fundamental foci that are common to all types and contexts of social work. The six concerns identified here are interrelated and together create a unifying narrative that demonstrates how, despite the diversity of social work with adults (and children), it is a profession with a shared identity bound together by its commitment to enhancing human wellbeing.

The six concerns raised within this chapter create a nautical star, the aim of which is to guide practice and, like the original, focus on finding ways to hold steady and move forwards in sometimes choppy waters. The star reflects the Professional Capabilities Framework (PCF) (BASW, 2018) and Social Work England's Professional Standards (2019), and the six concerns are woven throughout the book as they are discussed in relation to specific situations, through personal narratives, case studies, reflective exercises and other pedagogical features in later chapters. The figure below is a visual representation of the nautical star for social workers (Figure 1.1).

Prior to introducing the six key concerns in detail, it is helpful to provide clarity about what social work with adults is and how it has developed into a complex system of support, care and, potentially, control.

What is social work with adults?

Social work is a global profession focussed on human wellbeing and distress that works with often marginalised individuals, families and communities (IFSW, 2014). Social workers are located in a wide range of public service settings including hospitals, hospices and health centres, schools and colleges, charities and local authorities where they work with adults who have or may have care and support needs. Social work with adults

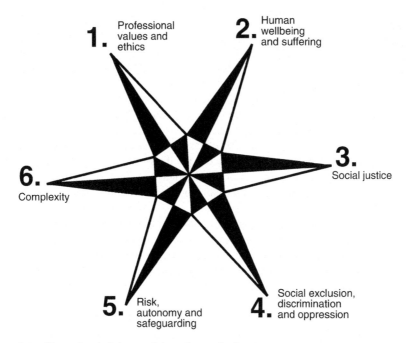

Figure 1.1 Six points of the social work nautical star

is an activity usually undertaken in partnership with individuals accessing services, carers and other services that the individual may be involved with such as health, education or the police.

The definition of social work published by the International Federation of Social Work (IFSW) (2014) and recognised by 122 countries worldwide highlights social work's multi-faceted identity. It is not one activity undertaken with a particular population but instead it is a practical activity, an academic pursuit and a profession seeking social change to enhance human wellbeing (Lee, 2022). The IFSW definition suggests to the authors that the head, hand and heart model (originally associated with transformative learning by Orr, 1992) is a helpful way to illustrate what social workers do and to establish at the start of this book the importance of practical wisdom and embodied knowledge:

Practitioners are social scientists using their heads to critically engage with knowledge drawn from multiple sources (social policy, human rights, research, theory, expertise of people with lived experience and their own practice wisdom) to understand and support people in their unique environments, but also to reflectively consider what and why they do the activities ascribed to the role of social worker.

Practitioners use their hands to undertake the practical and creative skills involved in enhancing wellbeing such as assessing for and arranging/enabling the provision of care and support, assistance with suitable housing, supporting economic wellbeing, employment, education and multiple other examples of the ways social workers provide practical support.

Practitioners use their hearts because practice is a form of emotional labour in which practitioners use themselves as a resource and an essential part of their practice toolkit. Social workers use their personal skills to build and maintain relationships and enable change. This may include sharing part of their own stories which enables individuals to recognise that practitioners are not solely figures of authority, but people with their own stories and experiences, some of which may resonate and support the building of positive working relationships within professional boundaries.

The head, hand and heart model also offers a useful way to understand social work's unique role in society and its holistic concern for the whole person: the head in relation to concern for people's emotional and psychological wellbeing; the hand in terms of people's physical, economic and social wellbeing, and the heart in terms of social work's care for human distress.

Social workers engage with diverse individuals, families and communities within their specific contexts and to enable practitioners to navigate contemporary problems and work effectively they need to understand the context in which practice takes place. This means using their heads, their hands and their hearts. This book provides information about how this is achieved in practice.

Social work in the United Kingdom is a regulated profession

Practitioners are required to register with Social Work England, Scottish Social Services Council, Social Care Wales or the Northern Ireland Social Care Council depending on their location. These bodies oversee professional standards and the standards of qualifying and post-qualification education.

In the United Kingdom, British Association of Social Workers (BASW) publishes the PCF (BASW, 2018) which describes nine domains of professional social work ranging from personal attributes of practitioners, such as integrity, to the knowledge, skills and professionalism required of practitioners. Each domain is divided into levels that describe the developing capabilities designed to enable social workers to know what is required of them throughout their career and for employers to be able to gauge the workforce's capabilities. This book is mapped to the PCF which can be found at: https://www.basw.co.uk/professional-development/professional-capabilities-framework-pcf/the-pcf.

Social work is political

Social work with adults is focussed on working with people to enhance their wellbeing. How this goal is achieved is context-specific, for example, in countries such as the United Kingdom, social work is generally part of the state-provided welfare system established via social policy. Social policy is created through parliamentary, political processes that are shaped by and express dominant social and political perspectives of the time. As such social work occupies a place between citizen and state with practitioners acting as the public face of policy. Locating social work in this intersection between citizen and state requires practitioners to critically engage with social work's political identity and to understand their role in implementing law and social policy which at times may feel contrary to professional and personal values. For example, implementing reductions in services due to austerity measures introduced in response to the global financial crisis of 2008 has been challenging for many practitioners (Grootegoed and Smith, 2018).

Social policy informs how social work is both organised and delivered and three strands of early forms of social work continue to underpin practice: firstly, individual casework, which originated in the work of the Charity Organisation Society (COS); secondly, welfare administration, particularly involving various forms of relief from poverty much of which originated from the Poor Laws of 1601 and 1834; thirdly, social action (Horner, 2019).

The commitment to social action as a core part of social work, in the United Kingdom, seems to have become a matter of individual choice rather than a key part of the identity of social work. The authors hope that reading about the key concerns will prompt readers to think about actions they can take to enhance and promote human wellbeing, be that by engaging with current affairs to writing to their MP about an issue they feel strongly about or supporting a campaign. In the UK organisations such as BASW (https://www.basw.co.uk/) and the Social Work Action Network (https://socialworkfuture.org/) run campaigns which you may be interested in.

Activity 1.1

This is a mini (non-scientific) independent research activity for you to complete.

1. Ask five people of different ages to tell you what they think social work is.
2. Analyse their answers by:
   A. Looking for similarities in the answers
   B. Looking for differences in the answers
   C. Note any points made by all your respondents
3. Compare the answers to the IFSW definition of social work at – https://www.ifsw.org/what-is-social-work/global-definition-of-social-work/

So far this chapter has considered the broad context of contemporary social work practice and it will now explore the six core concerns referred to earlier in more detail.

Key concern 1: Professional values and ethics

Social workers work with people to create positive change and enhance wellbeing; social work is therefore an ethical activity requiring practitioners to demonstrate integrity (Banks, 2021). Professional values and ethics are articulated in professional codes (BASW, 2012 in the United Kingdom) and standards (Social Work England, 2019), although such codes cannot provide detailed guidance for every situation, meaning practitioners need to operate as self-aware, ethically minded agents who maintain their professional standards to protect individuals who have care and support needs and carers from abuse and exploitation.

Returning to Activity 1.1, did any of your respondents refer to 'doing good', or 'promoting human rights' or 'helping people'? Did any respondent explain what they meant by such terms? Concepts such as 'good' or 'help' or a 'right' are more complex than at first appears and this is because the specifics of meanings given to such terms, while often shared within cultures and communities, are determined by the definer. How an individual or society defines meaning is influenced by their values, that is, what is cherished and believed to be worth maintaining. At a macro, structural level of society, values are expressed through and reinforced by social systems such as the law that sets out what is viewed to be valuable social goods and rights (for example, in the United Kingdom, law establishes its commitment to the value of the education of children in Article 2, Protocol 1 of the Human Rights Act 1998). At the cultural level, values are communicated and embedded through meso- and micro-level interactions and institutions such as communities, families and individual expressions.

Social work is a complex activity and its professional values and ethics have developed in response to wider events and social movements. The gradual shift away from society being underpinned by, and organised according to, faith-based traditions to more secularised forms of society mean that the (previously faith-based) obligation to do charitable works has weakened and other drivers for addressing distress have been needed (Barnard, 2008; Banks, 2020).

Analysis of the stages in the development of social work values and ethics by Reamer (2018) is helpful in appreciating how they have reflected changing social priorities. Reamer discusses how social work values and ethics have moved from a focus on the morality of individuals (or perceived lack of morality) and subsequent attempts to 'strengthen the moral rectitude' of 'wayward' people through work, to the **values period** of the early to mid-twentieth century when appreciation of the impact of structural problems such as housing, healthcare, sanitation, employment and poverty on people's wellbeing gained momentum following the two world wars.

Critique of the 'morality' and 'values' periods led to the expression of radical social work values in the 1960s and 1970s that criticised social work's role in ensuring a compliant and healthy workforce (Lishman et al., 2018). Radical approaches focussed emancipatory values (Barnard, 2008) including social equality, welfare rights, anti-discriminatory and anti-oppressive practice – values which reflected the changes in wider society led by civil rights, disability and female liberation movements. These radical values stimulated fundamental questioning of social work and its values, especially in light of perceived failings in high profile cases such as the death of Maria Colwell in 1973 and saw increased interest in applied values and ethics in what Reamer (2018) calls the **ethical theory and decision-making period of** the 1970s. Growing awareness and concern regarding professional negligence, legal accountability and liability in the 1990s led to what Reamer calls the **ethical standards and risk management period** when there was the expansion of ethical standards to guide conduct. At the same time increasing emphasis on professional capabilities such as trustworthiness and integrity emerged.

The influence of New Right ideology during the 1980s which has since become embedded within the UK political and economic system challenges social work values by again conceptualising social problems as the result of individual 'failure' or immorality, effectively expressed within public discourse and social policy (Morrison, 2019). Reamer argues we are now in the **digital period**, characterised by ethical dilemmas posed by the new technological environment.

Key concern 2: Human wellbeing and human distress

Activity 1.2

Get up, walk around the room and think about why you are a social worker/will become a social worker/are thinking about becoming a social worker, then complete this sentence 'I am/will be a social worker because...'

The recruitment process for students onto the social work qualifying programmes at Bournemouth University may seem a strange place to start a discussion about wellbeing, but it illustrates a fundamental and enduring concern of practitioners. As part of the interview candidates are asked 'Why do you want to be a social worker' (this question is preceded by candidates being asked to define social work and discuss the current challenges, leading me to always rephrase the question to: 'Why *on earth* do you want to become a social worker!'). This question elicits a range of answers that often draw on personal or family experience. However, there is a common theme in candidates' answers that is reflected in the authors' own motivations: the fundamental concern of one human being for another who is distressed, and the desire to express compassion, care and support.

Often this desire is articulated uncritically as a wish to help other people (the ways in which helping others is defined may be wrapped in layers of taken-for-granted assumptions, unconscious bias and social expectations that are subsequently unpacked over the course of the programme). The point being made is that social workers often share the motivation of care and empathy for human distress which leads them to seek ways to enhance wellbeing; it is something we *want* to do and are *required* to do by the IFSW (2014) definition of social work, national codes of ethics (BASW, 2012) and professional standards (SWE, 2019).

In England, the Care Act 2014 formally embeds the concept of wellbeing into social work with adults policy and practice (each part of the United Kingdom has its own equivalent legislation). The concept of wellbeing includes objective factors, such as good health, and the subjective sense of how a person perceives, and feels about, their life. The Act refers to nine domains of wellbeing which capture the subjective and objective nature of wellbeing and together offer an inclusive framework for assessment.

The domains of wellbeing listed below do not have a hierarchical order as all are equally important.

* Personal dignity (including treatment of the individual with respect)
* Physical and mental health and emotional wellbeing

- Protection from abuse and neglect
- Control by the individual over their day-to-day life
- Participation in work, education, training or recreation
- Social and economic wellbeing
- Domestic relationships, family and personal wellbeing
- Suitability of the individual's living accommodation
- The individual's contribution to society (Care Act 2014 [s1])

Because of the subjectivity of wellbeing, it is necessary for an individual to interpret and define what is important and the impact their unique physical, emotional and personal circumstances may have on their wellbeing. This personalised understanding makes the goal of enhancing wellbeing flexible (supporting diversity, for example, facilitating cultural differences), but potentially hard to measure, which can sit uncomfortably with systems of accountability required by local authorities.

Key concern 3: Social (in)justice

Activity 1.3

Listen to a song by a social activist like Billy Bragg (for example, *The Red Flag*) or Beyoncé (for example, *Freedom*) – what thoughts **and** feelings do you have after listening?

Social justice concerns the fair distribution of resources, opportunities and responsibilities (Lishman et al, 2018). It is concerned with different forms of inequality and deprivation such as unequal access to economic, education or health wellbeing (Pickett and Wilkinson, 2010). The concept of fairness is influenced by personal views about what is understood to be fair, views that are informed by a complex range of perspectives on human nature and society.

Societies are often structured in ways that privilege certain groups because the structures are 'expressions of cultural belief systems often based on political philosophy, values, and traditions which serve to explain (justify) why some inequality is seen as inevitable, natural, and right' (Lee, 2022, p2112). Inequality can become embedded over generations and seen as a social norm (Pickett and Wilkinson, 2010).

The negative impacts of deprivation, poverty and inequality continue to be central to social work. Such differing views lead to contrasting actions to achieve fair distribution of opportunities and economic resources (Levitas, 2005).

The profession's commitment to promoting social justice is clearly articulated by the IFSW (2014) and, in the United Kingdom, by the BASW (BASW, 2014, p8) which states that 'social workers have a responsibility to promote social justice, in relation to society generally, and in relation to the people with whom they work'. This means that social workers need to engage with social justice in their daily work with individuals, families and communities. To meet this responsibility, social workers must understand the causes and effects of social injustice and challenge taken-for-granted assumptions which reinforce embedded injustice and inequality.

The radical aspects of social work's identity are a reminder of the profession's important role in raising awareness of injustice and aligning with individuals and communities who are oppressed and marginalised. Social workers are society's 'awkward squad' reminding people that inequality is not good or natural but has negative impacts across the life course and for wider society (Pickett and Wilkinson, 2010).

Social workers promote social justice by working in anti-discriminatory and anti-oppressive practice ways which include proactively challenging discrimination, challenging unjust policies and practices, recognising diversity, distributing resources, and working in solidarity with individuals accessing social work services, carers and marginalised populations. This can be achieved through rights-based approaches to practice where the focus on human rights enables practitioners to ensure citizens are treated fairly. Human rights help social workers advocate for, safeguard and work towards better outcomes for individuals, but they rightly provide limitations to public authorities' (including statutory social workers) intervention in an individual's life (proportionality). In the United Kingdom, human rights are currently enshrined in the Human Rights Act 1998 (Lee, 2022).

Key concern 4: Social exclusion, discrimination and oppression

Social exclusion, discrimination and oppression are closely related to social justice but are focussed on how the organisation and structures of society can be exclusionary. Social workers work with people who are often marginalised and excluded from some or all family, community and societal networks because of disadvantage, unfair or unequal discrimination and oppression (Parker and Ashencaen Crabtree, 2018; Thompson, 2021). Social exclusion is both the cause and result of multiple personal and societal factors which have profound impacts on health and wellbeing (Marmot, 2010, 2020; Lee, 2022).

Discrimination in the context of social exclusion refers to unfair or unequal treatment and prejudicial behaviour towards individuals or groups who characteristically belong to relatively powerless populations. In the United Kingdom, the Equality Act 2010 makes it unlawful to discriminate directly or indirectly (for example, universal rules that disadvantage someone with a protected characteristic) against anyone on the grounds of protected characteristics including disability, ethnicity, gender or sexual orientation. Harassment and victimisation based on protected characteristic is also included within the Equality Act 2010.

Poverty is key to understanding social exclusion because it not only undermines inclusion and security but also creates stress, despair and frustration which may be expressed through violence (Shildrick and Rucell, 2015). Poverty is often passed from one generation to another, and its presence early in a child's life can have a harmful biological effect on their brain development and life outcomes (BASW and CWIP, 2019) resulting in relationship and family problems (Lansley and Mack, 2015). Social workers require a wider understanding of poverty as poverty is not simply the absence of economic means; poverty also concerns the absence of the means of participation (Lee, 2022).

Key concern 5: Risk, autonomy and safeguarding

To enhance individual, family, community and societal wellbeing, practitioners need to appreciate factors that put wellbeing at risk. The diversity of risk reflects the complexity of peoples' contexts and practitioner's understanding of what constitutes risk must be constantly reviewed because risk is a complex and multi-faceted process (Stalker, 2003, p211). Risk can change quickly or be an enduring threat to wellbeing. Risk can be rooted in the personal attributes of the individual, their circumstances and their social context, or come from external factors such as the processes of discrimination and oppression including violence and marginalisation (Young, 1990; Thompson, 2021). Good practice requires social workers to appreciate the diversity factors influencing and causing risk, and the experiences of and impact on the person must always be considered with every new piece of information received. This enables social workers to reframe and understand the person's experiences more effectively.

Activity 1.4

The word cloud below illustrates many risk factors. Think about your and your family's wellbeing, what factors might put those at risk?

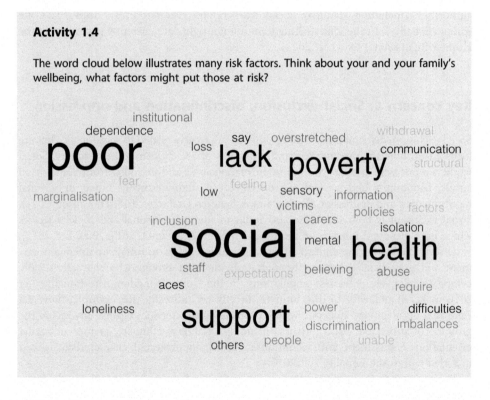

The wellbeing domains listed in the Key concern 2 section are helpful in enabling practitioners to frame the concept of risk as events or experiences that threaten those domains. The domains can be used to understand risk at the micro level of society such as individuals and families but can also be used to consider meso level of risk and the macro level of society's wellbeing.

The concept of human rights introduced in the wake of the Second World War means contemporary practice is now alert to threats to wellbeing created by public authorities including risk to autonomy created by risk-averse by practice. For example, policies and practices that over-emphasise control in the name of protection to the detriment of individuals, families and communities exercising autonomy. Exercising autonomy includes the freedom to make decisions and accepting that risk is an inevitable part of decision-making. Social workers work with individuals with diverse needs; for some people this means requiring support in decision-making, or who have a different perspective of risk (Faulkner, 2012). The Care Act 2014 provides a statutory footing for adult safeguarding in England and Wales which had previously been guidance only under 'No Secrets (2000)'. The Act requires individuals and organisations to work together to prevent and stop abuse and neglect.

Social work with adults therefore has a duty to safeguard an adult's right to live in safety, free from abuse and neglect. Safeguarding adults is about empowering individuals and aims to support balancing risk to the individual, family and community with their personal control and choice (Mandelstam, 2017; White, 2017). However, safeguarding practice is not simply about making people safe, instead it is an approach that enables choice and control and concerns genuinely listening to the person (Section 14.11 Care Act Statutory Guidance, 2022). It is underpinned by the policy Making Safeguarding Personal (LGA and ADASS, 2017) which is a personalised approach, meaning safeguarding is undertaken with the individual and not something done to them. This approach involves setting personalised and meaningful safeguarding outcomes with the individual and aims to address the criticism that social work practitioners and organisations are risk-averse, negatively impacting on individuals' decision-making and control.

Key concern 6: Complexity

Social work is the antithesis of simplistic or polarised thinking in which people, problems and solutions are divided into 'good or bad', 'workers or shirkers' and 'deserving or undeserving'. Instead, social workers work with nuance and complexity. Practitioners understand that people are complex beings who are situated within and influence interactions between the physical, psychological and social dimensions of human relationships linked through familial, friendship, work, leisure and other connections or systems (Faulkner, 2012). This understanding requires practitioners to use a range of theories, knowledge and approaches to understand and support people with whom they work. For example, Bronfenbrenner's ecological approach (1979) facilitates identification and consideration of an individual's complex networks by mapping relationships and determining the strength of each relationship (Bronfenbrenner, 1979).

Activity 1.5

Create your own ecomap. The illustration below is a simple model which you can adapt to include the relationships that are relevant to you. Add connecting lines using the key below. Once it is complete, reflect on the influence each relationship has had on making you who you are.

(Continued)

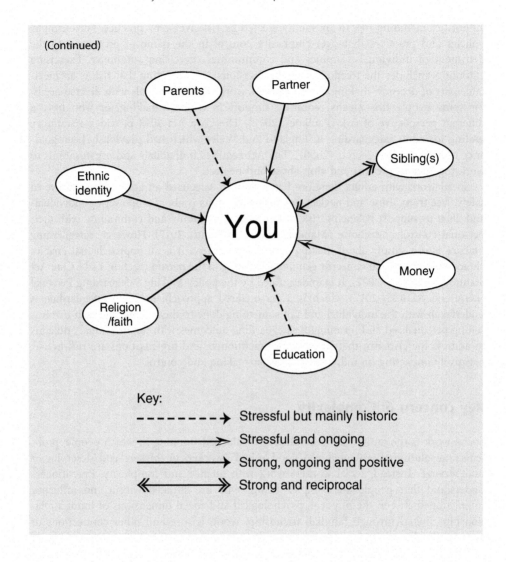

(Continued)

Key:

- - - - - - - → Stressful but mainly historic

————→ Stressful and ongoing

————→ Strong, ongoing and positive

≪————≫ Strong and reciprocal

Recent advances in knowledge in a range of sciences including neuroscience, developmental psychopathology and interpersonal neurobiology reveal the fundamental connections between human experience, biology, psychology and behaviour in relation to adverse experience (Van Der Kolk, 2014) which is key information for effective social work practice. In addition, increased awareness of diversity (for example, that 'women' are not a homogenous population) and recognition of the intersectionality of discrimination where different forms of discrimination or inequality compound each other (for example, discrimination based on an individual's gender, race, sexuality and disability) mean that practitioners can work in ways which navigate this complexity by addressing experiences of discrimination and inequality through anti-oppressive and anti-discriminatory practice which actively rejects the processes of discrimination and oppression identified by Thompson (2021) and Young (1990) including stereotyping, infantilisation, marginalisation and cultural imperialism (Lee, 2022).

Chapter summary

This chapter has discussed six key concerns the authors believe are at the heart of social work practice with adults. The key concerns offer a nautical star to guide practice which complements the PCF, SWE Professional Standards and BASW Code of Ethics to ensure that what matters to individuals accessing services, carers, families and communities is kept at the forefront of practitioners' actions. The chapter also recognises that social work is subject to societal priorities expressed through social policy. This means that practitioners need to be aware of the political aspect of their work and engage in creating social change to address human distress and enhance human wellbeing.

Annotated further reading

Morrison, J. 2019. *Scroungers: Moral Panics and Media Myths*. London: Zed Books.
   Morrison provides an engaging account of the history and enduring use of the concept of deserving and undeserving individual, families and communities through the theory and practice of journalism.

Useful websites

Several websites are important sources of news, information and guidance about social work with adults and these will be useful to readers throughout their studies and careers. It is worth exploring each of the websites and revisiting them on a regular basis:
   Social Care Institute for Excellence (SCIE) https://www.scie.org.uk/
   Community Care https://www.communitycare.co.uk/
   British Association of Social Workers (BASW) https://www.basw.co.uk/
   Each of UK social work regulators have websites where professional standards are published and other important information is available:
   https://www.socialworkengland.org.uk/
   https://socialcare.wales/
   https://socialworkscotland.org/
   https://niscc.info/

2

Assessment in social work practice with adults

Penny Riggs, Charlotte, Liz, Pam and Sally Lee

Learning from experts by experience

This chapter brings together the voices of Charlotte (anonymised), Liz and Pam, experts by experience having undertaken social work assessments. They are joined by Penny, who is a social worker, and Sally, a social worker and academic. This chapter emerges from conversations between Charlotte, Liz and Pam, experts by experience and Penny and Sally, social workers, and who have all participated in the assessment process as users of social work services or practitioners, or both. The chapter is in two parts; the first part offers insights and top tips from the lived experience to make assessment a meaningful and ethical activity. The second part explains the three Ps of assessment (Heslop and Meredith, 2019, p11): its **p**urpose, **p**rocess and **p**roduct. The chapter is purposefully structured in this way to prioritise learning from the lived experience and for readers to learn what experts by experience say before reading about the legal context and process of assessment.

Chapter objectives

By the end of this chapter you will be able to:

- Identify the key skills and knowledge required to undertake assessment
- Recognise the legal basis and process of Care Act 2014 care and support assessments
- Understand how assessment can be experienced by service users, carers and practitioners
- Start thinking about the influence of learning from lived experience on your assessment practice

Introduction

This chapter focuses on assessments as a part of the social work role. Assessments are conducted in order to gain a better understanding of the people they are working with. To gain an understanding of what is working well, what difficulties, challenges and risks they may be experiencing and ascertain what, if any, support is required. This is done through engaging first and foremost with the person the social worker is working with, then, as appropriate, family and friends as well as professionals working with them. This helps support a more holistic assessment. This chapter will explore the lived experience of those who have been involved in the assessment process and then focus upon the purpose, process and product of assessments. Throughout this chapter, we invite readers to reflect on ways to prioritise social work values within assessment and thereby humanise what can feel like a bureaucratic and administrative procedure.

Assessment practice: understanding assessment from people with lived experience and carers' perspectives

Practitioners should not underestimate the impact undergoing an assessment may have on an individual and the anxiety, effort and time people spent preparing for and completing an assessment, the consequences of which may influence their future life opportunities (Buckley and Lee, 2019). Practising anti-oppressively includes recognising that, while assessment is an everyday activity for social workers, this is not the case for most people. Charlotte, Liz and Pam highlight different insights as to what having an assessment means to them:

Charlotte: for me an assessment means a lot of work and looking at the effects of my disability.

Liz: Social Care assessments are, by their very nature, tedious. But the paperwork has to be completed to get support, so it's a case of just getting on with it. In our case there are two assessments that have to be completed for our sons and that doubles the workload.

Pam: Having professional business backgrounds means we have been able to understand how processes work and the way different documents need to be pulled together.

Charlotte, Liz and Pam's words illustrate that assessment and reassessment is a regular feature of their experience and requires preparation and organisation of information which is in addition to managing their care and support needs.

Understand power and promote empowerment

Awareness of the inherent power assigned to professional roles is an essential part of ethical practice (Dyke, 2019). One way to exercise this power ethically is to enquire what an individual hopes an assessment will be like, as Charlotte suggests:

Charlotte: I want it to build on what I can realistically achieve, like when I got assessed to go to college for it to improve my life outcomes. I would still be an independent person, but the support is to help me achieve my goals. I like doing assessments in my own home, I get quite loud, I struggle to talk about toileting to a social worker, so doing it in my own home, might promote a more open conversation. I might say I need help going to the loo and they might say what does help look like to you?

Maybe they should take the time to come in and not even do the meeting, just follow me and the PA around. The only way you are really going to understand my needs is by watching me do it.

Power comes from the legal basis and functions of social work, but also in the form of covert power, often ascribed to social workers. There are many negative stereotypes about social workers, such as their putting older people into residential care against their will or removing children from their parents without cause, and while social workers know such stereotypes are untrue, nonetheless there is an assumed covert power associated with the title and profession which practitioners need to be aware of to build effective relationships (Dyke, 2019).

Empowerment concerns supporting people to be active agents in their own lives through prioritising the person's voice, supporting their involvement, decision-making and control – no decision about me without me. Empowerment involves awareness of the multi-dimensional power dynamics occurring at the personal, cultural and structural levels of individuals' lives (Thompson, 2021), and these complex dynamics should be reflected within an assessment in order to accurately represent the individual's lived experience. Empowerment concerns creating rapport and building trust by being open and honest, approachable, reassuring and empathetic. Using jargon can be intimidating and confusing, therefore disempowering, whereas empowering language is respectful, inclusive, culturally sensitive and jargon-free (Koprowska, 2020, provides helpful information about communication and use of language).

Assessments often happen during periods of transition (for example, a disabled adult moving from the family home to their own property) or change (for example, an older person now requiring assistance with self-care). Transition and change create uncertainty which can be destabilising and experienced as loss (Brodie and Swan, 2018) and therefore emotionally intelligent communication, informed by psychosocial knowledge, is required, especially as many people will not have met a social worker or been assessed previously.

Liz: Being assessed is having something done to you. An imposition. An intrusion. But I always try to think that it is being done to us in order for someone to decide which needs are eligible for help.

Other people may have previously experienced assessment, and this informs how they anticipate current contact:

Pam: Our view of assessment is inevitably coloured by our past experience. Sometimes it has been accurate and effective in terms of services provided to support us in our family life together, and sometimes it has resulted in us challenging the understanding of the social worker and most frequently the amount of money it is considered adequate to cover the needs in question. It feels like we live in a different world to the social workers, or budget holders live in.

Strengths-based assessment that supports people to identify and build on their strengths is promoted by the Care Act 2014 (DoHSC, 6.63–6.64). Focussing on strengths promotes what a person can do, which can be empowering and supports positive risk enablement (Parker, 2021). However, individuals can be fearful of 'doing too well' and this impacting the level of support provided.

Pam: Assessments always concentrate on the negatives – you feel as a carer you cannot celebrate the positives in case it goes against the person you are caring for.

Charlotte: I think they tried to implement a strengths-based model, but it worked against me as it did not enhance my life by looking at my strengths. If I continue to do what I can do, how will I grow? They said that I could travel to uni on my own, and I can get to uni but we have had tutors who were really supportive. If I put that into the context of a job, which is my next challenge, then yes, I could get there on my own, but I cannot interact at the workplace… well, I would not hire myself on my coping abilities, put it that way.

Prioritise communication

Ensuring the experience of assessment is genuinely person-focussed, inclusive and humanising. Communicating well supports practitioners to demonstrate their professional values and goes some way in addressing the core concerns discussed in Chapter 1. Being authentically person-centred means empowering the individual to set the agenda as far as possible and with support. Using open questions during the assessment, such as TED questions (Tell me..., Explain to me..., Describe to me...) supports individuals to create their own narrative in words, or in other ways, that are personally meaningful.

> Liz: Although my sons do have some things in common the way they present within their disabilities is totally different. This is the important part of any assessment. They are brothers, they have very similar diagnosis, but they are VERY different in the way their characters and personalities shine through the medical labels. This is what I feel is really important to have recorded in assessments. I have learned over the years to constantly correct beliefs and ideas that others have about the boys based on just the basic information. Including 'they are not twins', 'they can't just share a support worker', 'Ben is hyper sound sensitive, Dan is not', 'Ben can cope with having small children around, Dan cannot'. The list is endless. But I know if I do not keep the focus in the right place for the right son things can go awry and assumptions are made.

Good communication starts prior to contacting an individual or their representative as it is important to check for any previous involvement with adult social care and gather any information available. Doing so enables practitioners to be informed about an individual's situation and reduce the likelihood, often described by service users as a burden, of having to repeatedly retell their story and, potentially, relive trauma (Hughes, 2019 provides multiple accounts from lived experience of the impact of social work interventions).

Considering the holistic needs of an individual including their cultural, social and health needs is essential to ensure practice adheres to professional standards (Social Work England, 2019). For example, considering prayer times through the day, taking account of when someone who has a cognitive impairment is most comfortable and able to engage with social contact, allowing the person to choose where to be assessed and who they may want to be present. There may be circumstances when it is not possible to fully follow an individual's wishes, for example, if the person is in hospital and unable to leave, but it is the practitioner's responsibility to ensure the individual feels as relaxed and as involved in the assessment as possible. This means being prepared, and while an individual may not express any preference, it is essential to check with that person what their wishes are in order to ensure practice is person-centred and inclusive.

Top Tip: Before an assessment visit it is good practice to make sure that a copy of the blank assessment is offered to enable the person to be familiar with the questions and prepare. Individuals can feel pressure to give information on the spot which could lead to important details being missed.

The COVID-19 pandemic led to a greater use of technology in assessment including completion being via phone or video link. Positive experiences include how technology has enabled individuals to be supported by family members that live too far away to travel for one appointment or enabling people to feel more comfortable when disclosing private information. Some people also find having strangers in their home intrusive and uncomfortable, at least initially, so an online or phone conversation allows rapport to start building before having someone in their home. But there have also been negative experiences, for example, the experience of online or phone assessments being impersonal or even impossible if someone struggles with technology. In addition, practitioners have expressed concern about risk from abuse or neglect going undetected or minimised without face-to-face assessment (Kingstone et al., 2022).

> *Liz: The pandemic and lockdown has created unique problems for us and when it comes to assessments. The whole issue is made more complicated by the need to communicate large amounts of confidential information via the phone or email. The longest session I had was two hours on the phone answering questions about one of my sons. I had a pounding headache and sore throat when we finished. The Social Worker had wanted to find the information out from my son directly over Zoom but both my husband and I thought the boys would just not cope with this method of communication. Eventually I asked the social worker to email me the forms in questions and I would complete them. Because the document format is web based when sent and transferred to a .docx document the layout went haywire, when received it was sixty-nine pages long. It took an hour to actually get the form into some sort of workable document.*

Manage expectations

Being clear from first contact about what is involved in an assessment and what it may lead to is an important aspect of open, honest and, therefore, ethical practice (BASW, 2012). Local authorities are required to publish accessible information about their services, such as online fact sheets that set out eligibility criteria, resources and links to other sources of support. Directing people to this information prior to assessment can help to manage expectations.

The reflections from lived experience in this and other chapters show that many of the issues raised by service users and practitioners concern limitations of the 'system', specifically the restricted resources and 'hoops' people must jump through to receive social work services. This, in part, is due to expectations raised by social policy. While in reality social care is characterised by long-term problems such as limited funding, staff recruitment and retention and increasing demand (Samuel, 2021). One of the most difficult parts of assessment is when someone is deemed eligible, but the budgetary constraints of the local authority limit possible options. Social workers need to be honest about finite resources and when options an individual may hope for are not viable, for example, someone wanting to remain at home, but the cost of care required being unsustainable. Pam adds a further perspective below.

> *Pam: It's quite challenging to be told that yes, there is a need for help/support but no funding to pay for it. This has happened several times to us. We have also been told that we should be very grateful for the level of help we receive.*

Assessed eligibility means an individual is entitled to care and support (Mandelstam, 2017), and it is therefore not a gift to be grateful for. Social workers can demonstrate their commitment to anti-oppressive practice by allying with marginalised people and seeking fair resource distribution within society so that care is adequately funded and respected. Enabling individuals to have the best quality of life possible should be at the heart of social work. This involves identifying and building on strengths, balanced with anti-discriminatory and anti-oppressive practice that require social workers to ensure people have equal access to services and resources whatever their strengths or needs and to do this without prejudice or discrimination (Thompson, 2021). As Charlotte describes: *When you have the right support, it doesn't take away the disability, but it enhances your life.*

Experts by experience have provided readers with insights into what assessment feels like which offers a lens through which to view the next part of the chapter that focuses on the 3 Ps of assessment: its **p**urpose, **p**rocess and **p**roduct (Heslop and Meredith, 2019, p11). This discussion provides readers with key knowledge for professional practice.

Purpose of assessment in social work practice with adults

The purpose of any assessment is to gather, interpret and analyse information and evidence to form opinions and make decisions (Heslop and Meredith, 2019). Assessment is something we all do as part of daily decision-making and happens at different levels of formality and conscious cognitive engagement:

Activity 2.1

Consider how you decided what to wear today. What factors did you take into account? Did you look at the weather? Check if something was clean enough? Or did you think about what makes you feel good? Maybe you have a pre-prepared outfit for each day of the week.

Deciding what to wear may feel largely unconscious, however, on reflection you are likely to be able to identify a range of knowledge, evidence and experience on which your decision is based.

Now think of a time when you have undertaken a formal assessment process, for example, in applying for a place on a university course. What knowledge, information and evidence did you assess to decide what was the right option for you?

Practitioners develop the skills of assessment by critically engaging with information and knowledge from diverse sources including social policy, the lived experience of service users and practitioners, along with academic study and evidence from research and theory (Fook, 2016). Critical engagement means examining evidence for its robustness and applicability to inform practice, but also being critically reflective meaning that practitioners consider situations holistically and look for 'underlying processes and influences' (Thompson, 2018) affecting peoples' lives, including the six core concerns of practice discussed in Chapter 1.

Social workers undertake a range of legally mandated assessments; therefore, practitioners require detailed knowledge and understanding of the legislation that informs their role and how this is applied in practice. The primary legislation underpinning assessment in social work with adults is the Care Act 2014 (section 9 care and support assessments; section 10 carers' assessments; section 42 Safeguarding Adults assessments), the Mental Health Act 1983 (Amended, 2007) (mental health assessments undertaken by specialist-trained Approved Mental Health Practitioners) and the Mental Capacity Act 2005 (capacity assessments and Liberty Protection Safeguards (formerly Deprivation of Liberty Safeguards) assessments). The latter two Acts are discussed in Chapters 5 and 6. This chapter focuses on Care Act assessments and therefore includes information specifically about this Act, but also discusses essential skills that are relevant to all types of social work assessment.

Process of assessment in social work practice with adults and the legal requirement to assess

The Care Act 2014 Section 9 (1) establishes the duty (which means **must do**) to assess an adult if: 'it appears to the local authority that an adult may have needs for care and support'.

Paragraph 6.13 of the Care and Support Statutory Guidance 2022 reinforces this duty:

> Local authorities must undertake an assessment for any adult with an appearance of need for care and support, regardless of whether or not the local authority thinks the individual has eligible needs or of their financial situation.

The Care Act 2014 Section 10 (1) also establishes the duty to assess carers when 'it appears to the local authority that the carer may have needs for support'. This will be addressed in Chapter 16.

This is again reinforced by Paragraph 6.16 of the Care and Support Statutory Guidance (2022) which states:

> Where an individual provides or intends to provide care for another adult and it appears that the carer may have any level of needs for support, local authorities must carry out a carer's assessment.

These are inclusive statements; however, eligibility for care and support services must be demonstrated.

Consent and assessment

The first stage of assessment involves ensuring informed consent has been given either directly or, if the individual has been referred by a third party such as a relative, by the referrer confirming that the individual has consented. The necessity to give consent before contact is made applies to everyone who has capacity unless there is risk of abuse when consent can be overridden (Brammer and Pritchard-Jones, 2019). If a person is assessed as lacking the capacity to consent information can be shared based on what is in the individual's best interests on a 'need to know' basis, therefore complying with the GDPR and Data Protection Act (Brammer and Pritchard-Jones, 2019).

Individuals are free to decline contact or, after initial contact, an assessment, and it is essential that the referrer is advised of this so that other sources of support and professionals acceptable to the individual can be alerted. Some individuals may accept an assessment but decline recommendations or the care and support plan, and it is part of the social work role in such circumstances to support the individual to reduce risks where they have mental capacity to do so (Parker, 2021). The Court of Protection, where a judge will ensure that all options have been explored, can also be referred to for guidance in cases where the individual has been assessed as lacking capacity in respect of the decision required (Lyne and Lee, 2020).

Focus on outcomes and wellbeing

The Care Act 2014 promotes an approach to adult social care that is focussed on the personal outcomes an individual wishes to achieve (DoHSC, 2022, section 1). Outcomes are not services or resources such as funding or equipment, but are the goals determined by the individual. Outcomes need to be clear, realistic and reflect the individual's actual circumstances for them to be achievable and meaningful (Heslop and Meredith, 2019).

Activity 2.2

Consider an outcome you wish to achieve, for example, improving your wellbeing by spending time with a relative or friend who lives in a distant location. What are the steps you need to take to achieve this goal?

The term outcome used in the eligibility criteria refers to specific outcomes identified in the Care Act 2014 regulations 6.106:

- Managing and maintaining nutrition
- Maintaining personal hygiene
- Managing toilet needs
- Being appropriately clothed
- Being able to make use of the adults home safely
- Maintaining a habitable home
- Developing and maintaining family or other personal relationships
- Accessing and engaging in work, training, education or volunteering
- Making use of necessary facilities or services in local community including public transport and recreational facilities or services
- Carrying out any caring responsibilities the adult has for a child.

The outcomes are broad descriptors, and an adult is deemed to be unable to achieve an outcome if they cannot do so without support, or causing significant pain, anxiety, distress, or endangering their, or others, health, or it takes longer than someone without the impairment or illness. The needs of people living with fluctuating conditions should be considered over a period of time to be representative of their circumstances. Eligibility is indicated by an adult's inability to achieve two or more of the outcomes above, providing there is significant impact on the individual's wellbeing. The 'impact' is not defined in the Care Act and the Care and Support guidance DHSC (2022), 6.109 but does state it should be understood in its everyday sense in at least one of the areas of wellbeing listed below:

a. *personal dignity (including treating people with respect)*
b. *physical and mental health and emotional wellbeing*
c. *protection from abuse and neglect*
d. *control by the individual over day-to-day life (including the type and way care and support is provided)*
e. *participation in work, education, training or recreation*
f. *social and economic wellbeing*
g. *domestic, family and personal relationships*
h. *suitability of living accommodation*
i. *the individual's contribution to society.*

(Mandelstam, 2017)

These nine domains of wellbeing, within the Care Act 2014, capture activities and experiences that research (Aked et al., 2008) identifies as being important to human health and wellbeing.

Exchange model of assessment

The purpose of an assessment indicates how best to plan and approach information gathering and analysis (Smale et al., 1993). The purpose of Section 9 and 10 of Care Act assessments is to enable decisions about eligibility, care and support. This is achieved in part through exploration of the individual's narrative biography (Dyke, 2019). Social workers must work, in partnership, with individuals and their networks of support, to identify desired outcomes, strengths, resources and needs. The exchange model of assessment (Smale et al., 1993) fits well with this purpose as it emphasises the expertise of the individual in their situation and conceptualises assessment as a potentially empowering mutual exchange of information, with the agenda led by the individual. The exchange model supports social workers and service users to explore the complex, multi-layered systems in which people live, as discussed in Chapter 1.

Top Tip: Tools such as the ecomap exercise from Chapter 1 can help in structuring this exploration and ensure it is person-centred. Parker (2021) discusses a range of diagrammatic tools and resources for assessment. Further resources from Research in Practice for Adults (RIPFA) to support assessment can be found at https://www.re-searchinpractice.org.uk/.

The product of assessment in social work practice with adults

The product of assessment is the document that records the information, analysis and decisions and may lead onto the development of a care-and-support plan. The assessment document is a decision-making tool not to be completed mechanically but instead used to support an assessment process that is responsive to the unique circumstances and needs of the individual and to ensure their maximum participation (Dyke, 2019). For example, proportionality is a key principle of the Care Act and must be considered during an assessment (DoHSC, 2022, section 6.35). This includes practitioners making professional judgements about what sections of the assessment document are applicable. Sometimes, assessments can be a snapshot and in other circumstances, an assessment is a process of narrative discovery that allows the individual to express what their life is like 'lived from the inside' (Galvin and Todres, 2013). As such, assessment skills include flexibility.

Chapter summary

This chapter has highlighted insights from the lived experience of service users, carers and practitioners into the skills and knowledge required for assessment to be meaningful and effective. In conclusion, it is vital that practitioners examine their values and ensure they enhance the experience of assessment by supporting people to define and work towards their best life. This means challenging stereotypical and infantilising views of people who have care and support needs or are at risk of harm. It is not for social workers or other professionals to tell an individual what they need or how they should live, balanced by the duty to safeguard and ensure individuals are as safe as possible and live free from abuse.

Annotated further reading

SCIE, Preparing for an assessment https://www.scie.org.uk/care-act-2014/assessment-and-eligibility/practice-examples/eligibility-adult-carer.asp.
   This information provides guidance on how to prepare for an assessment including asking preparatory reflective questions.

Killick, C. and Taylor, B. J., 2020. *Assessment, Risk & Decision Making in Social Work*. London: SAGE.
   This concise text provides a helpful overview to support social workers in understanding assessment and risk.

Dyke, C., 2019. *Writing Analytical Assessments in Social Work*. ST Albans: Critical Publishing.
   This book is a practical and values-based guide to undertaking assessments.

3

Trauma informed social work practice with adults

Jenny Bigmore, Amy Trim, Stefan Kleipoedszus, Sally Lee and Louise Oliver

Learning from experts by experience

This chapter has been co-authored by social workers from diverse practice backgrounds each of whom have expertise relating to trauma-informed practice. Their different perspectives from working with individuals across the life course have shaped this chapter to create a resource from practice, for practice informed by evidence and research. The chapter uses a case study from practice as the backbone for understanding the lived experience of trauma.

Chapter objectives

By the end of this chapter, you will be able to:

- Discuss the impact of trauma and neglect on brain development from conception through adulthood
- Explore Attachment Theory
- Consider the research on Adverse Childhood Experiences (ACES) and how these early experiences impact adult behaviour
- Explore Adult Attachment styles and consider the implications for social work practice with adults
- Discuss what we mean by Trauma-Informed Practice

Introduction

This chapter explores the importance of understanding the impact of trauma in working with adults in social care practice. The chapter aims to enable you to start your journey towards becoming a trauma-informed practitioner.

We will be using a case study as a framework for exploring some of the key concepts. Josie is a fictional character drawn from Amy's wealth of experience supporting young people in her role as a social worker working within a Child and Adolescent Mental Health Service (CAMHS).

What is trauma?

Trauma is a contested concept which involves the subjective experience of individuals (Mersky et al., 2019). Traumatic events are frightening, often life-threatening, or violent incidents – the consequences of which can profoundly affect an individual, families and communities (Levenson, 2017; Bent-Goodley, 2019). People in unsafe or traumatic circumstances can experience multiple traumas and have fewer resources needed for stability or recovery and this links to social justice and social exclusion (Mersky et al., 2019). Trauma is a natural emotional response to the types of event(s) that threaten or cause harm. It is a term that is often used interchangeably with adversity, and there is debate about whether trauma refers to the event or its consequences (Mersky et al., 2019). To aid clarity, the authors of this chapter argue that adversity and trauma are different concepts: adversity describes a difficult situation or experience, and trauma refers to its impact. It is also important that practitioners remember that not everyone who experiences adversity experiences trauma so each individual is approached without the presumption of trauma.

There are different forms of trauma including acute trauma resulting from a single event such as an assault; chronic trauma relates to repeated and prolonged exposure to traumatising events such as domestic abuse; complex trauma relates to exposure to varied and multiple traumatic events (Levenson, 2017). Trauma can also be experienced in different ways, for example, directly experiencing the traumatic event(s), witnessing in-person or learning about traumatic events that have happened to people to whom an individual is close.

Practitioners working with trauma, including social workers, can also experience secondary or vicarious trauma from frequent exposure to the traumatic events experienced by those with whom they work. The Professional Capabilities Framework (PCF) (BASW, 2018) and Professional Standards (Social Work England, 2019) both require practitioners to be responsible for their self-care and seek support as appropriate; good use of professional supervision is part of self-care.

What is trauma-informed practice?

Trauma-informed practice represents a paradigm shift (Middleton et al., 2019) away from a diagnostic model that asks 'what is wrong with you' to a way of working that asks 'what happened to you' (Penna, 2021). Instead of assigning personal responsibility to people who experience difficulties in their life, trauma-informed practice acknowledges that adverse experiences, people may have faced throughout their life, affect relationships, behaviour, and physical and mental health as adults (Felitti et al., 1998). In practice, a trauma-informed practitioner uses strengths-based, survivor-defined or empowerment approaches to establish a safe context that facilitates trust and mutuality (Gerassi and Nichols, 2018). Six principles are essential to trauma-informed practice (Waite and Ryan, 2019):

1. Safety
2. Trustworthiness and transparency
3. Peer Support
4. Collaboration and mutuality
5. Empowerment, voice and choice
6. Awareness of cultural, historical and gender issues

Based on these six essential guiding principles, a trauma-informed approach aims to be more supportive and less (re-) traumatising than more traditional services that lack an understanding of trauma and the impact it can have.

Activity 3.1

Watch two short films on YouTube, part one and part two, by Nathaniel Matanick entitled *ReMoved*.
   Part 1: https://youtu.be/lOeQUwdAjE0
   Part 2: https://youtu.be/l1fGmEa6WnY
   The films are about a child, but they powerfully illustrate how trauma impacts future behaviours and can be triggered at any time. They follow the story of Zoe, who has experienced trauma in her early years and her journey. . . . Take a look.
   These are a couple of quotes from the films.

(Continued)

(Continued)

Sometimes my life feels like a circle... and I don't know how to stop it or change it or break it. When I finally come close its starts all over again, a whirlwind, a tornado, set out to destroy me

(Zoe – ReMoved Part 2).

Did you know there are tornadoes in outer space? It's actually how stars are born

(Carer – ReMoved Part 2).

Keep these quotes in mind as we examine how trauma impacts people.

Adverse childhood experiences

Trauma-informed practice is based on research that shows how exposure to severe and pervasive childhood trauma (McKay et al., 2021) or toxic stress (Shonkoff et al., 2012) can change our physiology and social and emotional development and lead to poor outcomes in adulthood (Felliti et al., 1998; Harris, 2018). The most extensive study of childhood abuse, neglect and challenges in the family, the CDC Kaiser study (Felitti et al., 1998; Centres for Disease Control and Prevention, 2022), established a clear link between ACEs and wellbeing in later life. ACEs represent potentially traumatic events, like the experience of abuse, neglect or violence or witnessing substance misuse, parental mental ill health or parental separation (Waite and Ryan, 2019). These adverse experiences are not a definitive list, and more recently, an ecological perspective covering systematic oppression has been introduced into the discussion (Barajas-Gonzalez et al., 2021). These ACEs can significantly impact the child's development with long-lasting effects into adulthood, including heart disease, diabetes, suicide and common neurological conditions like dementia, mood disorders and post-traumatic stress disorders (Ortiz et al., 2022). ACEs are relatively common. According to Hughes et al. (2019), almost half of young adults in 10 European countries reported experiencing one ACE, and 5.6% reported four or more ACEs. These figures highlight social workers' importance in acknowledging past and current adversity people experience.

Activity 3.2

Visit https://acestoohigh.com/got-your-ace-score/ and find your ACE score. Before you do, think of any support networks you can rely on should this questionnaire trigger memories of past adverse experiences. Once you know your ACE score, consider what this means for you and your practice as a social worker. Remember, this score is only a guideline. It does not tell you whether you should seek support or not.

Knowing your ACE score can help you appreciate the effect adversity can have on a person and that this adversity is part of who we are, not only in the lives of those social workers we work with.

Stress

It is essential to understand that when we experience a perceived threat or danger, there can be a physiological stress or trauma response. Coping with adversity in childhood is an integral part of child development and how we react to threats is an important part of survival (Bryant, 2016). Think about what happens to you if, for example, you have a near miss in your car. Your heart starts racing; you may feel sweaty and shaky. This experience is because a reaction has been set off in your brain, sending messages to other parts of your body. The vital thing to know is that it involves what is known as the limbic-hypothalamic-pituitary-adrenal-axis (LHPA), (De Bellis and Zisk, 2014). When we experience stress, the hypothalamus, which is located just above the brainstem and controls the release of hormones from the pituitary gland, is activated. Hormones are released into the bloodstream to reach various targets, including the kidneys, which activate the adrenal glands. The adrenal glands activate the release of cortisol which then causes a number of changes to prepare the body to face the perceived threat, such as the release of glucose to give the body energy to face the threat.

Shonkoff et al. (2012) categorise stress as positive, tolerable or toxic. In our everyday life, stress is a healthy response that often comes with an increased heart rate and stress hormone levels. This positive stress is part of healthy development, and most children will experience this when meeting new caregivers or starting school. Occasionally, people face more challenging situations, like losing a family member or a friend or being involved in an accident. These situations trigger more serious stress responses that last longer but do not have long-term consequences if they are buffered by a supportive relationship that tolerates these stress responses. Toxic stress occurs when there is a 'prolonged activation of the biological stress response' (Ortiz et al., 2022, p539) due to multiple stressors like abuse, neglect, parental substance misuse or domestic violence. The latter is the link between ACEs and their effects on adult health, as this stress affects the developing brain. Toxic stress occurs when there is no parental buffering or someone to support a person through stressful events.

Activity 3.3

Take a piece of paper and draw yourself in the middle of it. Draw two circles around yourself, the first one very close to you. Write down things that cause you stress regularly outside the inner circle. Now, write down some of the rare stressful events that had a greater magnitude in your life. Next, write down the people (or agencies) that help you deal with every day and tolerable stress.

The effect of toxic stress on the developing brain

In the past decades, advances in neuroscience have provided a much better understanding of how the brain develops in utero and post-birth. At birth, a baby's brain, with a healthy in-utero experience, is ready to soak up the world around it. However, maternal stress during pregnancy impacts foetal brain development (Fitzgerald et al., 2020). The experience of babies in the womb subjected to trauma in the form of parental drug or alcohol use, violent parental relationships and extreme mother stress will already affect the brain's development. Toxic stress in young children can change the structure of the brain and the way it functions (Shonkoff et al., 2012). The experience of trauma in children and young people has the potential to disrupt the LHPA axis mentioned above and lead to permanent changes in the way people regulate psychobiological responses to stress. This can result in depressive and anxiety symptoms, disruptive behavioural disorders or anti-social behaviours (de Bellis and Zisk, 2014) and 'create a weak foundation for later learning, behaviour, and health' (Shonkoff et al., 2012, p236).

Activity 3.4

Read Josie's story below and consider how this relates to what you have learnt about stress and the impact of toxic stress on a child. What could impact Josie's development as a child and later in life as an adult?

Josie

I do not really remember when I realised my home life was not the same as everyone else's, maybe around the middle of primary school when I spent my first night at a friend's house. I had not been allowed before, and I was so shocked that there was no shouting; her mum did not cry all evening. My friend spilt a drink, but her dad did not hit her around the head for doing it. He helped her clear it up. At that moment, I realised things in my house might not be what they should be. I still didn't tell anyone what it was like; I loved my mum and dad and didn't want them to get in trouble.

I think there were probably lots of things that happened that I do not remember or have chosen to forget, but there is still plenty that haunts me even now.

Let's start with my early years from what I have been told and some memories. Mum and Dad used to shout at each other all the time, it used to scare me, but then I just got so used to it that I did not even react to it. That was safer; if I cried, dad would get mad at me, and he used to hit me.

Mum was often on her own with us, and she often hid in the bathroom and cried. I used to try and do everything I could to make her happy. She would sometimes forget to feed us or change my little sister's nappy, so I used to do it, it stunk, but she would cry so much I couldn't leave her. Mum never came when she cried.

(Continued)

Uncle Dave used to come over and look after me sometimes, and mum liked this cause it meant she could go out. Uncle Dave liked to have me sit on his lap whilst we watched television. It made me feel really uncomfortable, but I never knew why.

When I was 10, a strange lady came to our house and spoke to Mum. Dad was out, which is probably lucky because he wouldn't have liked the lady. Mum got really upset, and I overheard the lady telling mum that she needed to look after us better or we might have to go into foster care. I remember not knowing what that meant, but it sounded scary.

Soon after, Mum and Dad had a huge argument, and the police came. The house was a mess, and I had a big bruise on my face from Dad hitting me the night before. That night I left my home and never went back.

Reflections on Josie's story

When a child experiences the ongoing persistent abuse that Josie did, their brain will not respond to the external world rationally. The child's brain becomes shaped for offensive and defensive purposes to protect itself. A child-like Josie may begin to display symptoms that could include intrusive thoughts, flashbacks, sleep disturbance, hypervigilance, emotional numbing, avoidance, altered cognitive functioning, obsessions, behavioural extremes, regression and relationship impairments (Hughes, 2016). As you can see, Josie loves her parents but does not have a secure attachment style. Her internal working model is that the world is unpredictable and scary, and this will make her wary and untrusting in relationships.

As a social worker working with adults, having this baseline understanding of their past experiences and the subsequent effect on how the brain functions will help you shape how you interact with them and understand the underlying reasons for how they may react to the external world at times, as Zoe in *ReMoved Part two* tells us 'You see what I do, but you forget why' and 'you forget what I've heard, you forget my pain'. If you can train yourself constantly to consider the *why* and not just the *what*, you will be halfway to properly being able to help redress some of the damage the adults you are working with may have experienced.

What does this mean for social work practice with adults?

Trauma and adversity can lead to different forms of emotional distress, poor mental health, self-harming behaviours and physical ill health, all of which are relevant to social work with adults (Levenson, 2017). Chronic stress impacts on physical health, for example, potential link to heart disease, as trauma may be held in the mind and body (Van Der Kolk, 2015). The experience of trauma can also have societal impacts in terms of disrupted social connections and relationships (Levenson, 2020). The diversity of impacts and presentations mean that practitioners need to be attuned and sensitive to recognising patterns of behaviour, relationships or thought processes that might indicate an emerging, trauma-related response and presence of current or historic adversity.

This returns us to the principles of trauma-informed practice. First, creating a sense of safety is essential. Feeling unsafe may activate a fear response and, thereby, a traumatic stress response. Classen and Clark (2017) emphasise that talking about safety and the need to feel safe is critical to create a sense of safety. Simply asking what the person you are working with needs to feel safe and inviting the person to share personal experiences is an essential first step.

Second, it is vital to building trust, as trauma survivors are less likely to trust people. That requires the social worker to be 'reliable, predictable, and to have clear boundaries' (*Classen and Clark, 2017*, p524) and transparent in explaining interventions and their rationale. Third, offering the opportunity to collaborate in decisions likely gives the person a contrary experience to the disempowering experience of the trauma. That can easily be achieved by exploring the person's perspective regarding potential interventions and taking a strengths-based approach (Lishman et al., 2018). Together, these three principles result in empowerment (Adams, 2003).

By actively listening to the person, the social worker can help to identify goals that are important to them and 'the mere act of working to understand the survivors' goals and helping the survivor to articulate them contributes to the process of empowerment' (Classen and Clark, 2017, p526). All this needs to happen in a way that takes the ecological context, culture, gender and historical issues into consideration. That requires a competency that aligns the social worker's practice with the realities the person is experiencing (Gerassi and Nichols, 2018). Last, organising peer support is essential to facilitate mutual support among peers (Anyikwa, 2016).

Activity 3.5

Going back to Josie's story, imagine you are a practitioner in a mental health service, and you will meet Josie for the first time in your offices. Write down some ideas about how you can prepare for this meeting. What can you do to make Josie feel safe? How can you create a sense of mutuality?

How to plan a trauma-informed meeting

Planning is essential to prepare for any meeting in practice. Even though plans should allow changes at the moment and more often than not, the best laid-out plans are unlikely to be realised as they are. However, it will be challenging to achieve the six principles of trauma-informed practice without preparation. Being prepared shows the person that they matter.

🗸 You may want to consider the space where you are meeting for this meeting. Does it provide a sense of safety, or is it a space that feels cold and alienating? Consider what you can do regarding the layout of the furniture or items in the room that facilitate conversations.

🗸 You may want to consider the context where Josie is coming from to align with her cultural context and history.

🗸 Maybe you also want to prepare some ideas about possible interventions so you can offer some ideas that may start a conversation about Josie's preferred way of moving forward.

🗸 Most importantly, it would help if you got yourself into a mindset that focusses on the strengths of Josie rather than considering all the things that may not be right now.

These preparation tips will enable you to focus on the person in the moment.

Activity 3.5

Practising in trauma-informed ways is empowering for individuals, and the table below highlights some of the key skills and knowledge the authors have identified for social work practice with adults. Add your own ideas to the table about the skills needed to work with people living with trauma.

Knowledge	Skills
Understanding risk from the perspective of the person, for example, has their experience of trauma led to the brain not recognising risk?	Work in empowering, non-judgemental ways **such as**...
Knowledge to understand and analyse behaviour which may appear self-destructive, irrational, aggressive or irresponsible	Communicating the impact of trauma in ways that engage traumatised individuals **such as**...
Knowledge to understand and analyse the impact of trauma on psychological and physiological development	Working in ways which demonstrate your understanding of human development and behaviour **such as...**
Knowledge to understand and analyse people's stories and their sense-making	Use relationship-based skills to communicate the person is being heard and understood **such as**...
Knowledge to communicate with other agencies in ways which make sense, for example, accounts from lived experience	Working in ways which enable knowledge sharing **such as**...
Knowledge to inform people that trauma is a normal human response to abnormal events	Demonstrating humanising skills including reassurance, empathy and understanding **by**...

This activity encourages you to think about the practical ways you can demonstrate your skills as a developing trauma-informed practitioner. You might have thought of some of the following:

- Ground people by connecting them to the here and now – ask them are you thirsty, are you hungry – connect them to their embodied experiences
- Don't expect logical or linear accounts – listen
- Trauma-informed social work is aligned to relationship-based practice – uses the relationship between practitioner and service user as a conduit for change
- The emphasis is on empathy, respect of people's dignity, allowing people to tell their stories, and valuing their strengths.
- Supporting people to understand and reframe their trauma responses as normal reactions to threatening encounters, helping to gain a sense of control and hope (adapted from Levenson, 2017).

We hope this information enables you to reflect on how you will be trauma-informed in your work.

Chapter summary

This chapter explores how ACEs can impact people across the life course and into adulthood. These traumatic events, for example, abuse, neglect, violence or witnessing substance misuse, parental mental ill health or parental separation, can have long-lasting effects on human development, including brain development. This in turn can affect thoughts, mental and physical wellbeing and also behaviours.

This chapter explains that it is through understanding the past experiences of those worked with and the very real impact this has upon development and behaviours help the practitioner engage with them, in a way which recognises this and adapts their approach to working with the individual. For example, creating a safe space to meet and talk in, taking time to build trust and strengths-based, survivor-defined or empowerment approaches. We recommend that this approach is woven throughout social work practice when working with people who have experienced trauma.

Annotated further reading

Watch Nadine Burke Harris' TED Talk entitled 'How Childhood Trauma Affects Health Across a Lifetime'. Dr Harris explains how trauma in childhood has long-reaching impacts on health and wellbeing:

https://www.youtube.com/watch?v=95ovlJ3dsNk.
Parry, B. D. and Winfrey, O., 2022. *What Happened to You? Conversations on Trauma, Resilience and Healing*. Blue Bird. This book offers information from experts by experience to help you understand how people living with trauma can find hope and change.

Van Der Kolk, B., 2015. *The Body Keeps the Score*. London: Penguin. This book reveals through powerful human stories from lived experience how trauma impacts on the human body.

4

Decision-making in social work practice with adults

Stefan Kleipoedszus

Learning from experts by experience

Stefan is a social worker and academic who specialises in decision-making. The experience of Jo, a fictionalised person, who has been diagnosed with Alzheimer's, will be developed throughout this chapter. This provides the backbone for the discussion and reflection on decision-making in the context of a hospital discharge decision. The case study is constructed as a decision-making exercise (Klein, 2000; Crandall et al., 2006) to provide opportunities to learn about different decision-making theories and consider how these theories could be applied in practice.

Chapter objectives

By the end of this chapter, you should be able to:

- Explain what a decision is
- Understand different theories of decision-making
- Draw connections between these theories and social work practice
- Use this knowledge to reflect on your practice in supervision

---

Introduction

In this chapter, the reader will learn about what decisions are and explore different ways social workers make decisions. First, this chapter defines what decision-making means and how uncertainty in decision-making is a crucial characteristic of social work. Following on from this and depending on the preferred decision-making style of the reader, intuitive, rational and heuristic decision-making strategies can be explored in any order.

What are decisions?

Decision-making is an everyday activity at the heart of social work. The verb *making* implies that a decision requires an activity following a decision. As such, a decision includes a person allocating energy into actively following one of at least two options in order to achieve a specific desired outcome (Churchman, 1968). Therefore, the decision-maker has to define strategies that include actions required to reach the desired outcome (Fishburn, 1964). That means a decision is a conscious and deliberate choice between possible courses of action (Simon, 1960; Ackoff, 1978; Taylor, 2013). According to Holsapple (2008), decisions can be *structured decisions* routinely made in a stable context with well-defined alternatives and clearly defined criteria for choosing a course of action. Other decisions are infrequent, do not have well-defined alternatives and where choices are ambiguous. The first group refers to small-world decisions, environments where all variables are known and clearly defined. The latter refers to large-world decisions in which variables and some relevant information are unknown (Gigerenzer and Gaissmaier, 2011).

The latter is a much more accurate description of social work practice, as complexity and uncertainty resulting from the multi-dimensionality of human behaviour are common aspects of human life (Rosati, 2017). In the words of Ackoff (1978, p15), this decision context is a 'mess', a situation in which it is only known that a problem exists but where it is not clear what the problem is or what the best way is to resolve it. Even though the case study below has very limited information, it already includes a high level of complexity which makes it difficult to establish a clear course of action.

Jo

As a hospital social worker, you meet Jo, a woman in her 50s, to assess the situation and prepare a discharge plan. Jo had been diagnosed with Alzheimer's seven years ago and is in hospital after being hit by a car while walking around the town about two miles away from her home. The paramedics who attended the accident reported that she did not know where she was or how she got there. Jo had a concussion, some significant bruises on her back and legs, and minor bruises on both wrists but no further injuries. After three days in the hospital, the medical team believes Jo has no medical reasons to stay. The daughter and son of Jo, who visited every day, state that they think it would be best for Jo to go into a care home. Jo's husband and primary carer, who visited only once, wants Jo to continue living at home. When asked, Jo states that she wants to go home because her husband needs her to be at home.

Activity 4.1

- What outcomes do you want to achieve for Jo?
- Write down different courses of action you could take to achieve these outcomes.
- What is your preferred course of action?
- How did you make this choice?

The first challenge after establishing what courses of action are available is to choose the most desirable option. There are different ways in which people make decisions, and decision-makers likely use strategies depending on the case characteristics, the organisational context, the decision-maker's characteristics and external factors (Bauman et al., 2014). As a decision-maker, you probably already have an idea about your preferred way of making a decision.

Activity 4.2

Below there are three descriptions of decision-makers. Consider how you make most of your decisions and select the description of the decision-maker most aligned with your preferred decision-making style.

1. They work under time pressure and have experience with similar problems. They believe that waiting longer to decide is riskier than making a decision now.
2. They want to collate all information to weigh up their options and assess the possible risks of each one to determine what option has the greatest chance of achieving a desirable outcome.
3. They do not have enough time to collate more information, and the minimum criteria for choosing the option is clear.

That is a very rough description of different decision-making strategies, and in reality, the delineation between these different types is not as clear-cut as suggested here. If you choose type 1, you may prefer an intuitive decision-making style. The second type suggests a more rational approach that aims to maximise utility. The last option indicates a preference for accepting cognitive limitations when processing information and using heuristics or shortcuts to determine the course of action.

The following sections introduce each strategy, and you may want to start exploring the theories behind each by reading the section that is most aligned with your preferred strategy first.

Intuitive decision-making

Maybe intuition is your dominant way of making a decision, or you have found a piece of information that persuaded you to take a particular course of action, or you have arrived at a decision through rational decision-making. You somehow felt uneasy about the decision regarding Jo. Now your gut tells you that something is wrong even though there is limited information. That is what people refer to as intuition. In everyday language, intuitive decisions are often referred to as *gut decisions* and mostly have positive connotations. Hogarth (2001) explains that intuition is a process where a decision-maker reaches an outcome without knowing how this outcome has been achieved and intuition seems to be an effective way of responding to complexity. Cook (2017) shows that social workers use intuition in their first encounters with families. The *'emotional responses, "niggles" and "gut feelings" sensitised them to potentially salient information before it was rationally accessible'* (ibid., 2017, p431).

In a social work context, gut decisions are more likely to be seen as unfavourable as they do not fit into the paradigm of evidence-based practice and the ideal that social workers need to make unbiased decisions that can be explained rationally. When social workers make errors (Munro, 1996, 1999), critics (Gove, 2013; Department for Education (DfE), 2015) highlight the failings of intuitive decision-making. Nonetheless, intuition or practice wisdom (Samson, 2015; Cheung, 2017) is necessary. Compared to an analytical and deliberate strategy, intuitive decision-making requires little effort. Intuition is fast and can be easily adapted to decisions made when the presenting information is complex (Seligman and Kahana, 2013). For example, Wilson and Schooler (2008) highlight that people's judgement can improve when they use intuition instead of reasoning. Using intuition, decision-makers can adapt fast to even the most minor changes in a presenting situation, which is impossible in a deliberate, analytical approach based on defining explicit hypotheses about reality (Hogarth, 2001).

Even though skilled decision-makers seem to make intuitive decisions effortless, developing intuition takes the effortful development of expertise. According to Klein (2008, 2015), the foundation of intuition is the recognition of similarities in patterns that decision-makers had accumulated when they progressed from being a novice to an expert (Dreyfus et al., 1986). In their professional journey, decision-makers develop *'vast stores of prior experiences'* (Seligman and Kahana, 2013, p399) that represent a high level of expertise. Experts use their experiences to develop a growing list of particular cues to their field. Together with learning about positive and negative outcomes of choices, these form patterns that can be compared to the scenario that a decision-maker faces at any given moment. As a result, the decision maker does not have to evaluate alternatives and pick the best but can see if a pattern matches a problem that can then be resolved by using previously used strategies with only minimal adaptations. That means that expert decision-makers can make intuitive decisions with confidence but will find it hard to articulate how they came to make a specific decision.

Jo

Imagine you are talking to Jo about what she thinks should happen next. Even though you focus on what Jo says about her wishes to go home, you observe Jo rubbing her wrists regularly. You ask how she got the bruises on her wrist. She tells you that she does not know but thinks that she may have fallen and hurt her wrists.

Activity 4.2

Reflect on what your 'gut' tells you about what is going on. Write down the first thing that comes to mind about what you think could have caused the bruises.

There are many ways to explain the bruises you observed; some are more likely than others. However, the bruises on the wrist do not appear to result from the accident. Somehow, you are not 'buying' the story about the fall, especially as Jo appeared to be very eager to steer the conversation away from these bruises.

In my professional experience, I have seen similar bruises on people restrained with some force. Therefore, I am concerned about the safety of Jo and whether she should return home. These bruises would be something to explore further, and until there is some more clarity on this, I want to ensure that Jo stays in a place of safety until this clarity has been reached. That takes a more deliberate approach to determine the risks for Jo to return home in these circumstances, so you may want to assess each option's possible risks. This step helps to determine what option has the greatest chance of achieving a desirable outcome. Alternatively, given the limited time available as Jo needs to be discharged from the hospital, you want to make a quick heuristic decision and do a more comprehensive appraisal of options later.

Rational decision-making

You may have made an intuitive or a heuristic decision, and now you have been asked to provide a more detailed rationale. That is what Kahneman (2013) calls a slow decision-making process based on conscious deliberation in light of the available information.

Any decision regarding Jo's immediate future contains many uncertainties. Given the high stakes of this decision, there may be a tendency to collate more information to reduce the number of unknown variables. Regardless of how much information we gather, there will remain an uncertainty. That means that these types of decisions are similar to what the so-called Expected Utility Theory by von Neumann and Morgenstern (2007) describes as a choice *'between prospects or gambles'* (Kahneman and Tversky, 1979, p263) that are based on a *'discrete and finite set of mutually exclusive alternatives'* (Aliev and Huseynov, 2014, p304). From this perspective, social workers would choose the option with the greatest chance of achieving the best possible outcome. In practice, this would require measurable preferences between at least two options. In the case of Jo, a social worker must decide if Jo is safe returning home. Depending on what action a social worker chooses, they would take different actions leading to different states of the situation, and each state would have different consequences.

Activity 4.3

Draft a decision tree. Take a sheet of paper and on the left side of the paper write down the question: Is Jo safe to return home or not? Next, think of a necessary action you would have to take for each option and write them down next to the initial question. Next, think of at least two possibilities of what could happen. Write them down next to each option. Now think of one possible outcome of each of the possibilities involved. What is your most preferred option? What is the least favourable option?

Depending on whether Jo is safe to return home, there are different actions a social worker could take. If Jo is not safe, applying to the Court of Protection to determine if Jo has the mental capacity to decide to return home herself may be an action to take. If the Court of Protection agrees with your assessment that Jo cannot make this decision, there could be two states. The first could result in the outcome that Jo may be placed in a care home against her expressed wish but is safe from abuse that happened at home, and Jo is settling well into the care home. The second state would result in Jo living in a care home against her wishes despite no abuse at home. Jo would still be safe but potentially unhappy.

If you think Jo is safe to return home, you will start to organise the care Jo needs. As a result, the state would either be that Jo is at home and is well cared for or that Jo is at home and there continues to be a risk for her. In the first case, the outcome would be that Jo is at home and safe; in the second, she is at home, not safe and you may meet Jo again when new safeguarding concerns emerge.

Following the Expected Utility Theory, the first step to determining what a rational decision-maker should do as a rational agent is to assign a numerical value to each possible outcome to allow ordering the preferences for the outcomes (Farmer, 2015; Newell, 2015). Newell (2015) suggests assigning 100 to the most preferred outcome (i.e. Jo is safe and at home) and 0 to the least preferred outcome (i.e. Jo experiences further physical abuse at home). Values between 0 and 100 would be assigned to the other possible outcomes (i.e. 5 for Jo being unnecessarily and against her wishes in a care home, but at least she is safe). The next step would be to assign a probability for each state to occur (i.e. 56% chance that abuse happened), which is difficult to achieve due to a lack of evidence base for providing objective numbers based on available research. The expected utility is the sum of the numerical values for each outcome weighted by the probability of each state. According to von Neumann and Morgenstern (2007), decision-makers choose the act that promises the highest utility.

This theory has many problems, especially concerning the limitations of human cognitive abilities (Simon, 1955; Thaler, 2015). Research by Kahneman and Tversky (1979) and Tversky and Kahneman (1981, 1986), who observed decision-making in an experimental setting, contradict the expectations set by the Expected Utility Theory. Probably the most prominent example of such an inconsistency is the framing effect (Bazerman, 1984), which describes the observation that the way choices are framed, either positive or negative, can trigger risk-seeking or risk-averse behaviours. The framing effect is a breach of the axiom of invariance in Expected Utility Theory that states that a choice should not change regardless of variations in the way it is presented.

On the back of their research, Kahneman and Tversky (1979) developed Prospect Theory, a model of choice where the decision-maker evaluates potential outcomes that are *expressed as gains or losses relative to [a] fixed neutral reference point* (Bazerman, 1984, p334). In other words, the value of an outcome is a function of the current status quo and the size of the positive or negative change concerning this status quo (Kahneman and Tversky, 1979).

Regardless of this criticism, Expected Utility Theory helps to structure social work decision-making as it invites practitioners to make decision trees that can help to reconstruct the logic of decisions, at least retrospectively. As such, this is an excellent strategy to add a phase of more conscious deliberation after making an intuitive decision discussed in the previous section. However, given the complexity of human life mentioned above, it is challenging to ascertain a complete list of all possible acts, states and outcomes that make a decision.

Heuristic decision-making

Jo

You are talking to the husband of Jo, who is also Jo's carer, to find out more about Jo's care needs and establish some more background information. He tells you that Jo has spent some time in a care home while he was in the hospital and that her cognitive abilities did deteriorate fast in this period. While talking to him, you realise that what the husband is saying about the difficulties he faces daily reminds you of a case you have had before. In that case, the carer used to lock his partner, who also had Alzheimer's, in an empty bedroom to stop her from leaving the house at night so that he could go out occasionally. When challenged, this carer admitted to using physical restraint by pinning his partner to the floor when she tried to leave the room.

As a hospital social worker, there is bound to be pressure to get people out of the hospital. As such, there will not always be sufficient time to undertake an assessment that explores all aspects relevant to a case in detail. Social work represents a large world with a lack of complete knowledge about the world. Here, choice problems are ill-defined and mostly presented as verbal data, which is open to interpretation. This context means that too many cues have to be considered, which can negatively impact performance (Pitt et al., 2002) as it becomes increasingly challenging to choose the relevant cues to make a decision.

In response to these complexities, decision-makers tend to generate strategies that *'ignore part of the information, with the goal of making decisions more quickly, frugally, and/or accurately than more complex methods'* (Gigerenzer and Gaissmaier, 2011, p454). According to Tversky and Kahneman (1974, p1124), decision-makers use so-called heuristic principles to reduce the complexity of *'assessing probabilities and predicting values to simpler judgmental operations'*. These heuristics are tools specific to the goal the decision-maker tries to achieve.

Heuristic decision-making aims not to optimise possible outcomes, unlike Expected Utility Theory or Prospect Theory. In return, they do not require the decision-maker to complete an analysis of the factors that influence a choice problem. That helps the decision-maker to make *'fast and frugal'* decisions in varying environments benefitting from less-is-more effects. In these environments, *'less information or computation leads to more accurate judgments than more information or computation'* (Gigerenzer and Gaissmaier, 2011, p453). In other words, heuristics are the rules of thumb social workers use to navigate the complex decision-making landscape in a highly regulated context. Even though there is likely to be an infinite number of heuristics, Gigerenzer and Gassmaier (2011) suggest four categories of heuristic decision-making.

1. In recognition-based decision-making, the decision maker first searches for alternative cues to compare and stop their search when they recognise a cue. In the case of Jo, this could mean that the social worker recognises similarities between two different cases and uses these similarities to decide that the carer of Jo is potentially restraining Jo.
2. In one-reason decision-making, decision-makers search through cues in order of their validity and stop when they find a single cue that is good enough to make a decision. From the conversation with Jo's carer, this cue may be the information that Jo's cognitive abilities deteriorated when she spent some time in a care home.
3. In trade-off or tallying strategies, the decision-makers search through cues in any order and stop to weigh up pairs of cues until a cue appears to have more weight. In social work, this would be the strategy to write down a list of pros and cons for each alternative action you could take as a social worker and take the one alternative with the most pros on the list.
4. Decision-makers who use social heuristics look for similarities in the responses of other decision-makers and imitate, average the wisdom of others or jump to an existing default if one is available. For example, after talking to Jo's carer, you speak to a few colleagues in the office or call to arrange a planning meeting, discuss the case and follow the plan of action that the majority of your colleagues suggest.

Even though heuristics are a valuable strategy for making fast and frugal decisions in complex situations, there is also the risk of biases that can impact judgement in social work (Munro, 1996, 1999; Kirkman and Melrose, 2014), for example, the observation that a person's estimate of the probability of an event is heavily influenced by their ability to recall a similar event (Availability Heuristic) (Tversky and Kahneman, 1979). Other concerns are the tendency of decision-makers to stick to their initial beliefs even when there is clear evidence that challenges this belief (Confirmation Bias) (Janis and Mann, 1977; Baron, 2000) or the desire to avoid conflict and achieve agreement in a group at the cost of what the individual may believe to be a good decision (Groupthink) (Janis, 1983). Many more biases or systematic distortions of judgements, like a framing bias, risk perception or overconfidence (Acciarini et al., 2020), can affect general and social work decision-making. Critical reflection and supervision are key in social work practice to avoid these biases or minimise their impact on decisions.

Chapter summary: Working intuitively and deliberatively

The reality of social work practice is that there is not going to be a single right way of making a decision, and it is more likely that a blend between these strategies has a reasonable chance of making good decisions. There needs to be more than the three strategies outlined in this chapter to find the best possible outcome for Jo. To be a skilled decision-maker, combining these strategies to complement each other is vital. A purely rational approach based on decision trees or structured decision-making tools may result in defensible decisions but undervalues the human interactions and the emotional responses to changes in small details that the social worker observes. Just relying on intuition is a mirror image of that previous scenario. With deliberation in a rational approach, the decision-maker may avoid falling into the trap of different biases that can make social work decision-making prone to errors. Making fast and frugal or heuristic decisions can be effective in the short term when social workers are in the midst of a situation that is developing fast, but more is needed for long-term planning. As such, the plea of this chapter is to explore your decision-making styles so that you know how you make decisions and find strategies (like supervision) to widen your perspectives on your own decisions.

Annotated further reading

Cook, L. L., 2020. The home visit in child protection social work: Emotion as resource and risk for professional judgement and practice. *Child & Family Social Work*, 25 (1), 18–26.
   This article by Cook (2020) is a very insightful paper about the impact of emotions on social work decision-making.

Kirkman, E. and Melrose, K., 2014. Clinical judgement and decision-making in children's social work: An analysis of the 'front door' system. *In: Department for Education Research Report* (Issue April).
   This report gives a good overview of decision-making at the front-door of social work.

Sicora, A., Taylor, B. J., Alfandari, R., Enosh, G., Helm, D., Killick, C., Lyons, O., Mullineux, J., Przeperski, J., Rölver, M. and Whittaker, A. 2021. Using intuition in social work decision making. *European Journal of Social Work*, 24 (5), 772–787.
This paper provides a great discussion of the role of intuition in social work decision-making.

Part II

Working with adults in practice

5

Working with mental health issues

Sarah Lake, Hazel Mayall and Rosslyn Dray

Learning from experts by experience

This chapter is co-authored by Ros, who is a social worker and academic who has specialised in working with adults with mental health issues, and Sarah and Hazel, who are experts by experience and whose lived experience is woven throughout the chapter to make their voices integral to the writing.

> **Chapter objectives**
>
> By the end of this chapter, you will be able to:
>
> * Understand how mental health is universally positioned in social work practice
>
> *(Continued)*

(Continued)

- Understand the legal context of mental health in social work practice
- Reflect upon the impact of social work practice using two different perspectives provided by experts by experience
- Incorporate mental health and wellbeing in your conversations with service users and carers

Introduction

The chapter is framed by two stories of lived experience to develop understanding around mental health and social work practice with adults. With experience of being a social worker in adult mental health, I encountered many people who were referred, or self-referred, to services. There were people in a time of crisis, people with chronic difficulties with mental health and people who experience unusual, and sometimes distressing, phenomena. Some people desperately wanted help, some did not welcome or believe they needed support and some had experienced services and felt sceptical about what could be offered. For practitioners, finding the most effective way to engage with a person is vital. You need to remain aware; seeking help outside of your own resources and opening up your world to a stranger may induce feelings of vulnerability and disempowerment. This frames a core message of this chapter exemplified by Hazel and Sarah's experience, meeting with the person in front of you and trying to understand their world.

Before Hazel and Sarah introduce themselves, it is important from the outset to consider language around mental health. One can use terms interchangeably such as mental health, wellbeing or mental illness, and this has different connotations. For the purpose of this chapter, the term 'wellbeing' will be adopted as this supports the link to the primary legislation guiding social work with adults in England (Care Act 2014). It also acknowledges the broader focus of wellbeing and mental health rather than a purely biological perspective. It is important to acknowledge conversations about mental health and wellbeing should be as much a part of the professional encounter as oxygen is part of human existence.

Hazel and Sarah: who am I?

Hazel: 'My name is Hazel. I am an autistic woman learning to navigate a world in which there is little help for me. Ask the internet for help as an autistic person and you will find out how you, as a parent, should calm your child's "meltdown", how you, as a parent, can look out for signs of sensory overload in your autistic child, how you, as a parent, can access resources for respite. What is there for me when I want to know how to calm my own meltdown, or watch out for the signs of autistic burnout, a devastating symptom which can lead to all sorts of difficult experiences. Where is my respite from myself? This is my reality'.

Sarah: 'My name is Sarah and my mental health problems first became apparent at age 13 when I suffered with depression and self-harm. This continued throughout school and intensified at university, where I first sought proper help. I continued to struggle with self-injury and in my final term I took an overdose. Later that summer I experienced my first psychotic episode. I was referred to the Early Intervention in Psychosis Team, one of whom was a social worker. In subsequent years I went through more episodes and was heavily medicated, admitted to a psychiatric hospital on three occasions and underwent considerable amounts of talking therapy. My psychotic symptoms also caused my self-harm to take on a new level of severity, and on two occasions I had to undergo surgery'.

Understanding my world

Hazel: 'I lead as independent a life as I can make it, with the ongoing support from my partner. I get involved with as many activities as is possible with my condition. There are many hours of my life that I do not divulge even to friends and family; needless to say that when people meet me and inevitably are surprised to find out that I am autistic, a lot has happened underneath the surface that they will never see (if I can at all help it) that would very clearly indicate my neuro-divergency. This is a fact that mainly relies on my sexually dimorphic ability to mask my autistic symptoms which the male autistic brain seems to lack. I hide, in essence, my true self to fit in with the societal expectations that surround us all. It is a struggle to know when I can unmask.

I also struggle with depression and anxiety. It is akin to treading water – sometimes the ocean is calm and it's easy to lie back and watch the clouds drift by, and sometimes it is an all-consuming storm that threatens to push me under the waves. Some days are easier than others, but so far I have never yet set foot on the shore where others seem to be seamlessly enjoying themselves, although I know that appearances can be deceiving. There are days when I cannot help the overwhelming and relentless suicidal thoughts that assail my mind, but to all outward appearances I am quite happily working away at my desk. The anxiety, meanwhile, can be triggered by anything: a sudden change in my routine or an unexpected expectation that creates a towering pressure and launches me headfirst into an anxiety attack. The amount of bathroom breaks I must take on any given day, hiding away in order to remember how to breathe and convince myself against the feeling of impending doom or a heart attack or spontaneous combustion.

I feel my voice here, in all its seriousness and dripping with a lifetime of fighting to be heard, is lending a rather too sombre weight to this chapter. I would like to highlight some positivity. I am, at all times, hand in hand with my inner child. Given the opportunity to blow bubbles or eat ice cream or build sandcastles, you will really see me thrive. So many interactions with professionals are so serious and I feel there is room to bring back the joys I felt when, as a child, I would enter my appointments looking forward to the pile of teddies and toys that would help me physically process my thoughts as we discussed my wellbeing, my disability, my traumas. If you were to tell me that a part of you does not wish to still play with those wooden beads on colourful metal wires that sit in the children's section of every GP surgery, I would absolutely question it'.

Sarah: 'The main features of my psychosis are auditory hallucinations in the form of several voices that I hear outside my head, some visual and tactile disturbances, and various paranoid delusions. At their worst the voices are very commanding and play into my delusions, and I sometimes see and feel bugs crawling under my skin. This often results in extreme distress until I try to "remove" them. Even when I am "well", I still hear voices daily, though they are completely inane, often unintelligible, and have ceased to bother me. I have been through enough rough patches to notice my warning signs early and take steps. I no longer take medication and I'm able to hold down a part-time job alongside my own pet portrait business, which helps keep me focused and goal oriented. I've also found exercise extremely important in maintaining both my physical and mental health, alongside good sleep habits. Although my mental health issues caused a fair amount of chaos through my early twenties, all the struggling definitely allowed me to become intimately acquainted with myself and how my mind functions and reacts to things'.

Social work and mental health

Mental health social work covers a broad spectrum of roles, and for developing practitioners this may feel confusing. There are specialist roles within mental health settings, but the core message in this chapter is mental health is integral to overall wellbeing and should be considered in every practice context.

Social work is about life, and life is complex. When capturing the necessary advice required to work effectively with people's mental health needs, it is important to acknowledge a fundamental starting point. Social work is a relationship-based profession (Davies and Jones, 2016); therefore, through every human encounter you can expect to engage in conversations about mental health and wellbeing. This means developing practitioners must foster confidence in having those conversations and understand how adapting your communication to individual needs is part of recognising how this differs for every person. Both Hazel and Sarah offer two very different perspectives.

Services are set up to provide a consistent point of contact and equitable access to treatment and support. This works at odds with the diverse nature of the human beings who access them, however, where the uniqueness and diversity of human experience struggles to be confined to neat service areas, diagnostic categories and well packaged solutions. Professional practice offers the opportunity to be the intermediary to systems, both finding ways to innovate and personalise the experience people receive to improve their wellbeing, but also recognising and challenging limitations organisational systems present in both health and social care. This is why conversations about mental health need to be universal.

Core principles of the legal framework

In social work, practitioners must be aware of the legal framework mandating their practice. In England, this primarily, but not exclusively, relates to duties and powers under the Care Act 2014. The various pieces of legislation, including Mental Capacity Act 2005 and Human Rights Act 1998, need to be seen as a tapestry with threads that are connected and weave together to help shape our understanding of the whole in order to advance the rights, or understand the extent of duties and powers.

Consideration of wellbeing has become part of Statute in adult social care through the Care Act 2014. This creates opportunity to think about mental health and people holistically when assessing their care and support needs. Mental health is part of who we are. It is a kaleidoscope of elements including life experiences, personality, environment, biology, survival or adaption strategies and systems. Humans are incredibly complex and what underpins wellbeing is as individual as a fingerprint. We also need to consider the influences of culture and ethnicity on wellbeing and how mental distress is viewed.

Activity 5.1

Think about your wellbeing and then consider the following reflective questions.

- Identify three things essential to your wellbeing.
- Think about a time in your life when your wellbeing has been affected. What has restored a sense of wellbeing to you?
- How do you sustain this in your life to help you keep your wellbeing in balance both personally and professionally?

S1 Care Act 2014 contains the duty placed on Local Authorities to promote wellbeing. Significantly, this requires practitioners to consider wellbeing in a broad range of areas, including relationships, day to day activity, contribution to communities or groups, finance, housing and health, recognising wellbeing as a pattern of components unique to each.

While statute tells us what wellbeing should encompass, defined under S1 Care Act 2014, how a practitioner interprets this, and the emphasis they place on different aspects contributing to the service user's overall wellbeing, is where an objective and subjective tension exists within the assessment process. What a person experiences (the subjective) may be different to what a professional observes (objective) and interprets from the encounter. Finding a way to bring those perspectives together to achieve the best outcomes for service users and carers is where effective engagement and assessment skills are needed. Both Hazel and Sarah offer insights into what has worked well for them, but also where that tension has presented in their contact with mental health services.

My experience of services?

Hazel: 'My dilemma: I am in an appointment with a mental health professional who may be able to give me assistance. Do I stay masked in order to fully articulate my issues, knowing full well that it will drain me so completely of energy that I will likely be melting down for days afterwards, or do I unmask and show the physical extent of my disability? If I unmask, I will likely be non-verbal and will rely on my carer to speak for me. Health professionals do not seem to like this, pushing me verbally until I am forced to use everything I have to put that mask back on, and answer their questions. I live in constant fear of being told that I must be faking this, even though when, all alone, I cannot speak or move or do anything but cry.

I cannot make comfortable eye contact when I meet new people or am in anxiety inducing situations. For most of my life, therefore, health professionals would direct not only their eye contact but their statements and questions at my primary caregiver rather than myself. Despite not being able to make eye contact, I was fully aware of the assumption I was unable to participate in my own appointment'.

Sarah: 'The mental health teams I have been with have mostly been fantastic. The two Early Intervention in Psychosis teams I had threw every resource they had at my recovery. The specialised nature of these teams made them really efficient and effective, something made painfully clear when I eventually transferred to the Community Mental Health Team and the standards of care dropped dramatically. I was then passed between numerous student psychiatrists, seeing them once or twice and retelling my whole story with distressing frequency. Eventually I felt like I just needed someone to check in with every couple of weeks, but this was not an option.

Luckily, someone in the team recognised how close I was to moving on and saw me personally for a set number of meetings before my discharge. She also introduced me to a local charity who helped to set up my business, which has since become a huge source of enjoyment and pride in my life. Sadly, the solution that presented itself was by no means the norm; the lack of time and care available on the NHS is particularly difficult for many people. Having spent so long working intensively with the Early Intervention Team I was fortunate to acquire various skills for managing symptoms, so the disruptions to my care had a minimal impact.

At my most unwell I did have a few hospital admissions lasting 7–10 days each. I was fortunate to go to a hospital that was local to my family. Though there was limited psychological input during my stays, I was kept safe at a time when I was not. Optional follow up sessions at the hospital, including art therapy, helped me transition back into "real life" and gave me structure. I later found similar structure and social interaction in various courses run by the Recovery College. Throughout my treatment I've taken any course or therapy offered to me, including an intensive ten-week 1 to 1 mindfulness course, confidence and wellbeing, coping with distressing symptoms (i.e., hallucinations, etc.), and more art therapy. I was desperate to gain some control over my symptoms and my life and these all helped me get to know myself and my illness a little better (Figure 5.1)'.

What challenges have I faced?

Hazel: 'I will describe what an autistic "meltdown" is like for me. Almost otherworldly vocalisations, complete loss of mobility other than to lash out violently at seemingly

Universal	As individuals, we may all look at factors impacting our wellbeing and seek informal support, or make changes in our lifestyle / relationships to improve our mental and physical health. We may sometimes experience a temporary crisis. This may resolve itself, or resolve with some low level support / advice / guidance whether from our existing networks or from other sources.
Primary	Sometimes formal 'help' is needed. All social work practice with adults includes a focus on mental health and wellbeing to promote independence and enable people to have choice and control in their lives. If there are health needs which require a level of professional intervention, these may be met at a Primary Care level (GP). This may include access to psychological interventions to promote better mental health.
Secondary	Integrated health and social care services for people with severe or enduring mental health challenges. For example, ongoing or chronic conditions which may require specialist opinion / management, or conditions such as schizophrenia, personality disorder, severe trauma, Complex PTSD / PTSD, mood disorder or dementia related illness. This is called Secondary Health Care.
Tertiary	Specialist services where particular expertise is required e.g. for people experiencing eating disorders, peri-natal needs or Early Intervention in Psychosis. This may also include specialist intervention or assessments relating to arrangements regarding an individual's care e.g serious decisions such as medical treatment or residence in the scope of the Mental Capacity Act (Liberty Protection Safeguards - LPS) or specialist assessment via the Mental Health Act 1983/2007, for example Community Treatment Order (CTO) or S7 Guardianship.
Acute	Acute or emergency mental health intervention e.g. from emergency services for situations where there is an immediate risk to health and safety, or concern for the protection of others. This may include urgent intervention via a Mental Health Act Assessment, at which point an Approved Mental Health Professional will become involved. This is the equivalent of A&E for physical health and is for emergency or immediate needs.

Figure 5.1   Understanding levels of mental health care

random moments, the loss of physical control resulting in saliva dripping down a chin and the completely uncontrollable screaming. Often, I am dehydrated, overheated, or past the point of sensory overload and into a new realm entirely. I am unable to communicate these needs past grunts, wiggling a finger, or blinking, if I am at all able to communicate. Here is what I wish to stress to you, reader – this horrid experience (and it is horrid, to the viewer and the experiencer alike) is one I am entirely aware of.

Whilst all control of my body has left me, I am often aware of everything. Every touch, every sigh of frustration, every moment of anger. When you have had enough and decide then to restrain or move me into a better position, better for you but undeniably more painful for myself, I am screaming for you to stop. Inside my head, I think in a strong reading voice, "Please, get me water. Please, please don't touch me. Please, please, please do not be mad at me for what we both know I cannot control". It is like losing myself and watching that identity of an empowered, intellectually articulate young woman slip away'.

Sarah: 'The main hinderances to my mental health care have been around the diagnosis I received from the Early Intervention Team at the end of my time with them: Emotionally Unstable Personality Disorder, aka borderline personality disorder. It's not a diagnosis I've really been able to understand for myself and yet it has haunted me throughout my treatment as it is a highly stigmatised label. Regardless of whether it is correct or not, it is frustrating to have people involved in my treatment make assumptions on the basis of my diagnosis, as it inevitably impacts the level of care I then receive, as well as often causing my most prominent psychotic symptoms to be overlooked.

Research summary

The International Classification of Diseases (ICD) 11th Edition (WHO, 2019) presents diagnostic categories for all mental health and physical health conditions and is used widely by professionals. For medical professionals, this guides diagnosis. The 11th edition was adopted in 2022. New revisions take account of changing perceptions of mental health diagnosis, so read them critically.

Sarah talks about her diagnosis of Emotionally Unstable Personality Disorder (EUPD) which relates to a diagnostic category in the previous edition, the ICD-10 (WHO, 1990). Borderline Personality Disorder relates to the equivalent diagnostic convention used in the United States in the Diagnostic and Statistical Manual, known as the DSM-5 (APA, 2013).

In the ICD-11, "Personality Disorder" is now grouped under the overarching label of "Personality Disorders and Related Traits".

Personality refers to an individual's characteristic way of behaving, experiencing life, and of perceiving and interpreting themselves, other people, events, and situations. Personality Disorder is a marked disturbance in personality functioning, which is nearly always associated with considerable personal and social disruption. The central manifestations of Personality Disorder are impairments in functioning of aspects of the self (e.g., identity, self-worth, capacity for self-direction) and/or problems in interpersonal functioning (e.g., developing and maintaining close and mutually satisfying relationships, understanding others' perspectives, managing conflict in relationships). Impairments in self-functioning and/or interpersonal functioning are manifested in maladaptive (e.g., inflexible or poorly regulated) patterns of cognition, emotional experience, emotional expression, and behaviour.

(WHO, 2019)

Sarah (continued): Another aspect of my care that could be better is informed consent. When I was first unwell I was put on anti-psychotics, and I was already on anti-depressants. These were fairly well explained in terms of what to expect. However, at my worst I was also prescribed something extra to help with anxiety – it was added in as a "let's give this a go". It did help, however when I was coming off my medications I struggled for months to taper this one down and I feel like if I had been better informed I may have declined it.

Furthermore, if my team had managed my expectations regarding treatment I could have been saved years of traumatic medication alterations, but at no point was it suggested that my symptoms would not be eradicated by these pills. It may seem like common sense, but I was so unwell and desperate to be rid of my symptoms that I was seeking the impossible. No wonder no medication hit the spot – I went from one to the next, increasing up to the maximum dose each time. It was only once I accepted the symptoms would likely stick around, I shifted my focus to learning to live with them and get on with my life. Things started improving. The best decision I made was advocating to come off all medication, even though it took 2 ½ years. I've since had periods that required a low dose of anti-psychotics to keep me stable, but mostly I'm free of medication and the horrific side-effects. Now, when I do go on antipsychotics, I know exactly which works best for me; a general idea of dose and how long it will take for me to feel stable enough to come back off them'.

What works well?

Sarah and Hazel: 'What do we want the social workers of tomorrow to know about working with someone with mental health issues? It's a massive question, but here are things we think apply to anyone working in mental health, and to social workers'. Below you can find our top tips for making a positive difference to people with mental health issues.

Figure 5.2 shows a word cloud, summarising Sarah and Hazel's top tips and issues to be aware of in your developing practice.

Meet with the person in front of you

Sarah: 'This usually involves asking people to disregard my diagnosis as its unhelpful for the stereotypes to be applied before I can get a word in. Another example that is far too

Figure 5.2 Top tips to remember in your practice

common to mental health patients is having our physical needs (say, a broken leg) ignored or circumvented by irrelevant questions about our mental health ("have you taken your meds today?", "are you hearing voices right now?"). This is also applicable to everyday situations when our mental health can be used to gaslight us'.

Listen to the perspective of people with lived experience and use this to inform your practice

Sarah: 'When you need to know about mental health please go directly to the source! Textbooks, academics, doctors are fine as a starting point, but they will never be as well informed as the person themselves. When historians talk about history, we prioritise the importance of "primary" sources, as opposed to the retellings of historians living after the time. The world is full of primary sources on mental health – make use of us! In this technological world it is easy to make contact with people. While we are only experts in our own experiences, we can still give a powerful insight into the ways mental illness can impact a person's life'.

Avoid fuelling the barriers mentally ill people face

Sarah: 'People with mental illness are often discredited for showing symptoms ("too ill") but are also discredited when not visually symptomatic ("not ill enough") – this can silence an entire community. If you can advocate for people under your care, and not fuel stereotypes to reinforce negative experience, it is a step in the right direction. Be creative and open in how you facilitate care and support, use the expertise of the individual. Sarah says "The things that helped most were the Recovery College, the kindness shown by someone who broke the normal care recommendations to see me through to discharge, and the connection made with a local charity". Think creatively to see where you can connect people to other resources for example, charities, activities, websites, and mental health advocates. Then you will be providing them with options for progress and encouraging an active role in their recovery'.

Create a calm, kind environment

Hazel: 'Nobody truly comes as they are to an appointment. Note that when a social worker sees a person with disabilities for the first time, be they physical or mental, they are never just seeing the person as they are in that room.

The professional is seeing the impact of the late timings, the extra minutes in the waiting room, or the traffic preceding. They are seeing that person in a new place who is, in turn, seeing a new person. They are seeing a person with a history of never being listened to, of never having had a straightforward experience of solutions presented, of potentially knowing that there is no chance of any kind of "cure" only, perhaps, a lessening of symptoms, of knowing they will be told there are no resources available. They are seeing the overwhelming noises and sights and smells, the uncomfortable waiting room chair, the children that may have brushed past, the hopelessness, the anger, the pain.

Being aware of the appointment environment. Being aware that it may be difficult for me, and you will not get everything you want. You may not know how much anxiety you may be contributing to the situation, please be self-aware'.

Treat people with humanity

Hazel: 'Be kind. If you take nothing else from what I have written, remember this: treat people with humanity. Let kindness and patience guide you and let curiosity be your mentor. You do not know our world. You may be able to make it easier. Treat everyone as individuals, and every day, do better. If you don't know, please ask me. At the beginning of a new relationship ask, "what will make a difference to you" or, how do you feel about eye contact?'

Understand and use genuine empathy

Hazel: 'Empathy is essential. You would be surprised how rare it is for me to know the person I am speaking with is on my side. I have been treated with cold detachment, discharged from my community mental health team during serious crisis, and told that there is neither the funding nor the specialist knowledge to assist me. I have been told by a counsellor, who, by the way, was no more able to help other than through listening, that they are with me, that they think the way I am being treated is abhorrent. This lifted, strengthened, and empowered me'.

Empower me in my recovery

Sarah: 'It was always reassuring to have a list of pre-prepared directions giving details of how I wanted to be treated should my capacity to make decisions fail me. For me, this meant keeping an up-to-date care plan and a document listing my current medications and the contact numbers for my parents, who knew my wishes regarding my care. For some people, particularly those without the luxury of such a strong support system, this may require further consideration and the appointment of a Lasting Power of Attorney'.

We have collated our top tips into a simple model – **ENGAGE** (Figure 5.3).

Activity 5.2

Consider the following questions for reflection and action:

1. How do you want to be remembered by the service users and carers you meet?
2. How do you want your practice to be experienced and what steps can you take to make that happen?

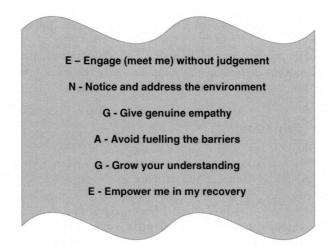

E – Engage (meet me) without judgement

N - Notice and address the environment

G - Give genuine empathy

A - Avoid fuelling the barriers

G - Grow your understanding

E - Empower me in my recovery

Figure 5.3 ENGAGE model

Chapter summary

Shaping your practice is a career-long endeavour. You will learn constantly and in unexpected ways. You may choose to specialise in the field of mental health practice, or another area of adult social work practice. However, in working with people, you will invariably encounter conversations about mental health.

This chapter has not been about providing a template for practice; it provides an opportunity for reflection. In concluding this chapter, we leave you with questions to reflect upon (see Activity 5.2).

We hope this enables you to think about how you want your practice to be experienced, and what you can do to make that difference to someone experiencing mental health difficulties.

It is with all this in mind that a social worker needs to approach meeting a service user, or carer, understanding nobody truly comes as they are in that moment. Seeking help exposes our vulnerability, but within any person looking for help, there is often a spark of hope that they will be heard and met with understanding. This creates an environment where positive outcomes can happen.

Annotated further reading

Hughes, M. (Ed.), 2019. *A Guide to Statutory Social Work Interventions: The Lived Experience*. London: Red Globe Press.
 This source provides further stories of lived experience in terms of the interface with Statutory Social Work Intervention. Essential reading for developing practitioners.

Kinderman, P., 2019. *A Manifesto for Mental Health: Why We Need a Revolution in Mental Health Care*. Switzerland: Palgrave Macmillan (Springer Nature Switzerland AG).
  This source provides a critical perspective on psychiatry to enable students to appreciate a bio-psychosocial perspective around mental health practice.

Tew, J., 2011. *Social Approaches to Mental Distress*. Basingstoke: Palgrave Macmillan.
  This source provides a social model perspective around mental distress and continues to be a key text in this area.

6

Working with the Mental Capacity Act 2005

Michael Lyne

Learning from experts by experience

This chapter is co-authored by Mike, who is a social worker, registered nurse and academic who specialises in the Mental Capacity Act 2005, and Zoe, who is an expert by experience. Zoe has experienced multiple involuntary admissions to hospital during which she has, on occasions, been assessed as unable to make certain decisions due to impaired capacity. This, combined with her mental health diagnosis, has had serious ramifications on her life. Zoe has shared her story with us to help illuminate the realities of this to support our understanding and learning regarding this very complex situation.

Chapter objectives

By the end of this chapter, you will be able to:

- Identify the five statutory principles contained within the MCA 2005 and how they apply in practice
- Understand the decision-making process in both straightforward and more complex situations
- Recognise the complexity of working with individuals who may not be able to make their own decisions
- Understand the need to keep the individual at the centre of the assessment and decision-making process
- Gain some understanding of the lived experience of removal of autonomy.

Important note: References to the law and Code of Practice are current at the time of writing. However, a revised Code of Practice is being consulted upon and is likely to be published in 2023. Content in this chapter might also be amended by the Mental Capacity Amendment Act (2019) when it fully comes into force.

Introduction

'Capacity' is the ability of individuals to make their own decisions. Decisions may range from simple everyday choices to major life changing decisions with legal ramifications. Making our own decisions is something many of us take for granted, and we practice decision making routinely without considering what might happen to us if we lose that decision-making ability. If that happens to us, we may need to fall back upon some of the provisions of the Mental Capacity Act 2005 (MCA or the Act).

The MCA has been described as 'a visionary piece of legislation' (House of Lords, 2014, summary). This chapter will look at the use of the MCA and will investigate the areas of practice which may be informed by capacity issues, the complexity of mental capacity work, how to remain person centred within the context of capacity and partnership work, including the role of the Office of the Public Guardian and the Court of Protection (CoP). It will draw upon the lived experience of a person who had their decision-making abilities removed upon admission to hospital.

The MCA Code of Practice states that everyone can assess capacity. It is equally true to say that capacity issues can affect everyone. Capacity and the MCA are often seen to be linked to older age groups and people with learning disabilities. This chapter will show that a far wider range of individuals may need to draw upon the Act's tools and mechanisms. While primarily reading this chapter from a professional point of view, it should not be overlooked that there is also a personal viewpoint that can be taken.

We will hear from Zoe throughout this chapter to learn from her lived experience:

I was put into a childlike state and before long you start to act like a child (Zoe talking about her experiences when decision making ability was removed from her.)

Using the MCA 2005

The foundation of the MCA are the five statutory principles to be found in Section 1. In brief, these are a presumption of capacity; the requirement to take all practicable steps to help the person make the decision; the understanding that an unwise decision does not indicate a lack of capacity; all decisions must be made in the person's best interests and consideration should be given to actions which are less restrictive of the individual's rights and freedoms (MCA s1 (2–6)).

When it becomes necessary to assess an individual's ability to make a decision, it is important to do this correctly. Following the decisions in *PC & NC v City of York Council [2013]* and subsequently reiterated in *A Local Authority v JB [2021]*, the process must start with the decision and whether the person can make it. Can they understand the information provided; retain that information; use and weigh that information and communicate the decision (MCA s3 (1) (a–d)). If they can do all those things, then they have capacity and should make the decision. However, should they not be able to do any of the above, then the assessor needs to ask, 'is this because they have an impairment or disturbance in the functioning of the mind or brain?' (MCA s2 (1)). If it can be shown that the inability to make the decision is because of the impairment, then the assessor will have displaced the presumption of capacity. This connection between the two parts of the process is known as the 'causative nexus'.

Zoe

Zoe relates an experience reporting an alleged rape to the police. Her complaint was taken no further after initial enquiries on the grounds that "she didn't have capacity to litigate." Unsurprisingly, Zoe feels this has had a profound impact on her life. "No-one listened to me, and no-one did a capacity assessment."

This feeling of not being listened to occurred frequently throughout our conversation along with Zoe's feelings that having a mental health diagnosis was taken as the equivalent of not being able to make her own decisions.

Once the presumption of capacity has been displaced, it will be necessary to make a decision on behalf of the individual. Professionals must check for the existence of an alternative decision maker before going any further. The individual may have donated Lasting Power of Attorney (LPA) for property and affairs and/or health and welfare to a family member, friend or solicitor, in which case the Attorney is likely to be the decision maker. The CoP may have appointed a Court Appointed Deputy in which case that person will be the decision maker. If the decision is in the realm of medical treatment, an Advance Decision to Refuse Treatment (ADRT) (MCA s24–26) may exist in which case, assuming it is valid and applicable, the ADRT holds the decision and must be followed.

Activity 6.1

Think about the steps you could take to identify the existence of an alternative decision maker. This might be particularly problematic in the case of ADRTs which, if not about life sustaining treatment, can be made verbally and are not required to be registered anywhere.

If the existence of an alternative decision maker is ruled out, then a decision will need to be made in the best interests of the individual (MCA s4). The decision maker will need to follow the best interests checklist set out in the Code of Practice. It is important to remember that the decision maker needs to consider the issues from the person's point of view rather than their own (*Aintree University Hospitals NHS Foundation Trust v James [2013]*).

For some decisions, if the individual is 'unbefriended' (DCA, 2007, 10.3), then the services of an Independent Mental Capacity Advocate (IMCA) will be required. And some decisions may well need to be made in the CoP. Therefore, capacity issues can affect most areas of practice. Professionals will be familiar with issues of capacity relating to adults with learning disabilities or with dementia, but it should be noted that the MCA applies broadly from the age of sixteen upwards. However, adults who have suffered trauma, Acquired Brain Injuries, serious mental disorders or a range of physical conditions may find their capacity questioned. In short, any situation which arises in which a person's cognitive processes may be impaired might give rise to questions regarding their ability to make their own decisions.

The principal areas where professionals may encounter decision-making difficulties are with health and welfare matters and in dealing with property and finances. The Courts have considered capacity in several areas. Ruck Keene et al. (2021) suggest that these areas include care, contact, contraception, deprivation of liberty, medical treatment, education, marriage use of social media and sex. They have very helpfully distilled information from various cases in court and have highlighted what information the court has considered relevant (and irrelevant) in those areas for assessment of capacity.

For instance, in relation to capacity to consent to marriage, information relevant to the capacity test is "1) the broad nature of the marriage contract. 2) the duties and responsibilities that normally attach to marriage. 3) that the essence of marriage is for two people to live together and to love one another and 4) that marriage will make any existing will invalid" (Ruck Keene et al., 2021, para 24).

It is important to ensure that you are providing the relevant information for the decision.

Activity 6.2

You decide to assess a patient's capacity to make a decision about going into long-term residential care. What information are you going to give the patient as part of the assessment in order to maximise their ability to choose?

(Read 39 Essex.com's Mental Capacity Guidance Note: Relevant Information for Different Categories of Decisions to check your thinking.)

The complexity of mental capacity work

Fluctuating capacity

In discussion with professionals, one area of difficulty which frequently arises is the area of fluctuating capacity. On the surface, assessment of capacity would appear to be straightforward. The assessor identifies the decision to be made and whether the person can make it using the four part 'functional' test set out in s3. If a best interest decision has to be made, this can be viewed as a 'cliff edge off which one falls into the clinging embrace of paternalism' (Ruck Keene, 2015). In truth assessing capacity can be a difficult and complex task.

> **Zoe**
>
> *Zoe started to significantly self-harm whilst in hospital when she started to feel powerless, and professionals made all the decisions on her behalf. She was told that she "didn't have capacity" and she relates this as feeling violated. "This (self-harming) was the only choice I could make" and "My major self-harming started when they took away my decision-making ability."*

For some people, capacity is not an 'either/or'. Capacity may be 'sometimes I can make my own decisions and sometimes I can't'. This is distinct from being able to make some decisions and not others. *In contrast to her comment above about professionals making decisions for her, Zoe also said that at one point when she was feeling suicidal, professionals told her that she had capacity to make her own choices. She questioned this at the time, 'have I? I'm suicidal!' and still questions it now, relating her feelings that the Act can be a 'bit of a joke ... they ask you to remember things. I struggle to remember what I had for tea'.*

The Act itself tries to anticipate fluctuating capacity by emphasising that capacity is time and decision specific (MCA s2 (1)) and that if a decision can wait, then it should (DCA, 2007, para 4.27). The speed of the fluctuation will be critical here. If it is fairly rapid, for example, some people may be at their best first thing in the morning before lunchtime medication, then the assessment should be undertaken in the morning. In situations of fluctuating capacity where the decision cannot wait then the assessor should carry out the assessment but record the need to repeat the assessment at a point when the person might have regained capacity (Farmer, 2017).

Executive dysfunction

'Executive dysfunction is a term for the range of cognitive, emotional and behavioural difficulties which often occur after injury to the frontal lobes of the brain. Impairment of executive functions is common after acquired brain injury and has a profound effect on many aspects of everyday life' (Headway, 2022).

This is also sometimes known as 'Frontal Lobe Syndrome' and can be another area where capacity assessment may not be straight forward. For example, George and Gilbert (2018) describe what they call the 'frontal lobe paradox' where the individual performs well in an interview situation such as a capacity assessment but shows impairment in everyday life. The intent may not match up with the action. They explain that difficulties will be more clearly observed outside of the interview setting. They also criticise the current process as assessing the individual's intent rather than their actual functioning. Ryan-Morgan (2019) suggests that it is important to observe the person in the situation the decision is being made about or interview those who have extensive knowledge of the person and about their behaviours in different settings.

Consultation with people who know the individual in daily life is, therefore, essential in order to be able to come to a conclusion regarding the person's capacity to make a decision. Ruck Keene et al. (2022) suggest that something which is essential to consider is whether the person is able to understand that there is a juxtaposition between how they may behave in a concrete situation when compared to talking about how they may react. This will impact upon the assessment of their capacity; if they cannot understand the information or weigh it up, if they are not able to put in place what they intend to do when talking/ hypothesising about the situation and if, in the moment, they are not able to put in place the information required, then they will be assessed as lacking capacity (Ruck Keene et al., 2022). An important codicil to this is that there must be a repeated mismatch between intent and action, and so repeated assessments of capacity are likely to be necessary.

Misunderstanding of the principles

In 2014, the House of Lords reported that:

> The presumption of capacity, in particular, is widely misunderstood by those involved in care. It is sometimes used to support non-intervention or poor care, leaving vulnerable adults exposed to risk of harm. In some cases this is because professionals struggle to understand how to apply the principle in practice. In other cases, the evidence suggests the principle has been deliberately misappropriated to avoid taking responsibility for a vulnerable adult.

(para 105)

This scathing comment refers to situations where professionals either assess individuals as lacking capacity when the professional perceives a need to get involved in that person's life or conversely where the professional states that the individual has capacity in order not to get involved in the person's life, something that Zoe has experienced. She feels that the Act is open to interpretation and could potentially be failing a lot of people. Zoe also questioned professionals' understanding of the difference between intelligence and capacity, saying, '*you know what to say to avoid professionals becoming involved*'.

As with many aspects of the Act, reference to the statutory principles can help navigate this issue. The starting point should be the presumption of capacity, but as the House of Lords points out, this can be problematic. To avoid this, professionals should remember that an assessment of capacity is not required unless two things exist. The first is that there needs to be a decision to be made. If there is no decision, then there should be no assessment of capacity. Capacity is time and decision specific.

The second thing that is required prior to an assessment is a trigger, a suspicion that the person actually cannot make the decision in question. A trigger may include an inappropriate response to a question, inappropriate behaviour in a certain circumstance or a series of repeated episodes of the above. In this category it is important to be careful of 'risk'.

Justice MacDonald stated, '. . .it is important not to use . . . repetitive risky behaviour to justify an assessment of lack of capacity' (*A Local Authority v RS [2020] para 52*). The judge also points out that, '. . .the repetition of risky behaviour can also indicate that a person has understood the risk, weighed it and decided to take it anyway notwithstanding the dangers' (2020, para 42).

In all circumstances, it is important to develop a relationship with the person being assessed as this is an effective way of understanding the person within their situation. In general terms, professionals should avoid assessing capacity on first meeting a person. A key skill here is listening. '*Nobody listened to me . . . I know what's best for me*' was a frequent comment in my conversation with Zoe.

And when an assessment of capacity is required, it is important to be honest with the individual. Zoe was told 'we're going to assess your capacity' on a number of occasions. Her response: '*What does that actually mean?*'

Family members and friends can be a useful source of support for the individual and a source of information for the professional. However, care needs to be taken to ensure that third parties are acting as support and not answering questions on behalf of their loved ones. A further area of difficulty here might be the use of coercion and control both by families and professionals. Individuals being assessed might want to 'please' the assessor or give an answer that they think the assessor wants to hear.

How to remain person centred when capacity is an issue

One of the easiest ways to remain person centred when using the Act is to practise using a human rights-based approach and to ensure that the five statutory principles set out in section 1 MCA are adhered to. As mentioned elsewhere, the primary purpose of the Act is decision making, and it must be remembered that if there is no decision to be made, then there is no need to assess capacity. This will help professionals avoid the trap of thinking that capacity must be addressed every time contact with an individual is made.

Section 1 (2) requires practitioners to assume capacity. This can be easier to say rather than to achieve. Getting to know a person on their terms and forming relationships, even if only for a short while, is always a good starting point in any practice setting. Within mental capacity work, it is that approach which may give rise to a suspicion that the individual is struggling to make a decision and that 'trigger' may then lead on to a formal assessment of capacity. What should not happen is a formal assessment of capacity the very first time the professional meets someone. Far from assuming capacity, this indicates that the professional believes the individual cannot make their own decisions and is setting out to prove it.

The second principle requires practitioners to make every effort to enable the individual to participate in the process. Professionals must consider what assistance the individual might need, and while some requirements may be obvious such as the use of interpreters with people whose first language is different from the assessors, other requirements may need the assessor to think much more creatively about potential solutions. The use of photographs, for instance, may be helpful if the individual is being asked to make a choice between one alternative or another. The key thing to remember is that it is what the individual themselves is going to find helpful, not necessarily what the professional believes should help.

The House of Lords was critical in its 2014 report about risk aversion in social care and paternalism in healthcare.

Activity 6.3

Are you a risk taker? Reflect on yourself as a person and practitioner. In your personal life, would you consider yourself to be risk averse or a risk taker? Repeat this exercise in your professional life.

Autonomy is a central facet of the Act. The freedom to make decisions or to appoint someone trusted to make decisions on one's behalf is perhaps the strongest aspect of the MCA. Professionals need to ensure that they are not removing this aspect by imposing either assessments of capacity or making decisions on the individual's behalf when someone else such as an Attorney is the decision maker. Zoe felt her loss of autonomy keenly and described turning to self-harm as the 'only thing I could control'.

Section 1 (5) reminds us that all decisions made on behalf of someone who cannot make it for themselves needs to be in their best interests. This applies to Attorneys and Deputies as well as professionals. But practitioners should not move directly from a finding of a lack of capacity to making a best interest decision. There is a stage to follow before this happens as shown in the flowchart below (Figure 6.1).

Checking for a valid and applicable Advance Decision to Refuse Treatment or for the existence of an Attorney is vital for ensuring that full consideration and weight is given to the individual's own wishes.

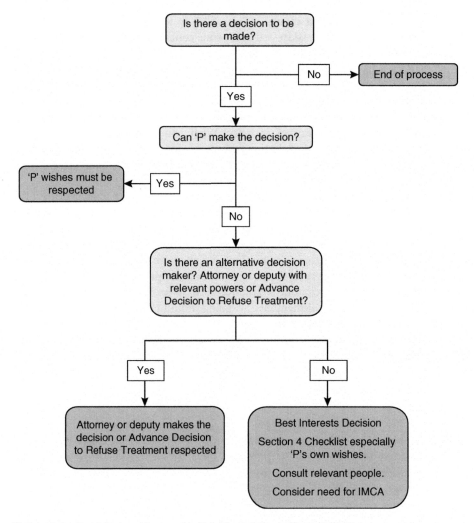

Figure 6.1 Decision making under the Mental Capacity Act 2005

In making any best interest decision, Baroness Hale, giving the lead judgement in *Aintree University Hospitals NHS Foundation Trust v James [2013]*, said,

The most that can be said, therefore, is that in considering the best interests of this particular patient at this particular time, decision-makers must look at his welfare in the widest sense, not just medical but social and psychological ... they must try and put themselves in the place of the individual patient and ask what his attitude to the treatment is or would be likely to be; and they must consult others who are looking after him or interested in his welfare, in particular for their view of what his attitude would be.

(para 39)

The importance of the words in bold reminds us that the best interests process needs to consider matters from the individual's point of view, not the professional or family member although family member's understanding of the person and what they would have wanted is extremely important. It is what the individual would have wanted which counts.

Partnership work including the role of the OPG (The Office of the Public Guardian) and Court of Protection

The MCA is designed to enable and protect individuals, but successful use of the Act requires an understanding of partnership work. 'Partnership' in this sense includes 'close relatives, friends or others who take an interest in the person's welfare' (DCA, 2007, p66). It also includes the individual themselves. Zoe's frequent complaints that she was not being listened to highlights the importance of this. Zoe also felt that having a history of mental health problems also counted against her: *'They believed other people rather than me because of my history'*.

Where the presumption of capacity has been displaced, professionals need to endeavour to understand what the individual themselves would have wanted in terms of decision making. This may not be easy to understand from the person themselves, and this is why consultation with other people who knew the individual is important. In *G v E (Deputyship and Litigation Friend) [2010]*, the judge reminded professionals that,

The Act and Code are ... constructed on the basis that the vast majority of decisions concerning incapacitated adults are taken informally and collaboratively by individuals or groups of people consulting and working together.

(para 57)

This collaborative approach extends to the two organisations which may provide a legal basis for action on behalf of a person who lacks capacity. The Office of the Public Guardian (OPG) 'helps people in England and Wales to stay in control of decisions about their health and finance and make important decisions for others who cannot decide for themselves' (https://www.gov.uk/government/organisations/office-of-the-public-guardian/about). The OPG does this in a number of ways including registering LPA and maintaining those registers, investigating concerns raised about Attorneys or Deputies and providing supervision to Deputies.

One of the most useful services that the OPG provides to professionals is the ability to ask for a search of the registers to discover whether an individual has a registered LPA or Court Appointed Deputy. This can be done by the completion of Form OPG100 available at https://www.gov.uk/government/publications/search-public-guardian-registers. There is also an urgent enquiries system for use, for example, in safeguarding cases.

The CoP makes decisions on behalf of individuals who cannot make them themselves in situations where a best interest decision may not be sufficient. Most decisions in the CoP are made by District Judges, but sometimes High Court judges can hear cases.

The types of issues brought before the Court include decisions regarding whether the individual has capacity or not, giving permission for people to make one-off decisions on behalf of an individual or appointment of Court Appointed Deputies for ongoing decisions, making decisions about Powers of Attorney and decisions regarding deprivation of liberty.

The Code of Practice suggests that an application to court may be necessary for 'particularly difficult decisions; disagreements that cannot be resolved in any other way or situations where ongoing decisions may need to be made. . .' (DCA, 2007, para 8.3). It is possible to make an urgent application to the CoP in cases relating to serious medical treatment, but even in those situations, the court expects family members to be involved in the hearing (CoP, 2020, para 24a). As a result of *An NHS Trust and others v Y [2018]*, it is no longer necessary to seek a court order confirming that it is no longer in an individual's best interest for life sustaining treatment to continue. This can now be made as a best interest decision although a court order will be necessary where 'the decisions is finely balanced, or there is a difference of medical opinion, or a lack of agreement as to a proposed course of action from those with an interest in the person's welfare, or there is a potential conflict of interest on the part of those involved in the decision-making process' (CoP, 2020, para 8 a–d).

Chapter summary

This chapter has considered the MCA in various areas of practice and highlighted some of the complexities that professionals may face. It has highlighted the importance of case law in changing practice and presented the reader with some questions to consider.

Zoe closes this chapter talking about the importance of getting to know the person being assessed: *'I don't think it's a good idea for tests to be done by people who don't know your normal behaviours. If I'm having a good day, then I've got capacity. But on my bad days I don't according to professionals. Police and medics don't care about capacity; it's social workers who are all over it'.*

Annotated further reading

Ryan-Morgan, T., 2019. *Mental Capacity Casebook*. London: Routledge.
   A collection of case studies providing practical guidance and legal commentary.

Farmer, T., 2017. *Grandpa on a Skateboard*. London: Rethink Press.
   More case studies looking at the complexities of assessment of capacity from a nurse's viewpoint.

Neary, M., 2013. *Get Steven Home*, lulu.com
   An account of getting the use of the MCA 2005 wrong and the impact on one family.

7

Working with substance use

Orlanda Harvey, Cathi and Seb

It all seemed normal to me.

(Seb)

Learning from experts by experience

This chapter has been co-written by Orlanda who is a social worker and academic and Cathi and Seb, experts by experience. It is impossible to do justice to everything social workers need to know about working with substance use in a single chapter. Consequently, by drawing on the belief that learning from the lived experience can help social workers develop a level of empathy around substance use, this chapter will be structured around the personal stories of the co-authors Cathi and Seb to support social workers to develop their understanding of the complexity of substance use.

Chapter objectives

By the end of this chapter, you should be able to:

• Explain how substance use can impact people in a variety of ways
• Understand some of the motivations for why people choose to use substances
• Explain why some people are more likely to be at risk for starting to use substances
• Explain some of the barriers for people using substances to access support services

---

Introduction

This chapter explores the impact of substance use on adults and discusses how the social construction of dependency affects service provision. Social workers from all areas of practice work with individuals affected by their own or other's substance use and sometimes feel unprepared to support this client group to manage risk (Galvani and Forrester, 2011).

For social workers, an understanding of substance use is important as people who use substances face risks to their physical and psychological health but may also take social risks such as driving under the influence, increased promiscuity and law-breaking (Heanue and Lawton, 2012). They could be at risk of harm from others, for example, being involved in sex trafficking (Walker-Rodriguez and Hill, 2011), experiencing domestic abuse (Stuart et al., 2009), or a risk to themselves from self-neglect or contracting blood-borne viruses (Nutt, 2012). There is also the possibility they may be a risk to others, for example, if they have children or are pregnant (Mactier, 2011). However, substance users should not be seen as a homogenous group. The risks that substance users face will differ depending on their substance of choice, knowledge of the substances, environment and network of support. Consequently, the purpose of this chapter is not to detail the range of substances used, the harms of each substance, or the interventions. Instead it will focus on the relevant practice-related issues through the lens of those with lived experience and explore the following themes:

• Motivations for Substance Use
• The Lived Experience
• Barriers to Support

Motivations for substance use

Substance abuse has been linked to childhood traumas such as sexual or physical abuse, bullying and neglect (Turner et al., 2013; Lindert et al., 2014). High-risk groups include the homeless, care-experienced children, sex workers, those excluded from school, young offenders, children whose parents use substances, those with mental health disorders and those who experience adverse childhood experiences (Lloyd, 1998; Villanueva and Gomis-Pomares, 2021). Cathi's story highlights the impact of adverse childhood experiences.

Cathi

I had quite traumatic childhood. My mum's last husband, my sisters' dad, died from a heart attack. I was 7 and my mum had a breakdown. He was the love of her life. I looked after my two little sisters. When I was 11, my mum got cancer, so I looked after her too. That responsibility was mine; there was no Race for Life, there was no facilities, no helplines, no support groups, nothing that there is now.

It was f*cking horrendous, I kept it together but there's only so much that someone can take. I had to cook. I didn't know where to go anymore, being so young and not having the tools to pay bills. How'd you do that? I did it, until I broke mentally. I just couldn't cope any longer. It was a facade I lied to the doctor and myself. I lied because I didn't want us to be split up and if we'd gone into care that would have happened. . ..
I became quite naughty, bunking off school. I had nobody to tell me to do anything. I was vulnerable. My mum was sick at home, so I listened to my record player and danced in the bedroom; it was my feel-good thing.

At 14, I met a man who got me involved in fraud. I loved dancing, so, I partied, smoked weed, hash and drank. I was living in a bedsit. I wasn't allowed back home; my mates were stealing food for me. My mum died when I was 16 and my sisters were placed with someone who physically abused them. I left my sisters; I've carried that guilt with me; it breaks my heart to think that I wasn't strong enough; still I was only a kid. I think if the right support had been in place then, my life might have been different.

A knowledge of risk and protective factors can enable social workers to identify potential risks related to substance use allowing practitioners to take both a preventative and harm minimisation focus. Risk factors of low self-control and peer drug use in young people can lead to an increased risk of using cannabis and alcohol into adulthood and protective factors; parent–child attachment, family church attendance can reduce risk (Lee et al., 2020). Cathi first encountered drugs through her love of dancing. Her initial motivations for use were a way to distract from the responsibilities she had taken on, to distance herself from the stress and trauma she was experiencing. Cathi notes that intervention at this time might have made a difference to her future. Seb had a different route into drug use but his motivations also link to his childhood experiences and social environment.

Seb

I was 10 when I started, I went to an All Stars training camp to play baseball and I blew out my knee, I had the worst day of my life. They gave me a load of painkillers. I felt bad about stuff in general and was very sad. I tried to talk to my dad about it. I said I'm depressed or something, and my dad, who is not the most supportive person in the

(Continued)

(Continued)

world, went 'maybe I'm depressed too', so there was no point talking to him. That was it when I took the painkillers I felt right. So, I started to take painkillers whenever I felt down or alone. When I was in my teens, my parents went through a nasty divorce, they pitted us against the other. I got drawn into arguments between them. My brother told me my mum asked him to live with her, but never spoke to me about it, so I told my dad I wanted to live with him. Then my mum, would walk into my room every morning before school and ask 'why don't you want to live with me, why do you hate me?' I wanted to get out of the house; so, I would go to school and wouldn't come home. I met guys from my neighbourhood who smoked weed, cigarettes and drank. They bought weed, and we all chipped in. I was good with money and thought well if I bought a bigger amount, I could sell to them, keep some and sell the rest. Inadvertently, I became a drug dealer. This was a thing I did; I made £120 working at a supermarket and £500 dealing drugs.

Relationship-based practice should be at the heart of social work, and embedded within this is the respect for the individual (Harrison and Ruch, 2007). In order to understand others, it is crucial that we also understand ourselves and are able to explore our own beliefs, values and attitudes fully. Activity 7.1 is a good place to start when it comes to understating our own beliefs and values around substance use.

Activity 7.1

Construct a mind map (Figure 7.1) with substance use at its heart: use it to map out and reflect on where your knowledge and understanding about substance use comes from, including:

- Your personal experiences
- Your family and friends' views
- The prevailing wisdom from your culture
- Your religion
- The influence of the press and social media
- Governmental policy

To effectively support people with substance use, it is helpful to understand their individual motivations for use (Galvani, 2015a) and to explore both the benefits and harms with them and their families; such an exploration also enables social workers to understand the person in their environment and the wider context of their lives (Galvani, 2015b). Cathi's and Seb's motivations for use are diverse and complex. Their stories share both the surface motivations aligned to how the drug use makes people feel in the moment and the sense of belonging to a social group, and the underlying motivations that come from a person's life experiences. The next part of Cathi's story highlights this:

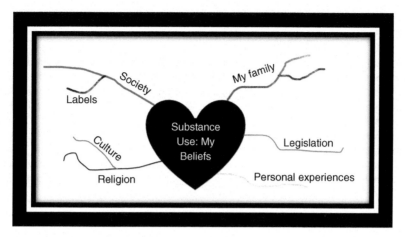

Figure 7.1 Mind map example

Cathi

Throughout my teens and twenties, I was on a roller coaster. After my mum died I went to Germany, to become an au pair. My brother lived out there. I went to a club, learnt to DJ and got a job DJ'ing. I met this American GI who was a drug dealer and money lender. That's when I started coke. I got nicked in Germany; luckily, I did just three months inside, but was banned from Germany for life. I returned to the United Kingdom and became a financial advisor in London. I went to raves and that was it; I started organising raves and selling drugs. It was fantastic. I was out every night, enjoying myself, being treated like a VIP.

I partnered with someone who left me in debt. I had a mortgage; I was going to lose my flat. I'd been a dealer before and saw a market. I was left to my own devices from a young age and I suppose taking chances was all I kinda knew and that's when I started smoking crack.

Here, Seb's story shows how someone's social circle can also influence a person's decision to use substances.

Seb

With my friends I was the butt of a lot of the jokes. The weed dealing died down. I still smoked weed and painkillers regularly. I started working the Doors at a club, working long hours, late nights and I noticed the guys were a lot bigger than me.

I was shredded solid muscle at 13 stone, I looked better than 90% of people there. I looked at some of the guys and their arms were huge. I worked in the most violent

(Continued)

(Continued)

nightclub in town, and everyone was on steroids. I didn't have much of a social life. The blokes I worked with took drugs, and one of the guys told me about how he trained and what he used. So, I started training and I got my steroids off a guy he knew. There were three or four of us who met weekly. We went into men's toilets and injected steroids.

I remember the first time I tried coming off drugs, I was in a car with a load of comedians doing a gig. One of them made a comment about how boring the journey was, and I thought when I'm on drugs, people think I'm a lunatic, I have fun; when I'm sober, not doing drugs, people think I'm boring and not fun to be around, that sucks; so I'll just do drugs and have more fun.

Seb's and Cathi's narratives evidence that once you learn that taking substances can help solve your immediate problems, then this reinforces substance use as a way to problem-solve across other areas of your life.

The lived experience

Learning from the lived experience of service users can help social workers to develop empathy connected people's experiences of substance use. Here Cathi's story gives us insight into what happens when a fun pastime becomes a dependency.

Cathi

Then the addiction set in. I was a closet smoker, no one knew I was doing it because it was seen as a dirty drug. I'd go out raving, up till 11/12 smoking, sleep, work, my health started to fail, I lost a lot of weight, started to get paranoid and aggressive. I could see my personality was changing, but I couldn't stop.

When you use coke, you can experience four hours of paranoia when you're coming down. Once you stop, you've got four hours minimum of mental torture, and that is where people then end up going out, robbing, ending up having the panic attacks in the hospital. You don't think of that when you want the high. In the beginning, you get euphoria, but the more you smoke, the paranoia sets in a lot quicker and it is horrible, senseless – that's when you know you're an addict.

It is worth noting that not everyone will become dependent and there is evidence to suggest that some people are more vulnerable to certain substances, as there are behavioural traits, environmental, age, and other societal and cultural factors that can impact (Nutt, 2012), and this seems to be the case for Seb.

Seb

I got bigger and people noticed. I got a lot of interest from girls. We had loads of fights all the time. I did not like violence growing up, but I was good at it and was known for violence. I'd had a group of friends who would take advantage of me, and I didn't want that to happen anymore. I thought if people saw me destroy others, then they would think 'that is someone who I would not want to mess with'. It was a defensive thing to keep people at bay. I think part of it was down to trust issues and people. The bigger I am, the more protected I feel, the more confident. It was like building my own personal armour.

I started using cocaine. I think it was because a girl in a bar had asked me back to her place, and then offered me some which opened the floodgates. I used about half an ounce a night. I took steroids weekly without really coming off cycle properly; we used cocaine whenever we partied two or three nights a week. I drank heavily. I was doing cocaine and painkillers all the time. I took Valium to come down so I could sleep. There were times when I wanted to end it all and would overdose on stupid amounts of Valium.

In Cathi's and Seb's stories we see two different perspectives on the impacts of dependency. Such complex and challenging narratives raise questions around both what support society can offer to people in such situations and also what might stop people accessing support.

Barriers to support

When it comes to our general understanding of drug use, we are impacted by our social and cultural environments. Views on different types of substance use can change over time, causing intergenerational judgements, as different perspectives are taken by each generation, for example, perceptions by some British Asian communities relating to Skunk cannabis is potentially undergoing a process of normalisation (Williams, Ralphs and Gray, 2017). Popular stereotypes of drug users are often influenced by depictions in the media, and the following activity gives you an opportunity to explore your own ideas about how substance users are portrayed in mainstream media.

Activity 7.2

Imagine you are a film maker and have been tasked with making a film about substance use:

- What would the plot be about?
- Which audience would you be targeting and why?
- What title would you give it?

(Continued)

79

(Continued)

- What angle would you take?
- What influences your creative thinking?
- What would be the main story arc?

Social media stories impact social problem construction around drug use and reinforce dominant constructions such as criminal punishment, enforced treatment and a form of 'badness' (Tiger, 2015). Some scholars, for example, Klein (2011) and Nutt (2012), argue that it is not just the Government, with their 'all drugs are bad' message and the negative depictions in the media that create a narrative of misunderstanding and fear but also some academic literature. Being labelled as chaotic or deviant can reinforce discrimination and lead to an internalisation of such labels which becomes a barrier to recovery and support seeking (Story, Shute and Thompson, 2008) and we can see this in Cathi's story.

Cathi

When I went to hospital, after experiencing a panic attack or for a drug related side-effect, the way they looked at me was quite judgemental. They didn't know me – or how I got to that stage.

Professionals need to have that insight to see that people have histories and not judge people just for the fact that they are taking drugs. Addicts come in all shapes, sizes, cultures, whatever, it's not just the homeless person in the street.

Stigma is one barrier for those wishing to access treatment services (Ezell et al., 2021), as accessing treatment can be shaming and shameful (Radcliffe and Stevens, 2008). There are also practical barriers such as conditions to attend counselling sessions to obtain methadone (Lloyd, 1998). Furthermore, the next part of Seb's story illustrates how professionals' attitudes and the very nature of support offered can also be a barrier.

Seb

I went to a couple of AA meetings with my friend, I'm not a religious person, and it was all about a higher power. I thought this ain't gonna work for me. My mum offered to pay for me to go to a proper Rehab Centre, where I could get counselling. And I just said no because I didn't want to explain to people why I've disappeared for four weeks to go there. It's not anyone's business, but mine. But you can't miss weeks of employment and not tell people.

Social workers need to know about the types of interventions that can be useful when working with people who use substances and that not one size fits all. Common interventions include individual support using change models such as motivational interviewing and peer support groups, and where resources allow 'live-in' rehabilitation programmes. For Cathi, her imprisonment was the catalyst for change supported by the regime of being in live-in rehab centre.

Cathi

Getting nicked the second time was the best thing that happened to me because then I went into the rehab for 16 weeks and got the help I needed. It was Monday to Friday, nine to four; it showed me where I was going wrong, what I was doing to myself and what I was doing to others. I'd had enough. I'd been a criminal from the age of 14–31; seventeen years was enough. I was lucky, a friend gave me a job and my life turned around.

For Seb, the catalyst was more of just a 'lightbulb' moment.

Seb

I was in the kitchen at a party, and I looked around and thought what are you doing to yourself? This is stupid, you need to stop. So, I stopped. I had one relapse since then. I now work as a trainee carpenter and restorer. I love it. It's a normal job. I've got two powerlifting competitions and a strongman competition coming up. I coach a certain group of MMA fighters the strength and conditioning work, I travel, do stand-up comedy and have written an autobiography (James, 2016).

I don't count steroids as drug in that sense; I now take very controlled doses and keep everything in balance. Everything I do is much like a professional athlete, I have recovery treatment, I have phases on, phases off, we do my aftercare correctly, we do my blood work, I see my doctor, I have a treatment protocol, and I don't take any painkillers. I've not done that in years. I stopped the cocaine. I wish I could do all the stuff I'm doing now without steroids to be able to say I achieved this naturally, that would be something.

Steroids helped take away a lot of other things for me that were far worse and far more destructive to my lifestyle and gave me something to focus my life on. I'm a lot more comfortable within myself.

The social constructions around drug use also impact on Government policy and service provision. Political decisions can hinder public health messages and will ignore scientific evidence if it does not align to social norms, political policy or strategy. For example, the challenges faced by services to fund evidence-based effective harm minimisation strategies such as the provision of naloxone (McAuley et al., 2012) or self-consumption rooms (Lloyd and Godfrey, 2010).

One of the major impacts of the negative social constructions around use is a lack of willingness to fund services as many in society do not see this group as deserving of support, and this is evidenced here through Cathi's experiences.

Cathi

There are not enough support workers. The majority of the services has to prioritise what they consider high risk, so someone who is kicking off, getting arrested all the time, but people who are deciding to rebuild their life and need some help in order to do that, there just doesn't seem to be anything there.

You go to hospital, they physically help you come down, you're offered some sort of help, but it never comes to anything, there is nothing there. What is needed is programmes where people can actually be looked after, receive guidance, support to attain an education or get a job.

You become vulnerable, you lose yourself when you're in that world; you're dealing with criminals and other drug addicts, that's your world. It's very difficult to go into normal society and have confidence to deal with normal people and do normal things. You need to change who you hang around with, otherwise you're just going to keep relapsing and there is no facility for that. I know that there are addiction groups but there is not a lot of people who want to go in a group setting, and having counselling once a week, that's one hour a week, what can you do with that?

Risk management

Social workers need the necessary skills and willingness to undertake the required research to manage risk and building a level of trust with the service user to gain an understanding of the use from their perspective. Key to risk management is to ensure we do not make assumptions about people, and to have an awareness that substance use is often overlooked in certain groups of people. For example, those with disabilities and older people, as these are outside the social norms. This relationship with those offering support is key as Cathi's perspective shows. If you now work through the related Activity 4.3, this asks you to reflect on your own development aligned to her expectations.

Top tips: Cathi's perspective

What should social workers know...

- **There is always hope**
- Never judge anyone: you do not know how they got where they are
- Listen and have empathy
- Be kind, patient and understanding
- Be informed of the help they may need
- Try to understand them as a person not just as an addict
- Often, drug users portray their addiction as not as bad as it really is
- They may relapse many times before getting clean, if at all
- **Do not make promises – this is key.**

Activity 4.3

Think about the statements from Cathi above related to the knowledge that the service user want from social workers. . ..

- How might you show some of the qualities needed?
- What challenges do you see in meeting these requests?
- What support might you need to do this?

Having the privilege of working with Cathi and Seb and hearing their stories has reinforced my own belief that having sense of curiosity and capacity for empathy are at the heart of social work practice.

In conclusion, the motivations behind people's choice to use substances are often complex and very individual. Social workers need to use a person-centred approach when working with people who choose to use substances and be aware of both the risk to starting and continuing use, aware of strategies to support harm minimisation and have an understanding of the possible comorbidities that often go hand in hand with substance use.

Chapter summary

This chapter explored how substance use can impact people in a variety of ways, and the lived experiences of Seb and Cathi highlight the complexity of motivations around why people choose to use substances. It discussed the risks for starting use and also explored the social worker's role in managing risk. This chapter also identified several of the barriers for people using substances to access support services. It highlighted the importance of having a knowledge of key interventions for working with this population and an understanding that due to the complexity of substance use 'one size' does not 'fit all'. The chapter concluded with an exploration of the skills that social workers need to develop when working with those who choose to use substances.

Annotated further reading

Nutt, D., 2012. *Drugs – Without the Hot Air: Minimising the Harms of Legal and Illegal Drugs.* Cambridge: UIT Cambridge.
   This text offers an accessible introduction to the different types of substance used and an exploration of their harms.

Crome, I., Chambers, P., Frisher, M., Bloor, R. and Roberts, D., 2009. The relationship between dual diagnosis: Substance misuse and dealing with mental health issues [online]. Available from: www.scie.org.

This short brief gives a clear explanation of one of the most challenging aspect of substance use and something that social workers needs to be very mindful of: the presence of underlying mental health problems.

Hughes, M., 2019. *A Guide to Statutory Social Work Interventions: The Lived Experience.* London: Red Globe Press.
This text provides real-life accounts of how it feels to experience statutory social work interventions within a variety of settings and is helpful to those seeking to understand and learn from the lived experiences of service users.

8

Working with marginalised adults

Chris Kidd with Jo, Keith and Marie

Learning from experts by experience

The authors of this chapter have worked collaboratively to share their lived experiences, and how their ethnic and cultural identity has impacted the way they access and engage with health and social care. Jo, Keith and Marie are members of Gypsy, Traveller and Roma (GTR) communities, and their voices are embedded in the main text and were especially keen to express top tips for practice. Lady-Jacqueline was a pillar of the Kennet and Avon boating community and is sadly no longer with us. Chris is a social worker with extensive experience of working with members from nomadic communities and in addition, the Gypsy, Roma and Traveller Social Work Association, of which he is a member, has contributed to the development of this chapter.

> ## Chapter objectives
>
> By the end of this chapter, you should be able to:
>
> * Identify some of the challenges that nomadic communities have in accessing care and support
> * Recognise how the Care Act 2014, and related legislation and guidance, can support members of Gypsies, Roma and Traveller communities access health and social care support
> * Identify top tips for practice to enable culturally relevant work alongside individuals and families
> * Understand the importance of the 'voice' and participation of Gypsies, Travellers and Roma in the way services are designed and delivered

Introduction

Social workers are required to challenge the ways in which individuals and institutions discriminate against others (BASW, 2014; IFSW and IASSW, 2018) and use their available resources to support marginalised and oppressed people (Baines, 2017; Ryde, 2019). This chapter will explore how social workers can work in anti-discriminatory and anti-oppressive ways with people from ethnic minority communities and specifically members of the GTR communities. This chapter has been written in partnership with three families from GTR communities who have engaged with services in Wiltshire.

GTR communities are some of the most marginalised and vilified in society (Mayall, 2004; Taylor, 2014). The Holocaust (Hancock, 2007), attacks on Roma across the former Soviet bloc, expulsion of Roma from Italy and France leading to statelessness (Gonzales et al., 2019), as well as high-profile evictions of Irish Travellers from Dale Farm in the United Kingdom (Tyler, 2013) all demonstrate how GTR communities' presence remains highly contested. We will now begin this chapter with a reflective activity focussing upon GTR communities and stereotypes.

Activity 8.1

At the start of this chapter, take a moment to list some of the different things you know about GTR communities. Has anything you listed surprised you? Where has your knowledge come from and are there any stereotypes from the media?

Key definitions

The term 'Gypsies and Travellers' encompasses a range of groups with different histories, cultures and beliefs including: Romany Gypsies, Welsh Gypsies, Scottish Gypsy

Travellers and Irish Travellers. Furthermore, there are numerous subdivisions based on family groups and religion; for example, ethnographers have identified 60 different Roma groups in Bulgaria (Revenga et al., 2002).

There are nomadic communities who do not fit under these headings, often regarded as 'cultural' rather than 'ethnic' Travellers (Belton, 2005). For example, New Travellers (also known as New Age Travellers) and Travelling Showmen or Fairground Travellers, who are commercial nomads moving from town to town during the fair season (Wills, 2020), and boaters or waterway travellers. In Britain, the term Gypsy/Traveller/Roma is often used inclusively and to highlight the history of the different communities. Most crucially, the definition should not exclude those who are currently settled and/or presently living in houses (Clark, 2006; Cemlyn et al., 2009; Ryder et al., 2014) because the lack of halting or transit sites has effectively forced nomadic communities into permanent accommodation. An estimated two-thirds of UK Gypsies and Travellers currently live in permanent accommodation. The transition away from a nomadic lifestyle is associated with the break-up of social networks and psychological distress, alongside difficulties in adjusting to behaviours associated with life in housing, such as requirements to pay household bills (Smith and Greenfields, 2015).

With the transition into housing, GTR become less readily distinguishable from the 'White British' population, thus diminishing awareness of their protected ethnic minority status (Bhopal and Myers, 2008). It is also important to note that both 'Gypsy' and 'Traveller' can be perceived as pejorative, and this can also change depending on circumstances. For example, Clark (2006, p13) notes that in the early 1990s some Scottish Travellers began to adopt and use the term 'Gypsy/Traveller' to distinguish themselves from the English New Travellers who attracted attention from the press and police.

The terms GRT (Gypsies, Roma, Travellers) and GTR (Gypsies, Travellers, Roma) are widely used and the debate on use of collective terms has been ever-changing; there is a perception that GRT is a term assigned by authority (Ryder et al., 2014; Corradi, 2018). It has been argued that the use of either acronym encourages Gypsy, Roma and Traveller communities to work together and recognise common traits and experiences. However, as noted in the Commission on Race and Ethnic Disparities (2021, p32) 'it is demeaning to be categorised in relation to what we are not, rather than what we are' and the use of an umbrella term can disguise the diversity (Ryder et al., 2014) and differing outcomes of these communities (Commission on Race and Ethnic Disparities, 2021).

For this chapter, GTR (Gypsies, Travellers and Roma) will be used as an inclusive term, which includes all ethnic Gypsies and Travellers plus members of the settled community who have adopted a nomadic lifestyle. This is not intended as a political statement but as a pragmatic recognition that nomadism or semi-nomadism presents certain common issues regardless of who is adopting that pattern of life.

Social work and the Gypsy, Traveller and Roma community

As with many other professionals, there is evidence of a lack of trust between social workers and GTR communities (for example, Cemlyn, 2008; Greenfields et al., 2014; Saltiel and Lakey, 2020). This is frequently due to ill-equipped and unsupported professionals who have limited cultural knowledge and training and work within the pressures of statutory time scales (Allen and Riding, 2018) alongside widespread discriminatory attitudes and stereotypes about both GTR communities and social workers (Allen and Hulmes, 2021). A lack of understanding and validation of GTR culture and lived experience can lead to poor responses and the problems the communities experience as only related to cultural and lifestyle issues rather than wider systemic problems (Cemlyn, 2000c). For example, the outcry when nomadic communities temporarily stop on unauthorised encampments and the concerns for those individuals and the wider public are highlighted rather than the structural issue that there are very few transit or stopping sites. Furthermore, an ignorance of cultural strengths (Cemlyn et al., 2009), such as kinship community support, is at odds with current focus on strengths-based practice (Saleebey, 2013).

Introducing Lady-Jacqueline Aster and her care and support journey

Lady-Jacqueline Aster was a pillar of the Kennet and Avon boating community for many years, living on Aster, a 72-foot canal boat. Aged 40, Lady-Jacqueline was diagnosed with adrenal cortical cancer and her subsequent experience of care and support helps us in understanding the ways legislation and social work practice can lead to a meaningful and personalised experience for members of GTR communities and other marginalised people.

Assessment of needs

As Lady-Jacqueline's condition progressed, a section 9 (1) Care Act 2014 care and support assessment was undertaken to identify her care and support needs and what outcomes could maintain or improve her wellbeing. The fact that Lady-Jacqueline is nomadic has no impact on who is responsible for completing this assessment, as unlike in other areas of social policy such as housing, it is not a requirement to be 'ordinarily resident' in the local authority area, that element is only dealt with if an adult has eligible needs (see DoHSC, 2022, paragraph 6.134).

Lady-Jacqueline was clear that she did not wish to continue with invasive medical treatment but wanted to be at home, feeling as well as possible for as long as possible. The assessment was conducted and showed that Lady-Jacqueline needed practical support to manage the day-to-day tasks involved in living on a boat as well as meeting her healthcare needs.

Following the determination of eligibility (detailed in Chapter 2), is establishing whether the adult meets the ordinary residence requirement (S 13 (4) Care Act 2014). Section 18 (1) (a) of the Care Act specifies that the local authority is required to meet needs only in respect of an adult who ordinarily resides in the authority's area or may not be settled in the area but is present there. The Care Act 2014 does not define ordinary residence, which can cause confusion when working with nomadic communities. The statutory guidance does, however, provide clarity as paragraph 19.14 (DoHSC, 2022) states that local authorities must have regard to Shah v London Borough of Barnet (1983) in which Lord Scarman defined ordinary residence as: 'a man's abode in a particular place or country which he has adopted voluntarily and for settled purposes as part of the regular order of his life for the time being, whether of short or long duration'. Lady-Jacqueline's allocated social worker was able to use the statutory guidance to evidence how regardless of her nomadism she was eligible for the provision of services.

Care and support planning

Care and support plans need to summarise all that has been decided in the previous stages of the assessment, as well as setting out how needs are to be met. The statutory guidance (DoHSC, 2022, paragraph 10.2) is clear that care and support plans should be person-centred and it should 'belong' to the person it is intended for.

Paragraph 10.48 (DoHSC, 2022) of the guidance stresses the importance of people being 'allowed to be very flexible to choose innovative forms of care and support, from a diverse range of sources'. This led to Lady-Jacqueline being one of the first live-aboard boaters to successfully negotiate 'reasonable adjustments' from the Canal & River Trust under the Equality Act 2010 on the grounds of disability, as the result of becoming ill. Having completed the assessment, Lady-Jacqueline was given a personal budget by her social worker. This worked well for Lady-Jacqueline:

> **Lady-Jacqueline**
>
> *I've got to the point now where I need carers, and they are all boaters. I employ them myself using the budget provided by my social worker. They know how things work on a boat. It's a completely different way of living to being in a house; you have to be careful not to use too much water or power. And emptying the chemical toilets ... I can't see an agency carer going 150 yards down the towpath with my bicycle and trailer and a plastic bucket of poo. There are jobs where you need to know what you are doing, like cleaning all the ash out of the stove and filling the coal scuttle up; carers have to be prepared to lift a bag of coal, and not mind if their hands get a bit dirty.*

Tips for the provision of culturally appropriate care and support

The following tips have been developed following conversations with those from GTR communities and the Gypsy, Roma and Traveller Social Work Association:

- Those from GTR communities often have a strong preference for carers from within the same community.

- Many GTR carers would not identify themselves as 'carers' and may not be aware that they themselves can receive support. Many GTR carers will not attempt to access support if they do not feel the service being offered is culturally appropriate.
- Those from GTR communities may have strong preferences around the gender of the person caring for them, especially if intimate care is required.
- Those from GTR communities can have limited literacy skills but may be reluctant to admit this leading to an inability to fill in forms, or, for example, menus to order food when in hospital.
- Do not underestimate the psychological distress and unfamiliarity for those from nomadic communities being placed inside bricks and mortar for hospital and palliative care.

The following activity is designed to deepen your thinking, understanding and reflections regarding cultural identity.

Activity 8.2

We all have a cultural identity and associated needs. For example, many people's diet is informed by religious or ethnic traditions. Identify a time when your cultural needs were not met; what were your thoughts and feelings about this experience?

The purpose of this exercise is to help readers understand a small part of the experience of discrimination and oppression members of the GTR communities face daily.

Tips around cleanliness and hygiene

- Gypsies and Travellers tend to maintain very high levels of cleanliness to prevent cross-contamination. For example:
  - One bowl for washing up, one bowl for cleaning trailers, etc., another for washing the body and some people keep another bowl for washing the face too.
  - Animals and other domestic pets would not normally be housed with the family
  - May use bleach in washing up, which can cause problems with other residents
- When staying in hospital, a hospice, residential care or other accommodation members of GTR communities may worry about not being able to stick to such standards. For example, staff breaching cultural hygiene rules if they place cleaning equipment on tables where patients or residents eat.

End of life care

Within a palliative and end-of-life care context, social workers may deploy a range of skills and techniques pertinent to the changing situation of the client. Sheldon (2000) identified six categories in the role of the palliative care social worker:

- A family focus – communication and relationship issues
- Influencing the environment – practical help and liaison
- Being a team member – role boundaries and collaboration
- Managing anxiety – of family, colleagues and self
- Values and valuing – non-judgemental, empowerment and anti-discriminatory
- Knowing and working with limits – assessment and open communication.

The list above is about professional values and methods of practice, and the following Activity (8.3) will engage you in the values you express through your practice and the way you build rapport with individuals and their wider networks.

Activity 8.3

Do an online search for Human Systems Emotion Wheels (https://humansystems.co/emotionwheels/). Scroll down and look at Emotion Wheel III, Uncomfortable Emotions. Consider a time when you lost a loved one or someone one close to you. Use the wheel to identify the emotions you experienced. If you were a social worker supporting someone in this situation, how would you want them to perceive you?

Lady-Jacqueline spoke about the importance of clear communication so she could be prepared for when her death was coming.

Lady-Jacqueline

I have asked for regular scans so I can be prepared, and at some point I'm going to look at a scan and know I haven't got long. I've got it all sorted, and I've had some laughs planning my funeral with family and friends. I will be supported to die at home, and then I want to do things the old-fashioned way: I want my body to be kept on the boat for a few days. I will go down the canal on my friends' beautiful wooden launch to trumpets played by musicians from the community and a procession down the towpath. I have friends who are performance artists and who have a hearse covered with skeletons and green lights, and that will take me from the canal to the burial ground. I can have it exactly how I want it.

In the last decade, there has been challenge to the model of hospice care for promoting the professionalisation of dying, and therefore, excluding family and community expertise (Brown and Walter, 2014). Many GTR families care for family members at the end of life (Okely, 1983; Liegeois, 2005). This might involve staying with loved ones in hospital although often caring for someone at home is preferred if the health condition will allow.

Barriers to good end of life care for GTR communities include poor provision for visiting family members, cultural clashes with staff and other patients, distress experienced by people with limited literacy skills, and unfamiliarity with being inside bricks and mortar (Jesper et al., 2008; CQC, 2016). These all contribute to members of the GTR communities frequently choosing to discharge themselves early from hospital as they feel like a 'fish out of water' (Jesper et al., 2008, p8).

Recognising that providing care to family members is an important part of the culture of nomadic communities means that social care and health providers need to enable people to care for their family members and not remove these duties and responsibilities away from them.

Tips for end-of-life care

- It is common for an extended family to travel to offer support and pay respects; make plans to support the extended family visiting where possible.
- Identify one family member who can act as a contact person for the wider family.

Traditions around death and bereavement

GTR families and communities live in close physical proximity; typically families will see each other daily, making the loss of a close relative particularly intense not just for the family but also for the wider GTR community (Rogers, 2016). This intensity of feeling makes death a very important part of GTR lives, demonstrated through a deep commitment to and respect for both those approaching the end of their lives and the dead. The increased practice of memory-making, previously the domain of pregnancy loss or the death of a child, for example, crafting hand or footprints, locks of hair and photographs as a means of connection and ongoing bond is helpful for families (Thornton et al., 2020; Fox et al., 2021).

When a member of the Gypsy community is dying or has died, the family will want to take the person or body home. The physical place of death holds particular significance for Gypsy and Traveller communities, in contrast to sedentary society where the place of birth is a primary marker for identity (Rogers, 2016). Death rituals and beliefs are influenced by cultural heritage and tradition, of which many are linked to religion (Okely, 1983; Liegeois, 2005). This is particularly evident among English Romani Gypsies and may include a strong belief in ghosts (or 'mulo'). Frequently, a vigil is kept over the body by family members, with the deceased usually laying in an open coffin so that the family can see their loved one for the last time and pay their respects. Following death and prior to a funeral, there will be a constant flow of visitors who come to pay their respects to the deceased and their family. Often death rituals are designed to protect the living from the return of the ghost or spirit of the deceased, as in the practice of 'sitting up' or not leaving the deceased alone from the moment of death until the funeral.

Historically all the possessions of the deceased would have been burnt, but today the trailer and any valuables are more likely to be sold to the non-Gypsy (Gorger) population. Furthermore, Okely (1983) suggests that the practices of the destroying possessions and the destruction of property are also linked to the belief that deaths (and birth) are polluting events and the burning of belongings is a cleansing process. Often, the deceased is not mentioned again by name after death, instead referred to by the relationship to another family member, such as Mary's dad. Photos of the deceased are also often removed from the public view, which Okely (1983) suggests is to prevent the return of the '*mulo*'. Close family members will wear black following a death in the family; this can often last for a year following the death of close family members. Women will often wear completely black and men will often wear a black tie or band.

The need for genuine community engagement

Community engagement has the potential to enhance trust (Gilchrist, 2019; Herbert, 2020) and ensure services are tailored to the needs of specific populations (Ledwith, 2016; McFadden et al., 2018). An example of good practice worthy of wider consideration is currently under development in Wiltshire, a county in South West England. In response to a recent Health Needs Assessment of the Gypsy, Roma and Traveller communities in the area (Wiltshire Council, 2019), the council has identified seven priorities for service development. Together, these priorities aim to enable the council to facilitate specific models of community engagement and promote sustainable opportunities for social change for Gypsy, Roma and Traveller people.

One specific project utilises an established Gypsy and Traveller Exchange model (Kings Fund, 2018). Advancing emancipatory theories of participation and co-production (Freire, 1972), the council is now supporting Gypsy, Roma and Traveller people to take a leading role in deciding how services should work, in planning what further research is needed and in agreeing what actions the council can take to achieve their service development priorities. For social work practice, the Gypsy and Traveller Exchange model is being embedded because of its potential to enhance trust and to ensure services are tailored to the needs of specific Gypsy, Roma and Traveller adults and their wider families.

Chapter summary

This chapter has highlighted some of the challenges people from ethnic minority communities may face when engaging with health and social care. This has been done through the lens of GTR, although the issues raised are applicable to a diverse range of people and areas of practice. Social workers need to do more to develop better practice with families from GTR communities. Lady-Jacqueline's story has demonstrated how, by using values from person-centred practice, social workers can work in anti-discriminatory and anti-oppressive ways with people from ethnic minority communities.

Annotated further reading

Bhopal, K. and Myers, M., 2008. *Insiders, Outsiders and Others: Gypsies and Identity*. Hatfield: University of Hertfordshire Press.
 This is a foundational text around issues of white racism and how this therefore impacts GTR individuals and their communities.

McFadden, A., Siebelt, L., Gavine, A., Atkin, K., Bell, K., Innes, N., Jones, H., Jackson, C., Haggi, H. and MacGillivray, S., 2018. Gypsy, Roma and Traveller access to and engagement with health services: a systematic review. *European Journal of Public Health*, 28 (1), 74–81.
  This article discusses how marginalised communities, specifically GTR, can struggle to access healthcare and could be enabled and collaborated with to change this.

Baines, D. (ed.), 2017. *Doing Anti-Oppressive Practice*, 3rd ed. Nova Scotia: Fernwood Publishing.
  This text includes a discussion about how practitioners can use their privilege and power as part of anti-oppressive practice.

9

Working with domestic abuse and supporting adults with care and support needs

Karen Maher, Serena and Michael

Learning from experts by experience

This chapter emerges from conversations between the authors, specifically between Karen and Serena, a disabled woman who has personally experienced significant domestic abuse and coercive and controlling behaviour, and Karen and Michael, the son of an older woman who experienced abuse throughout her long marriage. Serena and Michael have chosen pseudonyms to maintain their anonymity and, while their lived experience of domestic abuse and controlling coercive behaviour is unique to them, aspects of their stories are likely to resonate with readers working with, knowing or are themselves in similar situations. Their words are threaded throughout the chapter and provide key insights which Karen discusses and relates to social work practice.

Chapter objectives

By the end of this chapter, you should be able to:

- Identify domestic abuse and coercive controlling behaviour
- Understand the law relating to adult safeguarding
- Consider the impact of domestic abuse and coercive control particularly in relation to individuals who have care and support needs
- Understand how this type of abuse can present in many different forms.

Introduction

Before we begin considering our work with individuals experiencing domestic abuse, it is helpful as a starting point to think about what a healthy relationship looks like.

Activity 9.1

Take a couple minutes to think about this and write down a few key words to reflect what you think should be present in a healthy relationship.

Take your reflection to the next stage by choosing some of your keywords and draw or find an image which represents a healthy relationship to you. Keep this image close by as you read the chapter to remind you what characteristics you value.

When we (the authors) think about this, the words that instantly come to mind are balance, respect, trust and compromise.

Now imagine you need additional support to complete daily tasks and require someone to help you manage your personal care, medication or getting out of the house to meet friends and access community resources. Imagine you are in an intimate relationship and that person is also your carer; what characteristics would you want them to have and what would a healthy relationship look like in these circumstances?

The answer should, of course, be the same; however, for some people this is not the case, as their need for support can create a power imbalance which may place the person at greater risk of exploitation, abuse and harm. Social workers work with people with diverse support needs, and for practice to be effective in working with people in their unique personal contexts, it is essential that practitioners understand not only fundamental information about the phenomenon of domestic abuse but also the additional challenges resulting from individual support needs, such as a physical impairment, learning disability, a mental health condition or older age.

Unhelpful domestic abuse stereotypes

Domestic abuse is often hidden and unrecognised (LGA/ADASS, 2015) particularly among groups of people who do not match the stereotypical portrayal of perpetrators or victims. If you complete an internet search for domestic abuse images, victims are portrayed as predominantly white, young and female and perpetrators male. We are seeing a greater recognition of the wider representation and diversity of both victims and perpetrators, moving away from this 'extremely narrow conceptualisation of domestic violence' (Hine, 2019, p44). But caution must still be taken when reviewing data as these will not enable a full understanding of the 'prevalence and characteristics of victims who do not report domestic abuse or seek support' (Office of National Statistics, 2022). As Serena says:

My aim in sharing my story is to help readers think more clearly about the impact of domestic abuse and its presentation in often unrepresented groups.

Activity 9.2

Think of two fictional films which depict domestic abuse, google the films' promotional material and trailers: how are the victims and perpetrators portrayed? Do they represent diversity? For example, is there anyone portrayed with a protected characteristic as specified in the Equality Act 2010?

In completing this activity, you may have found that individuals with care and support needs are significantly underrepresented in mainstream media which impacts on perceptions of society. Older people, those who have a learning disability, mental health condition or physical impairment, are often stereotyped as being less competent and unable to make decisions and choices for themselves. This view discriminates and minimises the experiences of those who have been given a particular label within our society. Marson and Powell (2015) highlight an important point about how our understanding of relationships develop and are informed by our cultural norms and the primary frameworks of reference that shape and sustain our beliefs, attitudes and actions. This is highlighted in Serena's account of seeking support from service.

Serena

I have a physical impairment resulting from an illness in my early adult years. It led to me losing my job and my sense of self-esteem. I became addicted to prescription pain medication and led to depression. My physical health deteriorated significantly due to repeated infections which took long periods of time to recover from. As a result, I became reliant on others to support me to manage everyday tasks including things like my personal care, ensuring I had food, attending medical appointments and meeting with family and friends.

The intersections of gender, disability, age and ethnicity impact on both engagement and response from service providers potentially leading to domestic abuse being under-recognised, under-reported and under-recorded in other groups (Wydall and Zerk, 2017). This ultimately leads to a lack of understanding or alternative frames of reference and therefore lead to structural problems within supporting agencies (Wydall and Zerk, 2017) as different terminology such as, elder abuse, mate crime, neglect or carer stress being used instead of correctly identifying the abuse as domestic abuse and/or coercive and controlling behaviour (Bows, 2020). Michael shared his experiences of his mother's changing circumstances as she aged which led to changing methods of control and abuse developing.

Michael

As my mother aged and needed more support, this only served to create additional pressure and give further control to my father as she could not physically get out of the home without support.

Trauma-informed approach to domestic abuse

Experience of trauma can be a cause and an effect of abusive relationships; it can lead individuals to form and maintain attachments to abusive and controlling partners and be an outcome of being in an abusive relationship (Brandt and Rudden, 2020). Serena highlights how, as a person's situation changes, it may lead them to feel they need to accept the abuse to ensure their physical care and support needs are responded to.

Serena

My world became much smaller because the deterioration in my physical health impacted on my self-identity and confidence. I can see how this changed the dynamics within my relationships which were already characterised by coercive control and abusive behaviours but intensified further. For example, being ridiculed for being unable to complete tasks without support, asked repeatedly who would ever love me, screamed at when unwell and having faeces rubbed in my face. I faced physical and sexual violence and as my world became smaller, my partner gained more control. I knew this was abusive, but I wanted someone to love me and was afraid that the person who was my carer, as well as my intimate partner, would leave me alone and unable to cope. My partner was 'my life raft' despite the abuse.

Understanding the psychological impact of abuse requires a trauma-informed approach (Anyikwa, 2016) to practice and an awareness that people who commit such abuse often perceive themselves as being 'untouchable and immune from the repercussions of their actions' (Gravell, 2012 cited in McCarthy 2017, p599). This is highlighted by both Serena and Michael.

Serena

I eventually accessed support from a domestic abuse charity including access to talking therapies. It enabled me to recognise how my partner controlled my every movement including having to ask if I could go to the toilet and if I could eat. The relationship became so intense that everything about me smashed and despite knowing that my partner was dominant and narcissistic I became lost to the point that the trauma became comfortable resulting in the bonds with my partner tightening further.

Michael

My mother experienced domestic abuse throughout her marriage which spanned several decades. Watching the impact of domestic abuse all through my childhood and adult life made me feel helpless in enabling my mother to do something about it or protect her from harm. I constantly worried from child to adulthood about what to do, what to say and how to protect my mother.

As a result, it is often difficult for professionals and family members to identify domestic abuse, as perpetrators can groom and manipulate others skilfully. By its very nature, domestic abuse is about the ability to control the person in all areas of their life and interactions. As abuse evolves, it often becomes normalised and accepted, making it extremely difficult to leave (Thevenot, 2019). In Serena's words:

The abuse I experienced had been witnessed by professionals but as the perpetrator was also my carer this somehow minimised what was seen to be happening.

Bancroft (2002) cited in Brandt and Rudden (2020) refer to this as creating a sense of neutrality. This can also be referred to as seeking confirmation bias where we look for information or evidence to support and reinforce our beliefs or expectations. When thinking about carers we can make assumptions. Serena expressed her frustration that people thought 'oh look how good they are looking after me'. As a result, this means that we do not see, actively look for, or notice possible contradictory indicators which may need to be explored or acted upon.

As a system we can also become confused when people like Serena articulate, ask for help and support.

Serena

When I tried to get help, I was told I was complicated so many times. It left me feeling that I didn't belong anywhere because 'I'm complicated!'. I felt like I was in a constant battle with myself. I knew that I would go back to the abuse because it had become comfortable and predictable despite knowing that I would die as a person.

> **Michael**
>
> *When we did seek support from services, and my mother disclosed the abuse she was experiencing, it was difficult for professionals to provide the right support options to her. This isn't to blame anyone but is a recognition of the complexity of the relationship dynamics and of identifying the right support options for older people who find it difficult to see an alternative version of their lives having lived with domestic abuse for so long.*

Activity 9.3

With a colleague or friend, sit back-to-back and simultaneously describe how you reached your location today. Having not fully listened to each other, take turns to provide guidance about how to return home safely. What were your feelings as you were doing this exercise? Reflecting on the experience of this exercise do you think professionals always listen to ensure they have all the information needed to provide the correct guidance and support? What factors may prevent this from happening?

Developing knowledge of trauma bonding and trauma-informed practice includes understanding the impact of abuse on the person's ability to make free and informed decisions. Fear can become incapacitating resulting in an individual being unable to leave an abusive relationship. In this context the principles outlined in the Mental Capacity Act 2005 should be considered. The courts acknowledge trauma bonds, and case law demonstrates how the area of Mental Capacity and the complexities of domestic abuse have been addressed both in the Court of Protection and through the inherent jurisdiction of the High Court (e.g. A Local Authority v DL [2011] EWHC 1022 (Fam), Re FD (Inherent Jurisdiction: Power of Arrest) [2016] EWHC 2358 (Fam), Southend on Sea v Meyers [2019] EWHC 399 (Fam), Re BU [2021] EWCOP 54).

Ruck Keene likens this to a cliff edge and highlights that individuals who wish to leave an abusive relationship can be prevented from doing so because of a 'vacuum of support' (Kong and Ruck Keene 2019, p.128). There is also the danger that with a finding of capacity, practitioners and services could enable or allow the abuse to continue without any support to prevent the person from 'falling off the cliff edge' (Kong and Ruck Keene 2019, p.128). The area of mental capacity and domestic abuse represents a complex interplay of factors which requires more focus and consideration in the context of the decision and time-specific nature of the assessment process. Consideration must also be given to how the person's environment, relationship and social factors impact on executive brain function, creating an impairment and disturbance in the functioning of the mind or brain. This is an area which can be closely linked to self-neglect and repeated unwise decisions and patterns of risk resulting in the need to look beyond what the person is saying but observe their behaviours, especially if the person is repeatedly at risk from unwise decisions (Braye et al., 2020).

Relationship-based approach to working with people experiencing domestic abuse

The importance of relationship-based approaches is core to social work practice and pivotal to enabling difficult but supportive conversations to take place.

> **Michael**
>
> *My mother was assessed as having the mental capacity to make the decision to remain with her husband, but I recognised how her pride got in the way of her ability to create new narratives and routines to break the cycle of abuse.*

'Sowing the seeds' (SafeLives, 2016) highlights that by talking through issues and not walking away may well lead to a lightbulb moment for a person, where they recognise that they are experiencing domestic abuse and coercive control and want to do something about it. This requires a long-term relationship-based approach built on trust and respect as opposed to episodic social work where social workers dip in and out of people's lives at crisis points and often, with a different practitioner, resulting in the person having to tell their story repeatedly. Many may also have preconceived ideas about what support from a social worker will mean, and the use of the word safeguarding might create a sense of fear and lead to a reluctance to engage.

The 'sowing the seeds' message in conjunction with a relationship-based approach to practice which builds trust and confidence may lead the person to want to make changes in their lives including in older age, but while talking about this important message, Michael also highlighted the need to, 'please meet me at the garden gate so I know where I am walking to', to give the person more confidence and make them believe that there is a better life and support out there.

Responding to the complex nature of domestic abuse requires a consistent multi-agency, whole system approach and a cultural shift in perspective. Domestic abuse can affect anyone at any time in their lifecycle. While we are starting to see a shift in campaign imagery to heighten awareness of the diversity of victims, more still needs to be done to ensure all victims, no matter their gender, race, culture, religion, sexuality or disability receive the appropriate level of understanding, support and recognition. To understand the impact of oppression and marginalisation, we need to consider the effect of labelling people as being of a particular group with certain predisposed characteristics and challenge our unconscious bias in our responses to them.

How the Care Act 2014 relates to domestic abuse

The Care Act 2014 makes direct reference to domestic abuse and coercive control as adult safeguarding concerns. The connection between the two, however, 'lack(s) the conceptual framework to support practice around domestic abuse and safeguarding' (Robbins et al., 2016, p135). This is due to the limitations set by the act in respect of adult safeguarding with access to support from statutory services being determined by the presence of eligible care and support needs. This can seem confusing and at odds with domestic abuse pathways which are provided by a range of agencies both statutory and voluntary.

While the adult social care workforce understands its duty in respect of adult safeguarding and the responsibility to be involved in domestic abuse cases where the adult has care and support needs, McLaughlin et al. (2018) suggests that practitioners can sometimes become unclear about their role and 'the need to operate a parallel domestic violence and adult safeguarding approach', which can be further compounded by the 'complicated issues of mental capacity' (McLaughlin, 2018, p288).

A possible contributing aspect of this confusion relates to the presence of what often appears to be two separate systems. Adult social work promotes a strengths-based, outcome-focussed approach with risk considered from an enabling perspective rather than as a barrier (Department of Health, 2017). Risk is explored with the person to seek their views and support them to manage this both in the context of potential benefits and consequences to themselves and others. However, as Khalil (2013, cited by Robbins et al., 2016) highlights, this can lead to confused responses by practitioners attempting to work across what often seems like two separate and unconnected systems with two different languages.

When considering domestic abuse in terms of adult safeguarding, the Care Act 2014 is underpinned by six key safeguarding principles (Figure 9.1):

These principles have been established to ensure that individuals are supported, encouraged and asked their views and wishes throughout their safeguarding journey. This is an inherently strengths-based process which can achieve positive and life-changing outcomes. Making Safeguarding Personal (MSP) lies at the heart of multi-agency working and identifies that while safeguarding arrangements are there

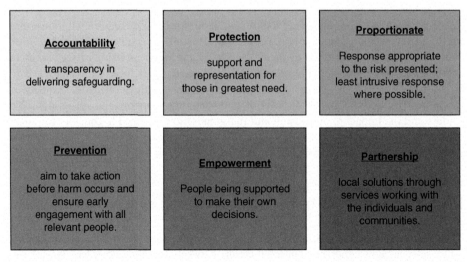

Figure 9.1 Six key principles underpin all adult safeguarding work (Care Act 2014, statutory guidance 14.13)

to support and protect people, we must also recognise that not everyone will follow the same journey through services or require the same support. Recognising difference is important and therefore overly prescriptive procedures and policies are unhelpful to positive engagement with individuals who need support and protection.

There are distinct categories for domestic abuse; however, the language of adult safeguarding promotes two perspectives: firstly, it gives 'emphasis on criminal or dishonest behaviours' (Robbins et al., 2016, p135) such as financial abuse, fraud, assault and secondly, the use of words such as 'victim' and 'perpetrator' in relation to domestic abuse emphasises 'power and intimacy' (Robbins et al., 2016, p135). The two languages do not align themselves sufficiently or enable practitioners to make obvious connections between adult safeguarding and domestic abuse which can lead to harm being categorised incorrectly. For example, the withholding of medication might be viewed and categorised in adult safeguarding as an act of neglect and omission when, in fact, it could be deliberately withheld and used as a means of coercive and controlling behaviour. As Serena says:

My partner not only managed my physical pain but my emotional pain also.

Therein lies the problem, if we do not recognise and identify abuse types correctly, we do not record them correctly and will not know the true prevalence of domestic abuse for people with care and support needs.

Michael

The nature of control and intimidation experienced by my mother was emotional and financial, and verbally threatening behaviour which at times also became physical. My mother had lived with it for so long, she had normalised his behaviour to such an extent that others began to see this as normal too. Resulting in an accepted viewpoint of 'well he's always been like that' or seeing him as old and vulnerable rather than seeing his behaviours as abusive.

The consequence of inaccurate recording and lack of recognition of prevalence is the inability of agencies to respond, adapt or develop support pathways effectively to ensure adults receive the right response at the right time.

The Domestic Abuse Act 2021

A further confusing aspect when working with domestic abuse results from the absence of a legal definition until the Domestic Abuse Act 2021, which has importantly changed the language used from domestic violence to domestic abuse to ensure all aspects of abuse are considered. This is important because it will encourage practitioners across agencies to think more broadly and to consider and observe not just the obvious signs of domestic abuse such as bruising and physical injuries.

Significantly, and in relation to Serena's and Michael's mother's experience, the Domestic Abuse Act 2021 brings the relationship between a disabled person and their carer within the definition of 'personally connected' which widens the scope and duty of support for victims. There is also no longer a requirement for abusers and victims to still be in a relationship or to live together as the offence of coercive control now also applies to former partners and family members. This is important because it recognises that those individuals who leave abusive partners can often continue to be subjected to sustained or increased controlling or coercive behaviour after they have separated. As a result, individuals can in fact be at a heightened risk of homicide during the period immediately after leaving (Monkton–Smith, 2019).

The Domestic Abuse Act 2021 is welcomed, but organisations including Women's Aid and the Legal Action Group (LAG) claim they lack the far-reaching impact hoped for as not all men and woman will be protected, for example, there has been a failure to provide protection and support to those individuals who are migrants and have No Recourse to Public Funds (NRPC). We also wonder if it will sufficiently support individuals with care and support needs to have their experiences recognised and acted upon and whether service provisions will change sufficiently enough to provide the same level of support as it does to those without care and support needs. To make a real difference to people's lives, it is important to challenge the stereotypes of what a real victim of domestic abuse is and understand that not everyone will always realise that they are in an abusive relationship.

Conclusion

As professionals working with domestic abuse, there is a need to ensure greater professional curiosity and that we have both the confidence and courage to ask difficult questions. Some may describe this as nosiness but what we are doing is using our communication skills to explore what is happening in the person's life and providing them with an opportunity to share their experiences, views and wishes. Developing and nurturing this skill is an important part of social work practice and integral to gaining a clearer understanding of what is happening in the person's life. It is fundamental in understanding and managing risk, as each interaction we have with the person provides an opportunity for us to receive information, and as highlighted above, 'sow the seeds' of disclosing and doing something about the abuse they are experiencing.

Professionals should always be ready to receive information, to believe and act upon what they have been told. Many professionals will worry about confidentiality and information-sharing but appropriate information-sharing is vital to ensuring the person is safe and the right support is provided.

Being professionally curious should be viewed as good practice and part of positive and effective multi-agency working. Similarly, having practice decisions and actions challenged by others should not be viewed as a criticism and lead to defensive practice but as an opportunity to consider and review practice with the shared aim of achieving the right outcome with the person by supporting them to be in control of their lives and enhance their safety and wellbeing.

Chapter summary

This chapter has explored:

- Domestic abuse and controlling and coercive behaviour and the experiences of individuals who have care and support needs.
- Societal conceptions of domestic abuse and intersectionality. How victim stereotypes develop and can be shaped by our cultural scripts or environmental frames of reference.
- The use of language and impact this may have on the availability of and access to the right support pathways and resources to support the person.
- Adult Safeguarding duties under the Care Act 2014 and the six safeguarding principles. The importance of Making Safeguarding Personal and relationship-based approaches.
- How the psychological impact of domestic abuse requires a trauma-informed approach to understanding the effect of and on the person.

Annotated further reading

Bates, E. A. and Taylor, J. C., eds., 2019. *Intimate Partner Violence: New Perspectives in Research and Practice*. London: Routledge.
   This text provides an opportunity to further consider domestic abuse from a holistic perspective by considering issues which are not part of mainstream discussion in more detail.

Thiara, R. K. and Radford, L., eds., 2021. *Working with Domestic Violence and Abuse Across the Life Course*. London: Jessica Kingsley.
   Explore the nature and impact of domestic abuse across the life course through three key themes: coercive control, developmental experiences of violence and an intersectional understanding of domestic abuse.

Access All: 'I wasn't allowed to look out of the window' on Apple Podcasts

   A short podcast which considers domestic abuse and disability.

10

Working with children (under the age of 18 years) who are abusive towards their parents

Louise Oliver with Katie Bielec and Gael

Learning from experts by experience

This chapter will draw upon the lived experience of a mother who has experienced child-to-parent violence and abuse (Gael), the expertise of a practitioner who specialises in working with family violence (Katie) and a social worker and academic who has worked with and researches child-to-parent violence and abuse (Louise). This has been done to weave together the different perspectives of child-to-parent violence abuse to help translate the theory to real life and vice versa.

Chapter objectives

By the end of this chapter, you will be able to:

- Define Child-to-Parent Violence and Abuse (CPVA)
- Understand the parental experience of CPVA
- Understand how CPVA presents
- Understand what the terms 'Power and Control' mean when talking about CPVA
- Understand what the impact of CPVA on the whole family
- Understand how age plays a part in CPVA

Introduction

This is a book which focusses on working with adults, but we wanted to include a chapter about children who are violent towards their parents as this clearly has an impact on the adult but often sits within children's social care. UK government guidance, suggests that in such family situations, a joined-up approach between children and families and domestic abuse services may be beneficial, to take a whole families approach, especially when the victim and perpetrator can both be experiencing adversities, including violence and abuse simultaneously. However, it should be noted that in order to write about CPVA, it is not possible to talk about the experience of the adult in isolation of the children and family. This chapter will, therefore, explore what CPVA is, how it is defined and how it impacts those who experience it, with advice on how to work parents/carers experiencing this.

To start with, we have chosen an activity to help you think about how children who are violent towards their parents are represented in film and fiction.

Activity 10.1

How many films can you think of which portray a violent child towards their parent? How do they depict the violent child and how do they portray the parent? How do you think that may influence the understanding of CPVA?

A few examples of books and films we thought of are: *We need to talk about Kevin* (Shriver 2003), *The Omen* (1976), *The Good Son* (1993), *Carrie* (2013), *The Boy Who Cried Bitch* (1992) and *Star Wars: Episode VI – Return of the Jedi* (1983).

I would now like to introduce you to Gael. She is a mother of adult twins, one of her twins started being violent towards her when he was in primary school and this narrative is centred around Gael and her son who was being violent.

Gael

I went to boarding school when I was 10, my mum used to drink and dad was away with work a lot. I would come home in the holidays or stay with friends, but really I was away from home from 10 years of age to 17 years. I still see my mum and dad but I have never had emotional support from them and it can be hard spending time with them.

Anyway, back to my boys. I met the boys' dad in a pub and we dated for a couple of years. We bought a house and after a while got engaged. I called the wedding off on one occasion because he drank too much and was violent. He would never hit me because he knew I would not stand for it, but he would punch and destroy our home, putting holes in walls and doors. We did get married in the end and I remember, he was so drunk on our wedding night and violent, it was not a good night, I wish I had hindsight.

The relationship ended when I was pregnant because he cheated on me and when I found out we both chose to end the relationship. I got a house for me and the boys and he got a flat near us. He continued to see the boys but tended to take them to the local pub. In the end, he was picking the boys up and he was drunk. Social Services got involved and were worried about the boys when with their dad. In the end, when the boys got a little bit older, they would phone me when with their dad, asking to be picked up. The visits came to an end, although, one of the boys has stayed in contact him, but the other chooses not to.

Then one of my boys started to struggle in school, he would get into trouble with the other kids. He then started to be violent at home, there were times when I was scared, not for me so much but for my other boy.

Trouble with defining child-to-parent violence and abuse

CPVA is generally understood to be when children (in the United Kingdom under 18 years old) are controlling, aggressive and/or violent towards their parent(s). In comparison to other forms of familial violence, CPVA continues to be under-researched and under-discussed, even with the more recent surge in research and publications.

Due to the understanding of CPVA being, in some regards, in its infancy, there remain some problems, specifically, that there is no consensus or legal name, or definition given to CPVA. This generates difficulties related to how CPVA is investigated, theorised, understood and worked with for both researchers and practitioners.

There are a few frequently used definitions within the body of literature (see Table 10.1). There is an issue, however, of not having a specific legal definition which addresses the uniqueness of CPVA, so that support can be given, and so people can be safeguarded appropriately.

Gallagher (2018) noted that not having an agreed definition demonstrates how little attention this issue has been given. This is when such definitions as Holt's (2016) help, as it shows some of the familial dynamics and starts to illuminate some of the complexities when working with CPVA. For example, in the United Kingdom, the government-led definition which guides practitioners when working with CPVA comes under the umbrella of domestic abuse (See Domestic Abuse Act 2021 in Table 10.1) and

Table 10.1 Definitions of CVPA

Reference	Definition	Application to practice
Cottrell (2003, p1)	Parent abuse is any harmful act by a teenage child intended to gain power and control over a parent. The abuse can be physical, psychological or financial	Focusses upon teenagers. Throws open a debate about 'intent'.
Holt (2016, p1)	A pattern of behaviour, instigated by a child or young person, which involves using verbal, financial, physical and/or emotional means to practice power and exert control over a parent. The power that is practised is, to some extent, *intentional*, and the *control* that is exerted over a parent is achieved through fear, such that a parent unhealthily adapts their own behaviour to accommodate the child	Includes children of different ages.

Includes family dynamics. |
| Domestic Abuse Act 2021 | Behaviour of a person ('A') towards another person ('B') is 'domestic abuse' if –

a. A and B are each aged 16 or over and are personally connected to each other, and
b. the behaviour is abusive. For example, physical or sexual abuse; violent or threatening behaviour; controlling or coercive behaviour; economic abuse, psychological, emotional or other abuse;

and it does not matter whether the behaviour consists of a single incident or a course of conduct (definition of 'personally connected' in relation to CPVA – 'they each have, or there has been a time when they each have had, a parental relationship in relation to the same child' | Age 16 years and above and deemed as domestic abuse. |

therefore the approach to working with families and any legal action is often one of domestic abuse (Bettinson and Quinlan, 2020; Holt and Lewis, 2021). Holt and Lewis (2021, p3) argue that 'representations of CPV [child to parent violence] as a form of domestic violence without informed debate about its contexts and correlates could have deleterious consequences for children and families'. As Bettinson and Quinlan (2020) note, there needs to be a balance between safeguarding the adult and finding an outcome which is also in the best interests of the child. Criminalising children for domestic violence and abuse may not be appropriate.

The new Domestic Abuse Act 2021, therefore, does not allow for the legalities, the bi-directional nature (as in how both the child and parent have an influence on each other) and complex family dynamics of CPVA. These inconsistencies and complexities affect policy and practice, especially for professionals targeting support for families experiencing this complex situation (Moulds et al., 2016). For example, Miles et al. (2020) drew attention to the tensions between recognising that adults need safeguarding and also seeing the child as vulnerable.

It is therefore important that practitioners working with families where CPVA is present are aware of the possible indicators that abuse is happening within the home. A parent being subjected to CPVA is not the same as an adult who is in an intimate relationship. There may be some similarities which present themselves; however, the complexities of working with a parent as a *victim* and then a child as potential *perpetrator* of abuse are very different.

It is important that you think carefully about the language you use with the parent who may already be feeling guilt and ashamed of what they are disclosing. Therefore, victim-blaming language should not be used within conversations or in any written reports. Children who are using abusive behaviours remain children and it is important for practitioners working with a family to remember this. Although there is a need to directly address the abuse, this needs to be carried out sensitively, and at the pace of the family (unless there is a significant risk of harm). We would like you to consider this further in Activity 10.2, especially in terms of how the UK society perceives family violence and abuse.

Activity 10.2

When you think of, or picture, a 'victim' and a 'perpetrator', what do you see? How then does this fit in with how you would approach working with a family experiencing CPVA, and why?

The dynamic of the parent–child relationship is different to those who are either experiencing domestic abuse by a partner or adult family member. The parent will most likely not want to criminalise the child, and the option of leaving the 'relationship' tends to not be open for a parent, especially as in the United Kingdom, the parent has a legal duty not to abandon their child.

Each risk factor needs to be addressed both with the parent to enable them to consider their safety, as well as the young person to enable them to understand the implication of their actions. Risk assessing is imperative with any intervention, and it is important to understand possible referral pathways available to all those involved. Practitioners will need to work with the parent to support them in understanding what they are experiencing and how to diminish any guilt, shame or blame. The parent may not recognise the behaviours, and therefore, motivational interviewing and open questions would be advised to create a safe environment to explore what is happening and for any disclosures.

The parental experience of CPVA

Now that you have an understanding of what CPVA is, we would like to bring Gael back into the chapter.

Gael

Their dad was always drunk and then not around to help and my parents do not understand and are not very supportive. I remember when my boy was young he tried to hang himself and he had a thing for knives and was self-harming, so we had to take away all the knives from the house. He would hit and kick me, threaten to kill me or himself. Support services became involved with the family to help and some were good and some were not. The practitioners who spent time to listen to him and take time with him helped the most but still little changed in terms of his behaviours.

When considering Gael as a single parent with limited support systems, as well as having experienced an abusive relationship with her son's father, it is worth drawing your attention to the research surrounding the parental characteristics of the parents experiencing CPVA. Many quantitative studies show that mothers are predominantly victims of CPVA (e.g. Condry and Miles, 2014; Purcell et al., 2014; Lyons et al., 2015). The context of the mother's role in a family is important as they are more likely to be the victim of CPVA simply because they are usually the primary carer, spend more time caring for children and are therefore more accessible. It is also usually mothers that tend to set children's behavioural boundaries. In these ways, women are more likely to be victims of CPVA than men (Routt and Anderson, 2011).

With this in mind, as mentioned earlier, when working with the parent non-blaming language needs to be used to build trust. When speaking with the parent, you should ensure that this is in a safe place, away from other distractions such as other children or family members.

TED questions such as:

Tell me what XX does to you,
Explain to me how that makes you feel,
Describe to me the impact that it is having on you

These will help open a conversation. You should avoid questions such as 'Why don't you do. . .?' and 'What did you do before they did. . .?'

Support services for CPVA

> **Gael**
>
> *Over the years I have had different professional support from different teams. Social Services have opened and closed our case so many times, even when I was asking for help, they were telling me to 'be strong', when I felt that I could not carry on anymore. I felt that they did not get it, that I needed help because one of my sons was being violent to me and most importantly being violent to his brother and I was scared.*

A parent who is experiencing this type of abuse may have feelings of desperation, of failure to their child/ren as well as fear from their child and the consequences of seeking support. Most parents will seek support when they have no other choice and are reaching for support for their child.

Any intervention needs to be carried out with the awareness of possible increase of risk to the parent. Those who are abusive may feel threatened if the 'victim' seeks help and support. Therefore, if there is a disclosure and possible intervention, safety planning needs to be explored with the parent in how they will try to keep themselves safe.

When considering a safety plan, a practitioner would benefit in asking the parent: 'What do you do to keep yourself safe?' From this, you can explore together what works for them and any risks that may present with different interventions. Workers should then be aware of and be able to offer a variety of different safety options available. Remember every family and every person will be different so not all safety planning suggestions will work with each family.

How does CPVA present itself?

> **Gael**
>
> *When my son is violent it is scary, it's like now when he has one of his, I call them meltdowns, because he just loses it. But most of the time he is lovely, but he's got very unpredictable because these moods just switch and I never know what mood he will be in when he wakes up. What worried me most was the fights between the boys. There was one time when he threw a mug at his brother, it broke, and his brother threw it back and it went in his arm and he had to have emergency surgery. I still worry about them now. Once they start, they won't stop and I try to get in the middle of them to stop it and protect them, it is hard, they are big and strong now.*

Experiencing CPVA can have a long-term impact upon children and families, and as you may be able to imagine, living with this level of abuse is likely to have a detrimental impact upon all involved. Clarke et al. (2017), in their literature review, highlight that CPVA could lead to parents developing mental health problems, negatively impact on familial relationships, lead to potential breakdown of relationships and financial instability. It is clear the detrimental impact that the abuse has had on Gael, as she talks about wanting to end her life because she could not cope anymore. For the child who is exhibiting violent and abusive behaviours, there is a growing body of evidence that they experience psychological distress, anxiety, depression and stress (Ibabe et al., 2014a, 2014b; Martinez-Ferrer et al., 2020). Gael explains this from her perspective.

> **Gael**
>
> *He does not leave the house now, he won't talk on the phone unless he has to. This anxiety may be coming from difficulties in school and he still has flashbacks. He worries every time I go out that I am going to die and he says 'if I die, he will kill himself'.*

The notion of a bi-directional relationship is not simple. Both the parent and the child experience adversities. As Moulds et al. (2016, p548), state; 'the idea that victimisation can be a shared experience, and cyclical in nature, has profound implications for how AVTP [adolescent violence towards parents] is recognised and responded to' (Moulds et al., 2016, p548).

Of course, not one case will be the same, and therefore, professionals need to use observational skills as well as speaking with the family to be able to identify abuse within the home.

A parent being subjected to abuse may present a number of ways such as:

- Fear
- Denial of the child's behaviour
- Justification of child's behaviours
- Minimisation
- Self-blame
- Lack of choice/agency
- Confusion
- Unable to engage/managing partner, services and other children
- Unusual behaviours (extraordinary cleaning regimes)
- Altered perception/reality (Gaslighting)

Those who are perpetrating abuse may present with:

- Entitlement
- Denial
- Justification
- Minimisation
- Blaming/denigration of parent
- Lack of empathy
- Arrogance/narcissistic traits
- Objectification
- Gender stereotypes
- Jealous/possessiveness

- Egocentric/me'ism!
- Isolating/controlling
- Unrealistic expectations on parent
- Shame
- Fear
- Guilt
- Confusion
- Isolation
- Rejection

(Adapted from Rock Pool, https://rockpool.life/)

Activity 10.3

Do any of these reactions resonate with you? Surprise you? Are there any you would delete or any you would add to the list? And most importantly, why?

What do the terms 'Power and Control' mean when talking about CPVA?

Gael

I was scared at times, he would kick me, hit me, threaten to push me down the stairs, kill me, get a knife and threaten me. It is emotionally draining to feel powerless. Sam would say when he was little that he was the man of the house, but you just feel helpless and I say, mentally drained, there were many times when I felt like ending it all.

The inclusion of 'power and control' is important within this discussion. Its usefulness lies in providing details of the different forms of abuse the family experiences. Although as Moulds et al. (2016) explain, difficulty lies in understanding what power and control actually mean in terms of the parent–child power dynamics. When looking at CPVA research, such behaviours are often seen as part of an ongoing pattern which, over time, renders the parent powerless. This situation often results in parents living in fear of their children (Holt, 2016; Clarke et al., 2017; Bonnick, 2019).

Calvete et al. (2014) show that the child may be proactively using power and control, through acts of aggression in order to have their demands met, for example, obtaining money. Such power and control changes parental behaviours to accommodate the child (Holt, 2016), leaving parents feeling as if they are 'walking on eggshells' (Clarke et al., 2017, p4), in order to avoid further violence or abuse. As Calvete et al. (2014) describe:

. . .the aggressions are described as a struggle for power and control. It is a power relation; practically all the time, they [adolescents] talk about 'them and us,' not letting the other win, not letting the other side get away with it. Furthermore, CPV often involves

self-defeating behaviours. In those cases, the goal is for the parent to lose, even though the adolescent does not win either.

(Calvete et al., 2014, p349)

Gallagher (2018) agrees that power and control is an important aspect within CPVA, but he argues that the child is not trying to gain power over the parent *per se*, but to disempower them, by weakening parental authority. To expand upon this point, Routt and Anderson (2011) explained that when a young person has been a victim of abuse, they view the world differently; they may develop a belief system much like the abusive adult, a belief system based on their own entitlement. For example, the child will feel a sense of entitlement leading them to talk to their mother in a degrading way, demanding respect and being dismissive of her.

It is important to also consider trauma-related behaviours, associated with mental ill health or a conduct disorder, and although the outcome may be the same, the intentions may differ. For example, a child who is struggling to manage their behaviours due to living with severe anxiety, may implement strategies to control their environment, such as using threats to harm others or harm themselves if their demands are not met. Research by Thorley and Coates (2019) supports this notion of the child needing to control a situation or environment rather than being seen as a 'personal attack'. Understanding such motives behind controlling behaviours may be different from a child using control over a parent for, say, financial gain, and therefore, support and guidance in working with either situation may need to be differentiated. When reflecting upon Gael's story, she has explained her son has a formal diagnosis of autism and has mental health problems which severely impact his life, and when thinking about this, she states:

My son would be mortified if he thought back to his behaviours when he was younger. When he has a meltdown now, he always apologies to me.

Thorley and Coates (2018) state, when addressing co-morbid conditions and dis-orders that 'the majority of children **do not intend** [authors emphasis] to behave violently or aggressively' (Thorley and Coates, 2018, p13). They conclude that families do not agree with the terms 'intent' or 'control' being used within the definition as they feel this does not describe their everyday experience (Thorley and Coates, 2019). Nowakowski-Sims (2019) discussing their research about childhood adversity, suggest that children who experienced abuse were more likely to develop reactive aggression rather than proactive aggression. Research by Papamichail and Bates (2020) also shows that children may struggle with controlling their emotions which then affects their behaviour. They state that participants reported 'feeling confused and afraid because they were unable to control themselves' (Papamichail and Bates, 2020, p14). In addition to this, Ibabe et al. (2014a, 2014b) and also Oliver (2019, 2021) show that children experiencing CPVA may themselves feel rejected, perceive a lack of parental warmth and experience internal hostility which illustrates the detrimental impact of CPVA upon the child.

Conclusion

The story of Gael and her son shows the very real and devastating realities of those experiencing CPVA, and their story is not a unique one. Through talking with Gael, we got a real sense of her commitment to her children, that she loved them and would stick by them no matter what, even when she felt like giving up. In writing this chapter it is clear that the different definitions of CPVA influence policy, legislation and funding for supporting families as well as funding for further research. The main issue in moving this debate forward is to further investigate and understand the lived experience of those experiencing CPVA, so that bespoke support can be developed for all involved.

Chapter summary

This chapter has explored the challenges of working with CPVA when there is not a legal definition to identify what CPVA is and therefore how to work with those experiencing it.

We discuss the Domestic Abuse Act 2021 and the connotations and complexities of working with CPVA under the domestic abuse umbrella, while recognising that when conducting risk assessments, some of the domestic abuse tools are useful.

We also drew upon the experience of those experiencing CPVA, including the long-term impact, and we gave suggestions of how we could work with those experiencing this form of family violence and abuse, in a non-blaming approach.

Annotated further reading

Bonnick, H. *Holes in the Wall*. Available at: https://holesinthewall.co.uk/.
This is a UK website which is filled with useful information, such as blogs, research, resources and events and training, focussing upon children who are violent towards their parents.

Holt, A., 2016. Working with Adolescent Violence and Abuse Towards Parents: Approaches and Contexts for Intervention. London and New York: Routledge Taylor & Francis Group.
This book focuses upon children who are violent towards their parents, both in terms of research and interventions.

Press, C., 2022. When Love Bites: A Young Person's Guide to Escaping of Harmful, Toxic and Hurtful Relationships. Sudbury: Cathy Press Publications.
This book explores harmful, toxic and hurtful relationships. It is an accessible guide, co-produced with teenagers.

11

Working with disabled adults

Josh Hepple and Sally Lee

Learning from experts by experience

The authors of this chapter promote partnership approaches to social work and to reflect that the contents of the chapter are presented in a way that amplifies lived experience. Each of the authors brings their learning and lived experience to co-create a shared perspective on social work with disabled adults.

Chapter objectives

After reading this chapter, you should be able to:

- Understand that disability is complex and diverse
- Recognise the importance of language in relation to impairment and disability
- Understand models of disability and their use in policy and practice
- Understand social care legislation and policy and how it can be used to support disabled people

---

Introduction

The term disability is used in social work to include people living with a wide range of impairments including:

- Motor impairments including congenital impairments such as cerebral palsy and neurological impairments such as multiple sclerosis
- Chronic illness
- Sensory impairments, specifically sight and hearing
- Acquired and traumatic brain injuries
- Severe disfigurement

The definition of disability used in social work policy and practice comes from the Equality Act 2010 s. 6 which states that a person is disabled if they have:

a physical or mental impairment which has a long term & substantial adverse effect on their ability out carry out normal day to day activities.

The definition locates 'disability' within the individual not their social or physical environment, and this chapter challenges this narrow definition while highlighting the complexity of disability. This chapter will, therefore, explore key models of how disability is understood within our society; these are the medical model, the social model and the affirmative model. The chapter will then consider how to apply different ways that social workers can uphold their professional values and standards when they work with disabled adults. To start with, however, we will explore how the environment in which people live can either disable or liberate people.

The environment in which we live

The activity below invites readers to imaginatively step into the shoes of someone disabled by their environment rather than their physiology.

Activity 11.1

In your imagination, step out of your shoes and into those of Kit, an astronaut who is stuck in zero gravity due to a system malfunction. Kit needs to get to the ship's main deck to reboot the computer. The engineers and designers have not prepared for this scenario and did not consult with Kit about the design of the ship. Kit's route to the deck is a wide, smooth metal tunnel with nothing to grab. If you were in Kit's shoes, how might you manoeuvre your way to the deck?

The point of imaginatively swapping shoes with Kit is to encourage you to think about how the physical and social environments in which people live can be designed and organised in ways that are disabling or liberating, that is, in ways that are exclusive or inclusive of diverse bodies. Inclusive environments address disabling factors, for example, automatic doors enable access to buildings that would otherwise be inaccessible to someone who uses a wheelchair. In Kit's situation, hand-holds were needed to traverse the route. You may be thinking that no matter how inclusive or accessible an environment is made, the individual will still have the condition or impairment and therefore continue to experience its impact (Kit will always be disabled by the lack of gravity no matter how many hand-holds there are in the tunnel). This is true and why it is important to be clear about language as Josh explains below.

Josh

I believe that my impairment is inherently part of my medical makeup whereas my disability is in my environment insofar as to say society has placed barriers which prevent my full participation. I am disabled until the barriers are removed from society/ environment. Cerebral palsy is an impairment not a disability.

An individual may be born with impairment or impairment may be the outcome of illness, accident, injury or a medical condition occurring at any stage of life; however, disability concerns the restrictions to the social and physical environment imposed on people living with impairments (Oliver, 2013). Below, Josh explains how impairment is often inappropriately assumed to mean a person is at risk of harm.

Josh

I have cerebral palsy and have too many signals from my brain to my muscles, but apart from that, there's not much pathologically wrong. At the start of lockdown in March 2020, the government wrote a list of almost every condition. Cerebral palsy was on this, yet after COVID-19 was better understood it was removed from the list rendering me high risk. I take pride in my general good health and have spent the last 30 years trying to convince people that I don't have a learning impairment. The pandemic has not helped this. It is

(Continued)

(Continued)

natural and understandable to see why people wish to protect those who may appear more vulnerable or disabled than others. Yet, at the same time, it's also really important to preserve agency and autonomy and understand that impairment does not necessarily equal high risk.

Language is value-laden meaning that personal, cultural and structural attitudes related to disability and impairment are expressed and reinforced through discourse (Thompson, 2020). The construct of disability is laden with discrimination and oppression and it is important that we understand the power of language, and how this can sustain certain believes and values, as Josh explains.

Josh

Many people tell me that I come before my 'disability' (person first language) and therefore I am a man with a disability. This arguably misses the point of the social model as disability in this context is synonymous with oppression. It wouldn't make sense to say 'woman with oppression' because society creates misogyny and patriarchy; it is not with the woman. Therefore, if you say that disability was always with the person who had the impairment, you would be suggesting that their oppression was an inherent characteristic of their personhood. This removes the onus on society to enable the person. I am a disabled man.

Social workers can demonstrate their respect of, and allyship with, marginalised people, and their commitment to anti-discriminatory and anti-oppressive practice by recognising the unique lived experience of each individual and by using language that acknowledges the extensive work undertaken by members of the disability movement. To further understand the complexity of disability, Josh explains that there are a range of models of disability identified by disabled people and discussed in the literature, which we will now explore in turn.

The medical model of disability

Josh

This model places the problem of disability with the individual and does not consider the environment. It suggests that someone is automatically disabled as a result of their impairment and if the individual wants to become an equal participant in their environment, they should seek medical intervention to change them rather than change anything around them.

(Continued)

The medical model does have some uses. As a social worker, you will be working alongside health professionals such as physiotherapists and speech therapists. Every morning I do 20 minutes of rehabilitation on a very complicated medical device which helps me with my movements. This is important so that I can make the rest of my day better and allow me to read a book without my head moving everywhere.

The medical model emphasises prescribed ideas about what 'normal' and 'healthy' bodies look and feel like (Swain et al., 2013, p23) and any problems experienced by the disabled individual are seen as the result of the impairment. The professionals' task is therefore to adjust atypical bodies into ableist conceptions of 'normal' and 'healthy' through treatment, rehabilitation or other interventions. This understanding of disability assumes that impairment is negative and leads to a poor quality of life (Swain et al., 2013; Retief and Letšosa, 2018; Oliver and Lee, 2020).

By focussing on the individual as the site of the 'problem', the medical model ignores the political, social and economic aspects of disability and undermines the individual's experience of their impairment (Oliver, 2013). In addition, the dominance of professional voices excludes the nuanced understanding and individual perspectives of disabled people themselves, including positive and creative experiences of disability.

The social model of disability

Josh

This model recognises that I have an impairment, cerebral palsy, but it places the emphasis on society in regard to whether or not I am disabled. To take a rather over-simplistic example, if the cinema decided to get a lift, they would be adapting to my impairment and they would be removing societal barriers. Going to a cinema exemplifies that in certain circumstances the medical model is highly offensive, whereas the social model can be empowering. The medical model answer would encourage me to only attend the cinema when I could walk, compared to the social model answer which would encourage the cinema to adapt such as by installing a lift. There are other types of barriers, for example, smaller print can disable people with visual impairments and can also be disabling to people with cognitive impairments.

The social model also has limitations: could I ever safely prepare a hot meal or go to the toilet on my own? Probably not. As social workers, you are very unlikely to create an environment where someone with an impairment could live entirely independently without being disabled in any way. As an activist I am a big supporter of the social model but also of the importance of looking at both medical advances and the environment together.

The social model recognises that bodily diversity is part of being human while also emphasising the social, economic and environmental barriers to participation in society due to ableist views of impairment that inform the organisation of society including the built environment, social structures, employment and relationships (Oliver, 2013; Swain et al., 2013). As such the social model shifts the location of disability away from the individual to the social disadvantages faced by disabled people (such as access to employment and housing).

Beyond the social model

The social model has influenced policy and practice in the United Kingdom and has become the unifying idea for 'collective disability consciousness' (Oliver, 2013, p1024). But it is not a static concept, and notions such as citizenship involving the rights and responsibilities associated with being a citizen are part of its ongoing development. Other models of disability such as the Affirmative Model promote the positive, creative and social identities of disabled people and counter the assumption that disability is always and can only be tragic (Retief and Letšosa, 2018). The affirmative model emerged from the disability arts movement in the 1980s which campaigned for the civil rights of disabled people and fought against their marginalisation in the arts and culture. Josh's award-winning play, *Animal*, written by Jon Bradfield is part of the tradition of the arts to challenge stereotypes and negative assumptions. It is a funny, uncomfortable and moving play and book about disability based on Josh's lived experience (https://park-theatre.co.uk/whats-on/animal;https://www.nickhernbooks.co.uk/animal).

Activity 11.2

There are many comedians, artists and actors who are disabled and reflect on their lived experience in their work. Search YouTube for Stella Young's TED talk 'I'm Not Your Inspiration, Thank You Very Much'. Read the comments under the clip and compose a comment you might make that is respectful.

Google the sculpture of Alison Lapper by Mark Quinn which was previously displayed on the fourth plinth in Trafalgar Square, London. Do you think the fact that the artist is non-disabled changes the impact of this statue or not? What are the reasons for your response?

The aim of Activity 11.2 is to encourage you to think about impairment and disability in different ways, and this is important because perceptions of disability and impairment and the models of disability inform the way health and social care practitioners approach working with disabled adults. As Josh explains each model includes aspects that can be applicable within social work practice. Mitra and Shakespeare (2019) argue that the most commonly used model of disability comes from the World Health Organization's International Classification of Functioning, Disability and Health (ICF). Although the ICF is a classification rather than a model, it is based on a bio-psycho-social model of disability that integrates the medical and social models. Mitra and Shakespeare (2019) state that the ICF needs revision to reflect current knowledge, and the authors of this chapter believe that it is an important model for practitioners because it draws on aspects of social model that align closely with social work values, for example, anti-oppressive social work practice, and it concerns working with every disabled person in ways that recognise their unique personhood, impairment and experience of disablement.

So far, this chapter has explored language, models and the social construction of disability, it now moves on to discussing ways in which social workers can ensure their work with disabled adults demonstrates their professional values and standards.

Effective social work practice with disabled adults

This section of the chapter will focus upon the application of anti-oppressive and anti-discriminatory practice, via effective communication; upholding dignity, choice and control; a critical consideration of anti-oppressive and anti-discriminatory practice will be given including recognising disabling forces within society. Starting with, communication.

Ensure good communication is central to everything you do

Josh emphasises how good communication is essential both to ensure the accurate exchange of information but also to work anti-oppressively by hearing and prioritising his voice. Clearly, not all disabled people's impairments affect their speech; however, the points Josh makes below are relevant to all communication skills.

Josh

Communication and practitioner confidence can create bigger barriers for me than anything structural under the social model. In other words, I would much rather communicate with someone patient and calm who didn't have an adverse reaction to my speech pattern as this can be more debilitating than physical barriers. Human beings are naturally social, and any barrier to that can be extremely debilitating and dehumanising.

While I acknowledge that my speech impairment may affect some of the understanding of what I am trying to communicate, I often feel that the other person's nerves and embarrassment get in the way of a good conversation. People often don't like to admit they haven't understood or tell someone that they got it wrong and don't know what to do. This is often what I find when I am trying to interact with someone who I may not have met before. Many people feel self-conscious asking me to repeat myself and I generally find this quite frustrating. But I acknowledge that I must be conscious of the fact that they do not want to offend me and find it hard to be honest about this.

Communication is important for all aspects of life and, as social workers, it is essential to write down the needs of a service user appropriately. If the service user has a speech impairment, you may need to think about giving them more time. Many disabled adults

(Continued)

(Continued)

are grateful when you're open and transparent about communication, as well as expressing when you are finding communication hard; let the service user tell you if there is anything that can improve interaction. In my experience, people and social workers often jump to ask whoever is with the service user to repeat and talk on their behalf. As an employer, there are financial and personal details of my life that my assistants need not be privy to and, therefore, it is sometimes necessary for me to talk with my social worker privately. On one occasion, my social worker was very pleasantly surprised to realise that he could understand me better than he thought he could. It was slightly tiring that it had to be me who sent emails before trying to reassure him that we would find a way to communicate, as I imagine that not many service users have the confidence to debate something personal with a social worker – such as the clarity of their speech impairment. This can be contrasted to police officers who in my experience are less likely to project their anxieties onto me or try to control the conversation.

This comes back to the social worker's nerves and anxieties. While we are all human and entitled to any emotions, it's important that these feelings do not hinder the relationship with your service user directly. This involves a huge amount of self-reflection and a very supportive team.

The necessity for good communication at a very personal level is highlighted by Activity 11.3.

Activity 11.3

Disabled people undertake invisible work including often having to give very detailed information to assistants and carers about tasks most people take for granted. With a friend or colleague, imagine you are each other's new Personal Assistant. Take turns to talk through your morning routines and how you like to do the tasks. How much detail is needed to make sure things are done the way you like?

Promote dignity, choice and control

Activity 11.3 reflects on the invisible labour associated with disability as well as exercising choice and control which is a prescribed domain of wellbeing in the Care Act 2014. For adults with assessed care and support needs, this includes choice and control over how and by whom care is provided. Direct payments, whereby individuals receive funds for assistance in lieu of services arranged by the local authority is one method through which disabled people can take control. However, social workers need to be aware of the labour direct payments create for disabled people, especially during a global pandemic as Josh explains.

Josh

As a disabled man who relies on others for care, I was affected by the pandemic in many different ways. My initial advice was to find someone who could isolate with me for ten days without any changeover. The care I need is quite intense and, for me to receive the best quality care, it is important that my PAs are not made to work 8–12 hours regardless of how skilled they are.

I feel that COVID-19 exposed many anxieties and vulnerabilities for some people, and this has caused friction with people who are naturally prone to taking risks. Naturally, I felt those assistants who were also living with someone vulnerable should not have been forced out, so I began to rely on three assistants for a few months. I was also very fortunate as many of my friends volunteered their time and two or three friends each week would volunteer a day shift. There was always the possibility that an assistant or friend may get COVID (as there still is).

As with any job, last minute cancellations are very disruptive and thoroughly discouraged, though this completely contradicts self-isolation rules. Assistants do not want to do unpaid standby work and my direct payments do not stretch to retain someone on standby. I am therefore really glad that I am quite a confident and very experienced PA employer and do not take my story as a general response to the pandemic for disabled adults. Yet, I often go two or three hours per day without help, which includes no access to food, water or the toilet. Cerebral palsy is not degenerative in any way but I know that I need people to help me with a lot. This involves being incredibly conscious my own health risk and what my body needs at any time.

Involvement with public authorities such as social work services can erode disabled people's privacy as Josh explains.

Josh

During the first lockdown in March 2020, there were lots of tense conversations about my private life and that of my assistants. For example, if I invited a friend over, was I legally obligated to tell my assistants what I did the night before? Did my assistants have to disclose their whereabouts on the days they were not working? How much did the pandemic remove my right to privacy and individuality?

Think anti-oppression and anti-discrimination

Social work with disabled people has a complex history which, on the one hand, has advocated for marginalised people, while on the other has reinforced ableist intolerance of physical difference and protectionist methods of social intervention, such as the institutionalisation of disabled people (Oliver et al., 2012). Social work has been part of the way the welfare state has 'managed' social need, and this 'management' has often been experienced as oppressive (Oliver et al., 2012; Horner, 2019). Awareness of the profession's dual and potentially contradictory role of care and control (Horner, 2019) enables practitioners to be alert to discriminatory and oppressive policy and practice and helps to navigate this dual role in ways that effectively promote social justice. This involves critical engagement with the socioeconomic context in which social work practice with disabled people takes place and the impact this has on individuals' health and wellbeing.

Evidence of health inequalities in the United Kingdom (Marmot, 2020) demonstrates that illness, impairment, disability and the causes of mortality relate to social as well as medical factors. Ill health and disability are socially influenced and distributed because the conditions that impact on health and wellbeing are unequally shared. This makes health and wellbeing a matter of social justice. For example, poverty leads to multiple negative outcomes including, but not limited to, poor living conditions, nutrition, education and social inclusion, all of which impact on health and wellbeing (BASW guidance on social work and poverty at: https://www.basw.co.uk/understanding-social-work-and-poverty). In addition, living with impairment or ill health costs more than living without disability. John et al. (2019) research reveals that disabled people have extra expenses amounting to £583 on average a month. This is likely to be much higher when rapidly increasing fuel and cost of living are taken into account.

The theory of intersectionality (first formulated by Crenshaw (1989) and subsequently developed by many scholars such as Goethals et al. (2015)) provides a further layer of understanding as it enables social workers to appreciate the often multiple levels of discrimination, disadvantage and marginalisation people may experience. Intersectionality concerns how an individual's multiple and intersecting identities, for example, their ethnicity, sexual orientation, age, religion, disability and gender are experienced simultaneously, and these characteristics form an individual's unique identity. Each characteristic might impact on their experience of discrimination and marginalisation, and the theory recognises that people can be privileged in certain ways and disadvantaged in others. This nuanced understanding of human identity enables social workers to work with disabled people in ways that recognises their complexity and diverse experience of discrimination and oppression.

Recognise disabling forces within society

Contemporary practice is informed by the work of the disability movement whose influence is evident within key legislation and policy underpinning social work practice with disabled adults. For example, the Human Rights Act 1998, the UN Convention on the Rights of Disabled Persons 2006, the Equality Act 2010 and the Care Act 2014 promote the rights of disabled people and the principles of independent living and personalisation. However, to appreciate the enduring nature of disability discrimination, this progress needs to be understood within the overarching social context of disablism.

To be effective, social workers need to be alert to the overt and covert ways disablism impacts on the lives of disabled people. Disablism is a socially constructed (meaning it has no foundation in evidence or nature) form of oppression which has become engrained within society (Oliver and Lee, 2010). The social model addresses the disablism that creates a cycle of disadvantage for disabled people as it both emerges from, and causes, discrimination and oppression. Thompson's (2020) Personal, Cultural and Structural (PCS) model discussed in Chapter 1 provides a helpful method of analysis to identify how disability discriminstation operates at three different levels, personal, cultural and societal.

Research uncovers evidence of disablism in the United Kingdom. For example, Scope's (2022) investigation into members of the public's **personal** attitudes towards disabled people which finds evidence of frequent and serious incidents of abuse and discrimination that have become part of many disabled people's daily lives. Examples of **cultural** discrimination and oppression are explored in research exploring negative representation of disability in mass media (Parsons et al., 2017). Evidence of **societal** discrimination and oppression of disabled people in the United Kingdom is found in the report of the CRPD (Committee on the Rights of Persons with Disabilities)(2017) following its first review of the government's compliance with the Convention and raised concerns on the UK Government's failure to implement the rights of disabled people (Abreu (2022) summarises the report and subsequent action).

Disablism denies disabled peoples' personhood and their full participation in the rights and responsibilities of citizenship. One aspect of which, and one that both authors have campaigned, written and advocated for, is the importance of sexual wellbeing (meaning a person's sexuality, sexual self-esteem and sexual expression) (Hepple, 2016; Lee, 2021). Disablism leads to sexual disenfranchisement which excludes disabled people from opportunities for sexual expression and services such as sex education and family planning, putting people at risk of abuse and exploitation (Owens and de Than, 2015).

The PCS model is again helpful in identifying and analysing different levels of discrimination and oppression in relation to disability and sexual wellbeing:

- **Personal**: Desexualised perceptions of disabled people lead to infantilisation and disabled adults being seen as children who require protection and whose expression of sexual identity is considered inappropriate (Owens and de Than, 2015).
- **Cultural**: Ableist constructions of attractiveness and the subsequent absence of disabled people as romantic and sexual partners in film and television (Andree, 2021).
- **Societal**: Exclusion of disabled people from sexual services (Owens and de Than, 2015).

The desexualisation of disabled people is a form of oppression and injustice that denies people's sexual rights and citizenship (Liddiard, 2021). Social workers can demonstrate their commitment to anti-discriminatory and anti-oppressive practice by recognising disabled people's sexual identity, advocating for their sexual rights and citizenship and supporting disabled people to participate in relationships and activities of their choice (Owens and de Than, 2015; Shakespeare and Richardson, 2018).

Activity 11.4

Watch the video made with members of the Bournemouth University PIER Partnership to hear stories from lived experience: https://www.youtube.com/watch?v=qV80f Fs5_xw.

(Continued)

(Continued)

- What are your thoughts after watching this film?
- What surprised or challenged you?
- What key messages will you take from the film into your practice?

Chapter summary

This chapter has discussed the skills and knowledge required in social work practice with disabled people including the legal definition and models of disability. The discussion has emphasised the significance of anti-discriminatory and anti-oppressive practice and informed readers about the diversity of disability and the uniqueness of lived experience. Josh has used insights from his experience to illustrate important information about how social workers can work effectively.

Annotated further reading

Josh's website has links to his publications: https://www.joshhepple.com/ including:

Hepple, J., 2016. *If You're a Disabled, Gay Twentysomething, Grindr Is a Godsend*. Available from: https://www.theguardian.com/commentisfree/2016/dec/01/disabled-gay-twentysomething-grindr-cerebral-palsy
  Josh's article in The Guardian *discusses his experiences of dating and using Grindr. He collaborated with Jon Bradfield to adapt these experiences into the award-winning play Animal referred to in the chapter.*

Lee, S., 2022. Disability and social work: Partnerships to promote sexual wellbeing. *In:* Shuttleworth, R. and Mona, L., eds. *The Routledge Handbook of Disability and Sexuality*. Abingdon: Routledge, 474–487.
  This chapter discusses how social workers can support the sexual expression, esteem and wellbeing of people who use social work services.

Retief, M. and Letšosa, R., 2018. Models of disability: A brief overview. *HTS Teologiese Studies/ Theological Studies*, 74 (1), 1–8.
  This article provides a succinct overview of nine models of disability illustrating the multi-layered construction of the term and lived experience.

12

Working with adults with learning disabilities

Robert Murray, Toby, Sue and Pam

Learning from experts by experience

In this chapter Rob has collaborated with Toby, Sue, and Pam who are experts by experience and share their insights from living with learning disability (Toby) and being a carer (Sue). Rob is a social worker with professional and personal experience of learning disability, having grown up with siblings with learning disabilities. This chapter is grounded in the voices of people who access or offer services to people with learning disabilities, and Rob draws on his professional experience to illustrate points with case studies and reflections on practice.

Chapter objectives

By the end of this chapter, you will be able to:

• Understand the difference between a learning disability and learning difficulty.
• Have an awareness of the wider professional involvement in working with adults with learning disabilities.
• Understand the importance of legislation that promotes and protects the equal rights of adults with learning disabilities.
• Identify the role of carers supporting an adult with learning disabilities.

Introduction

This chapter is not a 'how to' on working with every adult with learning disabilities, because each adult is an individual, and your approach should be person-centred to reflect this. This chapter is, however, designed to enable you to effectively engage with adults with learning disabilities and does this by focusing on communication and advocacy skills.

Defining the term learning disability

When defining the term learning disability, it is important to understand the difference between learning disabilities and learning difficulties. A misconception is that they are the same, but in fact, although definitions of both terms overlap, they are not the same. A learning disability is defined by the Department of Health in Valuing People (2001) as:

• *A significantly reduced ability to understand new or complex information, to learn new skills (impaired intelligence), with;*
• *A reduced ability to cope independently (impaired social functioning);*
• *which started before adulthood, with a lasting effect on development.*

Whereas the Foundation for People with Learning Disabilities (2021) explain how:

Unlike a learning disability, a learning difficulty does not affect general intelligence (IQ). An individual may often have more than one specific learning difficulty (for example, dyslexia and dyspraxia are often encountered together), and other conditions may also be experienced alongside each other.

This chapter focuses on social work and adults with learning disabilities rather than learning difficulties. I grew up with siblings with complex physical and learning disabilities and have always questioned what makes a person disabled, their impairment or the limitations they face because of the society they live in. My view correlates with the social model of disability (discussed in Chapter 11), which considers how external factors, such as the physical environment, create disability. Maclean and Harrison (2015, p60) discuss how 'the social model has made clear that society can make itself accessible to all people and disabled people have a right to equal opportunities'. I feel strongly that society should be organised inclusively.

Background information and statistics

Mencap (2022) gather population data and statistics across a wide range of reporting areas including health and governmental departments. The collection of this data is to help gain a picture of how many adults with learning disabilities are living in the United Kingdom. On these data, it is reported there are now approximately 1.1 million adults with learning disabilities in the United Kingdom. This figure indicates an increase that could be the result of better recognition, diagnosis and support for different conditions at earlier points in a person's life. This change is due to the introduction of strategies such as Valuing People (2001) and Valuing People Now (2009) that have contributed towards the promotion of individual rights of adults with learning disabilities. As demonstrated throughout this book, social work plays a significant role in promoting the rights of often silenced and marginalised people and relates to the professional commitment to social justice.

The social work role

Social Work England (2023) sets out professional standards for social work practice including the need to 'promote the rights, strengths and wellbeing of people, families and communities'. Within this standard, there is an expectation that social workers uphold the human rights of the people we work with, value their individuality, promote equality and inclusion and work in partnership to achieve the best outcomes for them. The British Association for Social Work (BASW, 2022) further recognises how social workers should promote the human rights for people with learning disabilities in the same way as we would for any other person and has issued specific capabilities around the promotion of this. This is important because assumptions are often made about adults with learning disabilities, including whether they may lack decision-making skills and have mental capacity (to make decisions).

Social workers working with adults with learning disabilities are generally part of specialist teams made up of a range of professionals including doctors, nurses, psychologists and occupational therapists. Being part of a specialist team allows for multi-disciplinary support for individuals accessing services and enables practitioners to share their knowledge and skills to focus on the person's specific and unique experience of learning disability, and any impact this has on their daily lives.

Thinking about the social work role with adults with learning disability, we will now explore a case study about Kate. Think about how you might work with her and what it might be like for Kate to work with you.

Kate

Kate is 24 years old and lives in a small care home for adults with learning disabilities. She has a severe learning disability and requires staff to assist her in meeting her care and support needs including personal care, eating and drinking and ensuring her safety. Kate used to enjoy swimming when she was supported by both her parents, who have sadly passed away, and it has been suggested that she would benefit from accessing the community pool.

Kate is unable to assess risk to herself as well as to and from others, for example, she has tried to lean forward from the backseat of a car to get the driver's attention and is unable to demonstrate road safety or stranger awareness and so requires assistance when she accesses the community.

Kate communicates verbally, however is unable to retain information and will often repeat herself, and although she has limited speech, staff who know Kate well are able to interpret what she is saying/wanting. Kate also experiences periods of anxiety and can become self-injurious, making loud vocalisations.

Kate is also diabetic and sometimes requires a wheelchair for long journeys on foot or in the car.

Activity 12.1

After reading about Kate's experience, consider how you might work with her to help meet her needs and uphold her rights, think about:

What plans are needed to support Kate go swimming?
What risks are there, to whom and from whom?
What plans might the staff in the community and swimming pool make?
Would this level of planning be needed for an individual without a learning disability to go swimming?
How would you go about working with Naomi to support her needs?

Social workers aim to empower adults with learning disabilities to achieve their desired outcomes and goals such as accessing education and/or employment, or in Kate's situation, attending her local swimming pool, by addressing the structural barriers to equality. An example of this might be sourcing resources in the community which provide 'Autism-friendly' services, for example, having certain times available for people with Autism to swim where there is less noise/disruption.

Anti-oppressive practice means ensuring adults with learning disabilities have the same life opportunities as people without learning disabilities. Doing this work effectively requires practitioners to think ethically about issues such as informed consent and risk to self and others as individuals engage in life opportunities. This point is especially relevant in relation to the right of adults with learning disabilities to have a private and family life under Article 8 of the Human Rights Act 1998. Article 8 includes the right to relationships and sexual wellbeing and to be parents. Social workers should advocate and promote opportunities for adults with learning disabilities to engage in healthy relationships, including sexual relationships, however, in practice this does not always happen, for example the case of CH v A Metropolitan Council (2017) where a delay in an adult with Down's Syndrome receiving sex education from the local authority resulted in a period of two years abstinence from their spouse.

When promoting people's rights, social workers need to engage with individuals to understand their unique lived experience and views so that the work is person-centred. Equally important is communicating what work you are doing with the individual and why this is required.

How to work effectively with adults with learning disabilities

Communication

Good communication is essential to anti-discriminatory and anti-oppressive practice, and the necessity of practitioners having effective communication skills within social work are an essential requirement and is written into Social Work England's (2023) Professional Standards. Communication should always be done in a way that the person you are working with can understand; this includes verbal and written information. Care should be taken to consider who you are communicating with and any communication needs they may have.

When focusing on effective communication with people with learning disabilities, social workers should be adaptable in their approach to meet the individual needs of each person. It is important not to assume that a person's ability may be similar or the same to that of someone you have previously worked with or known. It may be that they have a stronger level of communication, require additional support in expressing their needs and views or have additional conditions impacting on their ability to communicate effectively. The impact of health conditions or impairments on communication requires professionals to be fully informed of an adult's individual care and support needs and how they communicate best. For example, The Foundation for People with Learning Disabilities (2021) report that 'Around 40% (exact estimates vary) of adults with a learning disability experience moderate to severe hearing loss'. It is, therefore, important to consider whether the communication needs of an adult with learning disabilities is due to their disability or an impairment, such as hearing loss, and attention is needed to avoid oppressive practice based on assumptions.

Adults with learning disabilities often use communication aids such as the Picture Exchange Communication system and sign language, specifically Makaton and/or Singalong. The Equality Act 2010 sets out the responsibilities placed on public sector organisations to make their services accessible to all, including enabling effective communication. The duty to make information accessible to all ensures adults with learning disabilities are not disadvantaged, and Easy Read information is made available to the public to share with and inform those who may need additional support. There are many services that tailor this support including Easy Read UK (www.easyreaduk.co.uk), who produce resources and promotes the importance of wording being to the point and images used being relevant to the topic to enable the user to understand or associate the information being provided to them.

Tips on how to communicate effectively

Mencap (2022) have produced a guide on different ways to communicate with a person with a learning disability. Examples of good practice include:

- Going at the pace of the person you are working with and ensuring you are avoiding the use of jargon. Plan ahead your intervention, taking into account what you want to achieve and what the person might need support with.
- Acknowledge the person's body language. Can you identify social cues from the person such as whether they are engaged in the intervention or uncomfortable or distressed?
- Consider the environment in which you are communicating with the person. Is it too distracting or noisy for them? Do they have someone with them who knows them well who may be able to support them with any questions they do not understand?
- Allow time for the person to be able to give responses you need, and that they do not feel 'rushed'.
- Consider the balance of power. Is it fair? Is it more dominant towards you rather than equally with the person you are working with?
- Always ensure that you are not speaking about the person in front of them. While a person may have difficulty communicating themselves, it should not be assumed that this impacts their ability to understand what is being said in front of them.

Advances in digital and assistive technology are supporting the ongoing progress in communication for adults with learning disabilities as well as others who may experience communication difficulties. This includes the use of smartphones and tablets. Examples of this may be mobile apps that help a person with completing their food shopping with visual images, transcribing audio calls into written word or maps that help pinpoint accessible facilities. Not only can these assist a person with their individualised communication needs, but it can increase independence in meeting their own care and support needs. Sue and Toby contributes an example of **this** in the case study below.

> ### Sue and Toby
>
> Sue explained how good communication is fundamental to ethical and legal practice as her son (Toby) was reported to lack capacity to sign a tenancy as he was unable to confirm who the landlord was. Sue explained that the issue was not really about Toby's capacity but more about what work had been done to enable him to understand what was being asked and how information should have been worded to her son to enable him to understand. With a personalised approach using appropriate language, Toby

(Continued)

was able to sign the tenancy. Sue advised that professionals should 'listen carefully and make sure they (clients) comprehend what you're asking for'.

On speaking with Toby, and gaining insight into the lived experience, he was able to share with me what he thought was important, not just for Social Workers, but all professionals working with adults with learning disabilities. Toby and I spoke about including the person in decisions about their life as well as recognising individual communication needs and preferences a person may have, such as his friend who uses sign language, lip reading and pictorial symbols which Toby helps his friend with. Toby spoke about how if information has to be in written format, professionals should be mindful of how the person might want this to be, such as whether handwriting is joined up or 'spaced out' to make it clearer to understand. No assumptions should be made about how a person communicates. Toby also spoke about having patience with communication and avoiding the use of jargon.

Activity 12.2

Imagine waking up alone in a country you have never visited before, and the local language is not one you are familiar with. You need to find your way to the nearest airport to return home.

- How will you get to the airport and communicate with other people to get there?
- What difficulties might you face?
- How do you think you will feel?

NHS and publicly funded adult social care services are legally (S.250, Health and Social Care Act 2012) required to follow the Accessible Information Standard (NHS England, 2016) that sets out 'a specific, consistent approach to identifying, recording, flagging, sharing and meeting the information and communication support needs of patients, service users, carers and parents with a disability, impairment or sensory loss'. The standard requires organisations to provide accessible information and support, such as from a communication professional (for example, a Speech and Language Therapist).

Empowering adults with learning disabilities

Advocacy

The Care Act 2014 S.67 states the importance of local authorities ensuring access to independent advocacy for a person when certain conditions are met (S.67(4)). The legislation continues to address how in the event an 'appropriate person' is identified to represent the individual who does not professionally provide care or treatment to the individual; the duty to appoint an independent advocate may not apply. It is vital that the voices of people who may not be able to speak up for themselves are promoted and any anti-oppressive culture or practice is challenged. Advocacy should be introduced at the point a local authority becomes involved in a person's private life and is not limited to a person's care and support planning but can involve access to other services such as health and education.

Evans and Lee (2020) recognise the involvement of family as advocates for adults with learning disabilities, and sometimes the challenges that can be faced with this in respect of conflict of interest in their views over that of the person they are representing. An example could be an adult with learning disabilities wishing to explore supported or independent living away from their family home and a parent or sibling wishing for them to remain at home so they can care for them. As social workers, we should always be mindful of the purpose of advocacy being to support the person in being as involved as possible with decisions around their life and their wishes are vocalised on their behalf.

Pam

Pam fostered her son when he was two weeks old on a short-term fostering arrangement, and he is now 40 years old. Pam explains that their experiences of social workers have been 'mixed' being 'good and bad in parts'. 'I think the power imbalance comes over quite loud and clear. I don't feel it so much now as I've had over forty years' experience'. But power comes from the fact 'I don't know the system and the social workers do'.

Pam expressed that 'Social Workers do not have that much time and it's about continuity' and described the family's frustration with being asked to explain her son's complex medical conditions each time a new social worker was introduced. Pam explained that as an adult, her son 'has much more of a right to have a say about his care. It's difficult but we need to take careful notice about how a person communicates and give them all the opportunities to express what they like and prefer'. On speaking of experiences with social workers, Pam reported that their experience, as a carer, has 'on the whole been very good because mine and my husband's attitude is that we see you as part of our team. The only thing I would say is that there isn't much continuity'.

It is important that social workers do their preparation ahead of any planned intervention as it can be infuriating having to repeat yourself to a new professional each time they visit. From personal experience with my siblings, I know it sets a bad precedent and made me lose confidence that the social worker visiting my family member was competent in their role. Chapter 17 discusses the importance of working with carers further.

How legislation supports advocacy

The Care Act 2014 also establishes the importance of advocacy in relation to safeguarding and sets out the legal framework for professionals working with adults at risk to recognise their duties in safeguarding adults from abuse or neglect. When working with adults with learning disabilities, it is essential that social workers are mindful of the Human Rights Act 1998 and the Mental Capacity Act 2005 so they do not focus on risk at the expense of the person's decision making. However, this can create ethical dilemmas where an individual may seem to be making unwise decisions.

The Mental Capacity Act 2005 is clear in setting out that a person should always be assumed as having capacity unless proven otherwise; the diagnosis of a learning disability does not affect this legal requirement. Any question around a person's mental capacity should be 'time and decision-specific' and not generalised. Furthermore, just because a person may lack capacity around a certain decision, this does not itself exclude them from being able to make other associated decisions. For example, a person may lack capacity to manage their own financial affairs; however, they could make a decision to appoint another person to manage their finances on their behalf. Now consider the following case study of Steve.

Steve

Steve, who is an adult with learning disabilities, wishing to give money to a 'friend' in exchange for companionship. His sister Lisa raises safeguarding concerns about Steve managing his finances as large sums of money have left his account, which she reports he is unable to account for. Steve has a gardener who he pays fortnightly; however, Lisa reports that the gardener appears to have taken on additional responsibilities around the home such as window cleaning and doing shopping for Steve. Lisa believes the gardener is financially abusing Steve.

Activity 12.3

Reflecting on the case study about Steve, now consider the following questions:

What would you decide to do first?
What further information might/do you need?
What legislation would you take into account when making enquiries?

Public Health England (2020) reports that the number of adults with learning disabilities involved in Section 42 of the Care Act 2014, Safeguarding Enquiries increased from 2015/2016 to 2016/2017 before reducing from 2017/2018. This reduction could be evidence of an improvement in support provided to those with learning disabilities, particularly in the prevention of harm or abuse occurring in line with the six principles of Safeguarding under S14.13 of the Care and Statutory Guidance (Department of Health and Social Care, 2022). The Police and Criminal Evidence Act 1984 (PACE) was brought in following the murder of Maxwell Confait in 1972 (The Justice Gap, 2019) and includes access to legal representation and 'appropriate adults' who support young people and adults considered 'vulnerable' (the term 'vulnerable' has changed with the implementation of Care Act 2014, in which an adult who meets the criteria under S.42 is identified as an 'adult at risk' rather than 'vulnerable', although the latter is still used within other legislation). Despite Department of Health (2011) guidance for professionals who work in the criminal justice system which provides information about how to appropriately support adults with learning disabilities, the recognition and support for adults at risk remains an ongoing concern (NHS England, 2019).

Learning from serious case reviews

Reports from NHS England (2019) and the Local Government Association (2021) on the experience of the criminal justice system by adults with learning disability, autism or both indicate how gaps in service provision are a contributing factor in why they may find themselves within the criminal justice system more than might have been the case if support was provided. Findings include how a delay in assessment and diagnosis in earlier years reflects a later lack of understanding or support among professionals (NHS England, 2019) and the impact of budget cuts such as on support provided to individuals who are not deemed eligible for care and support under The Care and Support (Eligibility Criteria) Regulations 2015.

The investigation and response from the Department of Health (2012) following the abuse exposed at Winterbourne View Hospital (and subsequent cases) have highlighted the importance of recognising institutional abuse within care settings to vulnerable adults including those with learning disabilities. Failings made by agencies, like many Serious Case Reviews evidence, reinforce the importance of improved multi-agency working and communication.

In the wake of the abuse that took place in Winterbourne View Hospital, there has been a movement (NHS England, 2015) for adults with learning disabilities to be supported more within the community and not within inpatient units; however, in February 2022, there were at least 2,040 people with a learning disability and/or autism still in inpatient units. Fifty-six percent of those had been an inpatient for over two years and over 350 people have been in hospital for more than 10 years (NHS Digital, 2022).

While the number of adults with learning disabilities in long-term inpatient units has reduced significantly since Winterbourne View, the question should be asked on whether reasonable resources are available within the community to help further reduce the need for hospital admission. My Life My Choice (2019), a charity that is operated by people with learning disabilities, argues that inpatient units should be closed and that people with learning disabilities should be supported within the community as well as being closer to family and friends.

In July 2022, the Government published an action plan titled 'Building the Right Support for People with a Learning Disability and Autistic People'. The plan sets out commitments to be made in order to improve the lives of those with learning disabilities and autism. Within this includes the aim of reducing the number of people in inpatient care and more frequent reviews are undertaken to monitor this.

Chapter summary

In summary, it is important to always consider how the impact of the lived experience for an adult with a learning disability should not be valued any less of that of an adult without one and they can also be affected by the treatment they receive from professional services. A clear understanding and awareness of this will formulate effective strengths-based practice and ensure that we, as social workers, are able to uphold their human rights as well as anyone else we may support.

Useful websites

The Makaton Charity have a wide range of online resources and how the use of signs along with using verbal language can help in understanding the needs of a person where they have no speech, or where speech is difficult for them:

www.makaton.org
  Learning Disability Today provides a wealth of information around learning disabilities across the life span, including resources such as books, articles, videos, discussions and debates on current issues and challenges faced by people with learning disabilities:

www.learningdisabilitytoday.co.uk
  The story of Steven Neary is one of the most well-known cases in learning disabilities and is vital learning for anyone looking to work with adults with learning disabilities:

https://signalong.org.uk/
  Signalong provides training and resources to assist those with communication difficulties and English as an additional language.

www.39essex.com/cop_cases/london-borough-of-hillingdon-v-neary-2/

13

Working with older adults

Louise Downes and Jonathan Parker

Learning from experts by experience

This chapter is co-authored by Jonathan and Louise. Jonathan worked as a social worker before becoming an academic, and Louise is a social worker and now works in a workforce development team. Their approach to this chapter allows the reader to delve into different theoretical perspectives of working with older people, supported by stories and reflections from practice and their lived experience.

> **Chapter objectives**
>
> By the end of this chapter, you should be able to:
>
> - Identify some of the ways in which older people are viewed negatively and the potential impacts of ageism
> - Recognise some key theories of ageing and their relevance to social work
> - Understand the importance of the 'voice' and participation of older people in the way services are designed and delivered
> - Describe and apply your knowledge to social work practice

Introduction

Increasingly, social work is associated with safeguarding work, especially in respect of children. While social work has always contained an element of regulation and control, its history is very wide, and the clue in the first word of the name 'social work' is important; we practise with all members including those excluded from society, and we work at the interface of the relationships that make us all human.

In this chapter, we are dealing with social work with older people. Firstly, we discuss the socially constructed nature of the term 'older people' and then consider some of the implications of this for social work practice, dealing with ageist assumptions, policies and practices. We must do this in the context of who we are as people *and* social workers. If we are to work with older people, we need to appreciate some of the theories developed to help understand ageing as an individual and as part of a society. Following this we will explore the current context of social work practice, focusing on England but also looking at the other UK countries' practices. This will bring us to consider how and why social workers might be involved in older people's lives and what we might do in those contexts including the centrality of genuinely hearing the older person's voice within the professional relationship.

Reflections from the authors

Social work is fundamentally concerned with wellbeing – both of ourselves and that of others. Here are some reflections from us that link wellbeing and our own particular takes on life and social work.

> **Louise**
>
> I was fortunate enough to attend a music festival which is a great place for some people watching – a favourite hobby for most social workers. My observations started
>
> *(Continued)*

(Continued)

me reflecting on the individual nature of wellbeing. One gentleman (who could have been described as older) was going for a run around the site one morning. I occasionally can bring myself to go for a run but prefer a dance class; I would never consider going for a run at a festival, which is for me about relaxing, but for this gentleman, I assume it was part of his routine that he could not manage without. As I walked to get my breakfast, I passed a line of people queuing to access the few showers that were available. Again, for me, this is something I can manage without for a few days but for these people having a daily shower was clearly important enough to queue and wait for. As I sat and munched my bacon butty, I observed someone going into the tent that sold essential items and came out with *The Observer*; this I can relate to! I was imagining as these individuals get older, these things that were a priority for them at a music festival will remain a priority. As social workers, we need to make the time to get to know the individuals we work with, to understand what these priorities are and what we require for our wellbeing. For me, I won't need to access a shower everyday, but I will need access to a range of music.

Jonathan

I have been in university life for many years now, but beforehand I was a social worker, working in many roles and finally settling into a specialist position with, mainly, older people living with dementia. This sparked an enthusiasm for ensuring that people's voices that were often ignored began to be heard, that a human relational perspective was introduced centre stage when working alongside people living with dementia and their carers. This enthusiasm continued into academic life and remains with me as I, myself, grow older. Now, coming to the time in which I am contemplating retirement, the needs of older people (and one in particular!) are seen through a different lens. The experiences I have had throughout life, whether in work or outside, have coalesced to give me a sense of the individual within a social context and to note the indivisibility of the person and the social world he or she inhabits. Continued opportunities to think, study and create will remain central to my wellbeing as I age.

Social work and older people: an ageist exercise?

Social work with older people sparks controversy by its very name. Why should older people be singled out as a group in need of social work; is it suggested that all older people require social work assistance; what constitutes an older person and what distinguishes them from adults not considered 'older'? Of course, similar questions might be asked of social work with children and families and other groups seemingly homogenised in this way. However, asking the questions is important when we come to considering social work with adults who are deemed to be 'older'. They are important in highlighting the inherent and often unspoken ageism prevalent within society and replicated through social work and other public services.

What is ageism?

Ageism is unfair discrimination against a person on the basis of their age. While this can relate to people of any age, including children (see Young-Bruehl, 2013), the concept was first used to illuminate rife discrimination against older people (Butler, 1969). This discrimination can be reflected in differential treatment, services, access to services and through the tacit acceptance of social expectations and assumptions made on the basis of a person's age. Age is a protected characteristic under the Equality Act 2010, and therefore age discrimination is against the law.

Before we look at some theories that are useful for social workers to know when working with older people, attempt the following activities which ask you to reflect on your thoughts and views of ageing.

Activity 13.1

Without thinking write down all the words you can think of to describe or which you might associate with older people.

Draw a circle round all the words that could be ageist or represent age discrimination.

What does this say about older people in society, and what does it say about your views of older people?

Comment

You may have come up with terms such as elder, wise old (wo)man alongside the more pejorative terms such as coffin-dodger, wrinkly, grumpy. We suspect that you may have identified more words that could be discriminatory than neutral or positive ones. This perhaps says a great deal about our society which, in many ways, works against older people as full, valued human beings and consigns them, often, to a role as troublesome, needy, requires protecting or in death's waiting room!

Activity 13.2

Consider the following saying: 'A ship in the harbour is safe but not what they are built for'. We invite you to apply this saying to your own life and what this might mean to you in terms of life choices. Now please reflect on how your thoughts might have an impact on you as a social worker and what it might mean for your practice.

Comment

This activity will help you go into greater depth in understanding how our society may be ageist and work against the interests of older people.

Carney and Nash (2020) explore a range of critical questions we need to ask ourselves when considering older people. They point out the social changes that are happening including rising retirement ages, explore the adequacy (or otherwise) of pensions and, therefore, the possibility of retiring and the wider state of social care for older people. Care-giving needs do rise in later life; however, the majority of that care is still provided in hidden or unacknowledged ways by family members, friends and others within the community. More formalised social care, which may involve social work to assess eligibility and arrange services, is increasingly expensive and delivered at a time wherein local authorities have seen a real decline in the funding they receive from central government. While social workers may be responsible for undertaking comprehensive assessments and ensuring that people apply for the right benefits and Personal Independence Payment (PIP), there is much more to the role that we need to explore and the human, relational elements need to be seen alongside the technical and practical aspects of helping.

Categorising older people is immensely difficult and often involves homogenising very different individuals and groups of people over a 35–40 year span. If we, in the United Kingdom, arbitrarily consider old age to start at 65 years, or even 66 years when the state pension starts currently, then attempts to collectively group people above that age will necessarily rely on stereotypes and prejudices. In reality, of course, people over 65 years old reflect different genders, sexualities, health, disability and employment statuses to name a few. It is often suggested, as well, that older people may be less radical in their thinking than those who are younger and that there may be conflict between generations. While life experiences may lead people to be more nuanced in their deliberations as they grow, and some level of disagreement is evident between different generations, this seems more of a myth than a reality and something that, again, feeds a gerontophobic and ageist beast – something social workers need to identify and challenge.

By association with people defined as being older, social workers who practise with them specifically are often similarly marginalised, stereotyped and ignored. It is important for social workers to be well versed in understanding the worlds in which they practise. Theories to help navigate this are crucial and it is to these that we now turn.

Theories of ageing

Theories of ageing are often seen within biological, psychological and sociological domains (Phillips et al., 2006). However, it is important to add a spiritual dimension as it is increasingly recognised that how people make sense of their lives and experiences is central to the ways people act, adapt and reflect their needs and wants in life (Szto, 2020). You should keep these four aspects of what it is to be human in mind while you read this chapter and, especially, when acting as a social worker with people. In this section, we will provide a brief overview of some of the key theories social workers should be aware of that will help you understand and plan your work with older people.

As we grow older our bodies change. Our senses begin to decline with sight becoming less acute, hearing loss affecting the ways we hear and interpret sounds, olfactory and gustatory loss may limit our enjoyment of eating. A decline in the sense of touch may demand new ways of approaching situations that rely on touch and grip; it may even lead to falling. The build-up of bodily injuries or trauma (known as physiological insults) over time may also increase with age as may illnesses such as cancer, heart disease, stroke and, of course, dementia (Sauvain-Dugerdil et al., 2006). These changes can lead to gerontophobic responses in the general public (Carney and Nash, 2020), but also in professionals and policy-makers as part of biological reductionism (Biggs, 1993). However, it must be remembered that these changes are not always catastrophic, do not affect everyone in the same way and that there are many things that can be done to mitigate them. As social workers, we need to have an awareness of these changes so we can identify when people may need more help, and so we can work more effectively with those concerned with individuals' bio-medical health and also so we can promote individual differences to others (Parker and Ashencaen Crabtree, 2020a).

Psychological and functionalist sociological approaches to ageing share much in common and cover disengagement theory, activity theory and continuity theories. The focus in psychological terms relates to the adaptation of the individual to the changes involved in growing older, while functionalist sociology emphasises adaptive responses that keeps society functioning in the best way possible. This approach sees disengage-ment from society and functional roles as a step to allow new and younger 'blood' to assume positions of responsibility and power and that this reflects the expected pattern of life. It is developed in the work of Cumming and Henry (1961) who considered decremental decline in all life's areas is inevitable.

Activity theorists are more fluid but still believe that change and decline are inevitable as people age. However, they suggest that different roles and tasks can be undertaken at different points in life (Havighurst and Albrecht, 1953; Lemon et al., 1972). This adaptation also forms part of continuity theory and adds that ways of making mean-ingful lives, as far as possible, can be emphasised when working with older people (Onega and Tripp-Reimer, 1997). It differs from activity theory in being holistic and continuous rather than linked to life stages.

Functional and psychological theories such as those we have introduced focus on decline and the inevitability of losing health, status and meaning. They miss, therefore, some of the more positive benefits of ageing that can also be highlighted such as taking on new roles, tasks and enjoying an active old age replete with meaning. This has been widely taken up in the concept of active ageing (Gomez-Jimenez and Parker, 2014). However, while this approach encourages wellbeing and healthy behaviours, it does seem also to be predicated on economic savings by reducing the health and social care burden and retaining active informal carers and workforce. So we would argue, as social workers, that we need to take a questioning and critical approach, recognising that healthy lives and ageing are good things but also that these may be used in ways that take advantage of people or create unfair expectations because of age.

Critical theories of ageing have developed to explain some of the ways that thinking about ageing can create societal myths that become accepted without question and influence public perspectives and service development, provision and delivery. The assumptions made can affect jobs, gender, health and care among other things and is something to be aware of in social work practice (Parker and Ashencaen Crabtree, 2020b). Grenier et al. (2017) talk about precarious ageing as a counter to the sometimes over-optimistic accounts of active ageing, suggesting that older people have been alienated from the workforce, excluded from planning for the risks of the climate crisis, do not always have the pensions or resources popularly associated with the 'boomer' generation and where deep old age combines a fear of these structural problems with the possibilities of biomedical need, especially in respect of dementia. However, such structured dependencies do not affect all older people, and postmodern approaches have challenged an approach that solely focuses on political economy. Gilleard and Higgs (2000) proposed the concept of cultural gerontology as a way of exploring living in and making sense of the world and contextual environment and sought to replace structure with agency.

Biographical approaches to ageing take into account all these perspectives and see the meanings created by ageing in the life course, stories and experiences of the older person (Gubrium and Holstein, 2003). Clearly grounded in sociological theories such as symbolic interactionism, phenomenology and ethnomethodology, this approach connects well with relational social work practice (Parker, 2012). It illustrates the interactions between a person in history and structure, their contexts, and their biographical narrative, or stories and meanings made through life. Life narratives are explored and (re)created through talking and actively engaging in conversations about the person's life in a respectful and dignified way that ensures the person is at the centre of those discussions (Parker, 2012). Milne (2020) continues this biographical approach through her life course focus on mental health and ageing. She believes the life course approach presents real importance for social workers as it recognises the significant impact that experiences in life can have on mental health, susceptibility to mental ill-health and wellbeing in later life. The central place of structural and social issues on the interpersonal and intra-psychic functioning of people, as we age, is important and helps us in recognising that each individual is complex, has their own stories, make up, wants and needs.

So there are many theories relating to human ageing. Some have more relevance than others for social work practice, but an awareness of the range helps us to understand other professionals' perspectives and also gives insight into what people may be experiencing and why, and some of the ways in which older people may be perceived.

Social work with older people

The Care Act 2014 in England, Social Services and Well-being Act 2014 in Wales and the 2022 National Social Care Bill in Scotland keep a focus on wellbeing and involvement. This is perhaps more pronounced in the Welsh and proposed Scottish legislation. The Care Act 2014 is important as it has collated legislation relating to adult social care in one place. Section 1 of the Act emphasises personal wellbeing, attention to the needs and goals of people, as the key principle central to care and support. Wellbeing is recognised as a complex concept but includes personal dignity; physical and mental health; emotional wellbeing; protection from abuse and neglect; having control over one's everyday life; being able to participate in work, education, recreation; social and economic wellbeing; having a positive domestic, family and personal life; having suitable accommodation; being able to contribute to society. Local authorities are responsible for personalising services depending on circumstances, needs, goals and wishes and for recognising social work cannot be delivered as a 'one size fits all' service.

The Care Act principles reflect the *Knowledge and Skills Statements for Adult Social Workers* (Department of Health, 2015a). When assessing, or planning for care and support, social workers should:

- start with the assumption that individuals can best judge their own wellbeing;
- take individuals' feelings, wishes and perspectives into account;
- prevent or delay the impact of needs for care and support;
- be comprehensive in their assessments;
- encourage participation of people in the process as far as that is possible;
- negotiate a balanced approach between an individual's needs and those of carers and friends;
- prevent abuse and neglect;
- minimise restrictions of rights and freedom.

These are useful principles to keep in mind when working with older people. However, they remain professionally led and are not themselves co-created or demo-cratised. We need to include the views and perspectives of older people themselves. Louise reflects on her experience in working with older people.

Louise

Older people are the largest users of social care but get the smallest allocation of resources and qualified social work input (Milne et al., 2014). When you consider the multiple com-plexities and dimensions of working with older people, I would suggest that you need skilled professionals to support. In my career, many of the older people I have worked with have lived through the war and this impacts on their life experiences and resilience. I recall one lady when I was completing a mental capacity assessment and explaining the concerns her family had for her safety at home, telling me that she had lived through the bombing in the war hiding under the table and therefore, wasn't afraid of having a fall at home. The experiences of older people in the coming generations will be different and social workers will need to adapt and work with an increasingly culturally diverse older generation.

Reflecting on your role as a social worker with older people

Social work is a reflective profession in which you are encouraged to consider your position in life and how this affects those with whom you work. This is why we started with a reflection from ourselves as authors, which positioned each of us, our concerns, wants and needs. We invite you now to consider the following activity and think about how it affects your role as a social worker.

Activity 13.3

If you were talking with a social worker about your needs. What would you like them to know about? What would you not want them to know about, but is still important in meeting your needs? And how would you want someone to talk to you about this?

No one individual can ever be 'representative' of the whole group. However, everyone has a valid viewpoint and perspective. So we asked an 'older person' the following questions:

1. What do you think is important for social workers to consider when working with older people?
2. What knowledge and skills should a social worker have before working with older people?
3. What does 'ageing well' mean to you?
4. Anything else you think is important to share?

The comments and answers give us an insight into some of the things that can be important to consider when working with older people, but it is important to remember this is one person's views and everyone you work with is unique.

*   *When visiting an older person, prepare first by making sure that the older person knows you are coming and why.*
*   *Check that the time and day is suitable for their routine. Reading any background information or notes.*
*   *When you arrive identify yourself and show your ID badge* (one older person suggested that the ID badges should be made bigger they can be hard for an older person to read).
*   *Adapt the way you communicate depending on the older person. Asking,* 'am I talking clearly enough' *is much nicer than* 'can you hear me alright'.
*   *Determine how the person would like to be addressed as not all older people like the informality of using first names although some do.*
*   *Establish the purpose of the meeting and that your aim is to help.*
*   *Avoid jargon, gobbledygook, keep things clear and simple. But ensure you are not being condescending, maybe ask about previous employment showing an interest and establishing that you understand they have not always been an* 'older person'.
*   *At the end of any meeting ensure you sum up and agree a shared understanding of what has been decided. Provide written contact details, preferably with a direct line contact number.*

Responding to a question about ageing well, one person said: *Advice from health and social care is important for many of us in order to assist in ageing well. Advising older people to take an interest in and control of their health and wellbeing can prevent*

Knowledge:	
Health services how to refer and access Local community clubs and groups Have read background information, if the person has a health need or diagnosis do your research, what impact might that be having on daily life? Understanding of impact of ageism and discrimination. Knowledge of grief and loss	**Skills:** Empathy Cultural competence Patience

Figure 13.1 Considerations for working with older people (see capabilities statement for social workers in England who work with older people, BASW, 2018)

isolation and loneliness as well. Introduction to groups and clubs can also help, so try to make sure you are fully armed with local information. But it was also considered important to work in partnership with older people to encourage self-empowerment. Utilising an exchange model of assessment (Smale et al., 1993), which treats the person as an expert in their own situation and builds on their knowledge of resources, services and so on, helps this process.

It is important that social workers have understanding and show empathy. By keeping abreast of theories and knowledge as well as of local resources and services and the biographies of those people with whom they are working, they can demonstrate this.

Distilling some of the key elements from our own experiences and practice, and from the views of older people, we suggest the following practical approaches when working with older people – see Figure 13.1.

The central message coming from all of this is that the key role of the social worker with older people is to support them in having a voice. Louise supervises a group of ASYEs and the common theme that comes through from their work, whether in hospitals, community or work with learning disabilities, is that without them (social workers) the people they work with would not have had a voice. Other professionals and often families may take a paternalistic attitude towards the person, understandably wanting to protect and keep them safe. As social workers, we understand that life cannot be without risks and that we all live and embrace risk in our daily lives. Social workers need to work in partnership with older people to understand their wishes, feelings and what wellbeing means to them, supporting those around them to understand and hear what they want.

Chapter summary

In this chapter, we have introduced some of the myths of ageing and older people, theories that can help guide you in working with older people and what social work has to offer in this area. You should now be able to identify ageism and some of the negative ways in which older people are portrayed; recognise the relevance of some key theories of ageing for social work; understand the central importance of the person's 'voice' and participation and describe and apply your knowledge to social work practice.

We are concerned to debunk stereotypes and to prevent unfair discrimination resulting from ageing, and sometimes it is suggested that grouping older people together as a field of social work practice might add to that. However, we would argue there is a need also to promote the rights of older people, to ensure they receive appropriate and respectful services and that social workers are aware of some of the specific needs that arise through living a long life. We are passionate about social work in this area and hope to encourage you as the reader to consider this as your career.

Annotated further reading

Carney, G. M. and Nash, P., 2020. *Critical Questions for Ageing Societies*. Bristol: Policy Press.
   This book provides a wealth of information on aspects of ageing societies that we need to know as background to working with people who are ageing.

Milne, A., 2020. *Mental Health in Later Life: Taking a Life Course Approach*. Bristol: Policy Press.
   This marvellous book explores the ways people's life experiences and the structural aspects of the societies in which they live interact to create their biographies and the ways in which mental health is affected.

Parker, J., 2012. Landscapes and portraits: Using multiple lenses to inform social work theories of old age. *In*: Davies, M., ed. *Social Work with Adults*. Basingstoke: Palgrave Macmillan, 285–299.
   This chapter outlines key theories that have been developed to understand the ways in which we age. It provides information concerning the ways other professionals might understand the ageing process which is very important in interdisciplinary practice.

14

Working with adults living with dementia

Jemma Goddard

Learning from experts by experience

Jemma is a social worker with extensive experience in working with people of all ages and who live with dementia. Jemma introduces us to Henry, who is based on the lived experience of people with whom she has worked, and his story is woven throughout the chapter.

Chapter objectives

By the end of this chapter, you will:

- Understand how social care supports people living with dementia.
- Understand the importance of applying person centred, strengths-based approaches and positive risk taking in care planning and decision making.
- Have an awareness of how communication skills can support a person to communicate and express their wishes and views.
- Have an awareness of the social care role in multi-disciplinary settings.
- Recognise and understand the importance of supporting people to make decisions about their own lives.
- Identify the role of the carer when supporting an adult living with dementia.

Introduction

Currently in the United Kingdom, it is estimated that there are around 944,000 people living with dementia, and with two thirds living in the community there is an estimated 700,000 unpaid carers supporting those living with dementia (Alzheimer's Research UK, 2022a; Social Care Institute for Excellence (SCIE), 2022a).

It is important to remember that dementia is an umbrella term used to describe abnormal changes in the brain such as memory loss, changes in thinking, perception, behaviours and language. There are many forms of dementia, with the most common being Alzheimer's disease, vascular, frontotemporal, and then other less common dementia such as young/early onset, Lewy Body and alcohol-related dementia which can lead to Wernicke-Korsakoff (Alzheimer's Research UK, 2022b).

Everyone's experience of dementia is unique to them and how it impacts them varies; how you work with one person will not be the same as someone else. While it is useful to understand diagnosis and symptoms, it is far more important to get to know the person and who they are. Activity 14.1 encourages you to explore this further.

Activity 14.1

Exploring dementia

Explore the Alzheimer's Research UK webpage Types of Dementia to see different types of dementia and lived experiences at:
https://www.alzheimersresearchuk.org/dementia-information/types-of-dementia/
Did anything surprise you about the diversity of dementia? Take time to consider how the different types of dementia might impact a person.

When working with older adults, it is very common to work with those living with dementia, including the less common dementias. Having an insight into different forms of dementia, therefore, will support with your ability to understand a person's experience.

A journey through hospital discharge

It is estimated that just under half of the unplanned hospital admissions for people over 70 years old have a dementia, with at least a quarter of hospital beds being occupied by people living with dementia. Furthermore, the statistics evidence that people living with dementia who are admitted to hospital can experience increased confusion, disorientation, increased risk of falls or hospital acquired illnesses and longer stays than those who do not have dementia (Royal College of Psychiatrists, 2019; NICE, 2022). Hospital settings and processes can be difficult for anyone to navigate, but even more so for someone who is experiencing memory loss and disorientation to time, place and person. People may be supported by their loved ones, but often they are unpaid carers and may be experiencing carer stress or strain themselves. Therefore, it is important to recognise the additional stress a hospital admission can bring, as well as the relief it can afford some carers and how these impact on the decisions made when planning discharges.

This chapter introduces you to Henry and takes you through his journey as he navigates the hospital discharge process; many of the examples and scenarios in his story are equally relevant in community settings and, therefore, support readers' understanding of how social care supports people living with dementia.

Henry

Henry is 87 and he lives at home with his wife Ruby, and they are both supported by their daughter, Ava. Henry is living with Alzheimer's disease, which was diagnosed two years ago following increased confusion, disorientation and short-term memory loss. Henry has also experienced several falls in the past six months, with the most recent fall leading to a hospital admission.

The hospital staff and Ava have concerns about how he has been managing at home and the carer stress that Ruby and Ava are experiencing. The hospital has recommended that Henry requires residential placement, and that returning home is not a safe option due to his high risk of falls, carer strain and risk of self-neglect.

Information gathering and person-centred approach

It is important to recognise that when someone is in hospital there is pressure to work in a timely manner to support with discharge; hospitals are acute settings which we know have a negative impact on a person's physical and mental health the longer they remain

(NICE, 2022). However, there can be many complex factors that contribute towards a delayed discharge, often this is surrounding social concerns such as how the person will manage or be supported once discharged. Often people living with dementia may be admitted to hospital, and it is the first time that social services are aware of this person, so a period is required to understand that person's situation from their views and others, and any concerns raised.

Working in a person-centred way means that first and foremost it is important to establish Henry's views. Person-centred approaches in dementia care focus on the individual and their values and beliefs, unlike the medical model which focuses on treatment and processes. Taking a person-centred approach is about considering the relationship you build with a person, how you communicate with them and supporting the person to make decisions about their lives (Fazio et al., 2018). Kitwood's (1997) focus on a person-centred approach in dementia established fundamental principles in supporting personhood, starting with love and branching off to comfort, attachment, inclusion, occupation and identity. These all contribute to supporting a person to retain who they are and what is important to them while adapting to how dementia may impact on their life and self. However, it is important to ensure that these aspects are meaningful to the individual person and do not become tokenistic.

Donnelly et al.'s (2018) study explored how people living with dementia are involved in care planning and decision making. It identified that social workers find that involving the person in the care planning meetings can often feel tokenistic; in that they are invited but plans continue to be made not involving the person. This could be due to the person's cognition/ability to communicate or inclusion of family members and relying on them to be the decision makers. Consider this further in Activity 14.2.

Activity 14.2

How would you ensure the person is at the centre of their care planning and decision making, and ensure that inclusion is meaningful? What communication techniques might you use (think creatively) and who and what might you involve in enabling a person to be meaningfully involved?

We are already aware that Henry is living with dementia, but this does not mean that he is unable to make decisions or contribute towards his care planning; it is important that this assumption is not made. In accordance with the principles of the Mental Capacity Act 2005 capacity should be assumed, as well as a person being supported as much as possible to make their own decision beforehand (discussed in detail in Chapter 6). Case law has shown the importance of ensuring the person's needs are taken into consideration and they are afforded the right amount of time, supporting aids and information to consider and understand the situation and decision (CC v KK and STCC [2012]). Furthermore, it is important to remember that in relation to capacity assessments, a person is found to lack capacity to make a decision not because they have an impairment of the brain or mind but because this impairment causes them to be unable to make a decision. A practice example of this is when I have worked with a person, who had a significant decision to make about where they should be living, but this came with different complications and considerations. I found that the person did not lack capacity but was still unable to make this decision; the reason being was due to the weight of the decision and the lack of information and understanding they had of their options in general terms, not because their impairment meant they could not understand or weigh the information. So, it is an important aspect of considering someone's capacity to make decisions about their lives, ensuring that it is because of their impairment and not just because they have one.

With consideration of the points above, unless it had previously been specified otherwise, it is important to have a conversation with Henry first, before approaching his family. Henry has the right to privacy, and data protection means that I would need consent from Henry to speak with his family first, something that can often be overlooked. This also adopts the person-centred approach and assumption that Henry can make decisions about his own life. From the initial conversations that I have with Henry, I would hope to be able to gather information about what is important to him, what he wishes to happen and his perspective of the current situation, as well as building a rapport.

Communication

Each person's communication skills may vary regardless of if they are living with dementia or not, and there should not be any pre-assumptions about someone's ability to voice their wishes and views. However, it is helpful in being able to identify how you might support someone with communicating, for example, does someone feel more comfortable with a family member present or does walking and talking work better than a more formal approach. From practice experience, often those living with dementia may find it more difficult to communicate or understand the conversation being had. In these circumstances, I have found that not having an agenda and being flexible to have conversations about what that person understands and wants to talk about can be a good steppingstone to building a rapport. When someone feels more familiar with you, it may be less concerning to them to have such personal conversations, and it also allows you as a professional to assess their understanding of the information.

Henry's medical notes suggest that he has difficulties communicating his needs. People living with dementia can often experience language or communication difficulties; Alzheimer's Society (2022a) identify that the person may:

- *not be able to find the right words*
- *use a related word (for example, 'book' instead of 'newspaper')*
- *use substitutes for words (for example, 'thing that you sit on' instead of 'chair')*
- *not find any word at all*
- *not struggle to find words, but use words that have no meaning, or that are jumbled up in the wrong order*
- *go back to the first language they learnt as a child. For example, if they learnt English as a second language, they may forget how to speak it.*

When visiting Henry, I noticed that he often used the wrong words to describe things and lost concentration in our conversation; this with Henry's increased confusion about his situation and his short-term memory loss made it more difficult for him to recognise why I was visiting. What is important in these scenarios is to not assume that Henry is unable to participate in meaningful conversations, but to adapt the way that we as professionals communicate. Start by trying to understand how Henry is feeling and other factors that may be having an impact; he is currently in a busy ward setting with constant noise and movement; he is not in familiar surroundings with his family. By understanding and recognising this, you have an opportunity to make changes to support Henry to feel more comfortable and able to communicate. Henry found it more calming to move to a quiet area, and we took the picture he had of his family; this was a good conversation starter, and something that Henry enjoyed talking about.

I found this quote by Mick R [a person living with dementia] helpful to understand practitioner's roles in supporting people with communicating:

You have the task of fishing around in this murky mind of mine.

(Mick R, SCIE, 2020)

When you start to 'fish around' you start to create a rapport, and by taking the time to understand a person's past and present and making connections and links between these, you may then start to have an understanding of what their reality is and how you can communicate in a meaningful way. Activity 14.3 and 14.4 will support you in considering ways of communicating.

Activity 14.3

How would you expect someone to speak to you?
  Often, I have seen people talk about a person right in front of them or speak to them in a childlike manner. At times we need to adjust how we communicate, but this needs to be done in a dignified and person-centred way. Think of ways that you can adapt the way you communicate.

Activity 14.4

Where is home?

We often need to gain the wishes and views of a person regarding where they want to live, or where home is to them. When someone says they want to go home, where do they mean?
  Where is home to you? What makes your house a home; is it the bricks and water, the people you live with, the belongings in your home, the décor, the area or the place you grew up in?
  How would you work with someone to establish what they mean by home?

Approaches to care planning

When we work with people living with dementia in the community or hospital settings, we often work alongside other professionals in a multi-disciplinary approach or team (MDT) such as Doctors, District Nurses and Occupational Therapists. Each professional brings their own expertise which contributes to a holistic assessment and support network for the person. Although the approach to risk and care planning has started to shift, especially with the introduction of the Care Act 2014, there is still a culture of 'paternalistic' or 'risk averse' that exists (Morgan and Williamson, 2014). From my practice experience, paternalistic approaches are often found in hospital settings and when we consider that the MDT in hospitals is mostly made up of health professionals, social workers may have a challenge to support other professionals in considering how we maintain a person-centred and strengths-based approach to risk and care planning.

I'm not dying of dementia; I'm dying of cotton wool.

(Brian, SCIE, 2020)

Brian's quote is not dissimilar to that of Lord Justice Munby (2007):

What good is it making someone safer if it merely makes them miserable?

Social work values are embedded in human rights and are reflected in practice models such as strengths based (The Policy, Ethics and Human Rights Committee, 2015). So how social workers view risks may differ to that of health professionals, and I would suggest that the understanding and tools social workers have enable us to support others to consider the positive outcomes that can be achieved by assessing and working with risks.

Henry is currently in a position where the medical professionals feel he requires long-term residential placement to remain safe and well. Henry's views are that he wishes to return home. I have often found that social workers are the 'voice of reason' in discharge planning meetings; often reminding others, including family, that we always need to consider the less restrictive options and consider how we can balance risks and the persons wishes and choices (MCA, 2005).

When we talk about someone moving to residential care because the risk is perceived as too high for them to return home, we also must consider how moving to such an environment may impact on that person's overall wellbeing; they may be physically safer but what impact will this have on their emotional or mental wellbeing? When we reflect that the Care Act 2014 places an equal measure on all aspects of a person's wellbeing, we then need to consider if we as professionals are putting more emphasis on one aspect than another, and possibly examine our own values and how this impacts decision making (McNamara and Morgan, 2016; Beckett and Maynard, 2017). For example, in Henry's case, are the health professionals placing a greater consideration towards his safety around falls risk than they are his wishes to return home, whereby he feels safe and connected to his family? A common practice and ethical dilemma can be balancing the need to safeguard those living with dementia from harm against their right to liberty and autonomy. Therefore, to avoid risk adverse practice, an approach of supporting a person to identify, weigh up and acknowledge risks will allow them to make informed choices, apposed to attempting to control aspects of individuals lives (Kemshall et al., 2013).

> *Being able to make mistakes is really important – otherwise how do you know what you can and can't do? I understand that people don't like to see me struggle, and don't want me to be in danger, but you need to get the right balance.*
>
> (Stan, SCIE, 2020)

Often when supporting people with assessments and support planning, there are a range of several approaches or models that social workers can draw on; the Care Act 2014 puts an emphasis on using people's strengths to support them in achieving their outcomes. Strengths-based approach can support social workers and the person to explore what capabilities, resources, knowledge and skills they have as a person, within their social network and community to use to meet needs and achieve outcomes (SCIE, 2022b). Positive risk taking, alongside a strengths-based approach, can be used in enabling a person to continue to use their capabilities to live their lives, while understanding and looking to reduce the risks around a person, but this does not necessarily mean avoiding risks. As McNamara and Morgan (2016) identify, positive risk taking is not about enabling risks but exploring and understanding the value of taking such risk to achieve a positive outcome for the person. Therefore, the word positive is meant in relation to the outcome, not the risk.

In Henry's case, his wishes and view of a positive outcome would be to return home. Taking a strengths-based approach to assessment can support with how we explore the risks needing to be considered to achieve the outcome. We are aware of the risks posed to Henry if he was to return home, falls, carer breakdown and self-neglect being the ones identified by the hospital. With careful consideration with Henry, his family and the MDT, and using his known strengths, and the support network of his family and community, we can start to build a support plan to bring together these resources while having open conversations about managing risks, expectations and ensuring that Henry remains at the centre of support planning and decision making. It is also important when we consider supporting people in the community that we consider the support provided by unpaid carers, and the impact of this role has on their wellbeing, including their relationships with their loved one, social wellbeing and physical health (Alzheimer's Research UK, 2015).

Being creative and resourceful

With the current 'care crisis' that we are experiencing (Age UK, 2022), now is such an important time for social workers to draw on the resources and support that is available within our communities and continue to build on these. While the pandemic had a devastating impact on the social care system, it also had a positive impact on how local communities came together to offer support, with many neighbourhoods creating volunteer services and support, and some of which have continued to operate (MacInnes et al., 2021). Services such as these enable people living with dementia to stay connected with local support and greater chance of living independently at home, as well as moving away from traditional care services, which do not always fit in with people's lifestyles and needs.

Assistive technologies can also offer people living with dementia additional support at home while maintaining skills and independence, and there are many forms of technology that may be useful (National Institute for Health Research, 2018; Alzheimer's Society, 2022b). However, there are also everyday technologies that can be used, such as smart voice-controlled speakers (e.g. Amazon Alexa or Google Nest); I have been able to use these in practice to support people to remember medication, appointments, to allow family to easily 'drop in' and offer social and emotional support. Consider that if Henry were living alone but required support in managing his medication, he would be reliant on carers visiting four times a day, whereas reminders could be set up using a smart device, which not only enables Henry to remain independent, but supports him in creating routines in his own home.

Activity 14.5

Consider the technology that you use daily; how does this support with your daily living? For example, would you be lost without your electronic calendar or Google maps?

Chapter summary

Dementia is not a natural process of ageing, and while there are health and government initiatives to support healthy living and early diagnosis of dementia, we continue to experience a growing population of people living with dementia along with people living for longer into older age. Dementia is always unique to the individual and while understanding the impact dementia can have on a person, it is far more important and relevant to get to know each person who we work with, to gain a true understanding of their wishes and views. By doing so, social workers can continue to work in person centred, strengths-based approach to enable people to create positive outcomes and remain a part of their care planning and decision making.

Annotated further reading

Leach Murphy, L. and Patel, J., 2021. *Living a Good Life with Dementia*. St Albans: Critical Publishing.
    Practical guide and explanations of the concept of Self-Directed Support and Care for people living with dementia and links the various Person Centred approaches within dementia care with Person Centred Planning and Community based approaches.

Useful websites

Alzheimer's Society and Alzheimer's Research both websites provide up to date information and guidance in relation to dementia & Alzheimer's for the public and professionals.

https://www.alzheimers.org.uk/
https://www.alzheimersresearchuk.org/
   Social Care Institute for Excellence, 2015. *Care Act guidance on Strengths-based approaches* [online]. Social Care Institute for Excellence (SCIE). Available from: https://www.scie.org.uk/strengths-based-approaches/guidance.

An easy guide to navigate to support with understanding of strengths based approaches.

Department of Health, 2015. *A Manual for Good Social Work Practice: Supporting Adults Who Have Dementia.* London: Department of Health. People living with dementia: social work learning resource – GOV.UK (www.gov.uk)
   A manual relating to dementia support in social care, which has lots of useful information and links to other resources.

15

Working with adults at the end of life

Jo Jury, Sally Lee and Louise Oliver

Learning from experts by experience

This chapter is co-authored by Jo, a social worker who specialises in palliative care, and Sally and Louise, social workers and academics. Jo draws on her extensive practice experience with many individuals and their families to provide stories from lived experience of working with death and dying. Jo, Sally and Louise layer the discussion with theory and research to deepen your understanding and practice knowledge about this sensitive and often avoided subject.

Chapter objectives

By the end of this chapter, you will be able to:

- Identify the role of social work in palliative and end of life care
- Recognise the physiological, social, psychological and cultural dimensions of death and dying
- Critically consider how the ways death and dying are conceptualised may impact on lived experience
- Start thinking about how awareness of discourse surrounding death and dying can inform social work

---

Introduction

This book has informed readers about ways in which social workers encounter people at every stage of the life course, and this chapter now focuses on the care and support practitioners offer to individuals, carers and families as the end of life is reached. Death is a natural part of the human journey, and one of the privileges of social work practice is to accompany an individual as they complete their personal journey and face the next stage, depending on their personal beliefs. Death, dying and bereavement are part of social work practice with every service user group and in all settings; after all death is about endings and everyone experiences endings, whether that is the end of a relationship, a job, a home or the end of life. There are, however, specific social work roles where death, dying and bereavement are fundamental aspects of every-day practice, for example, roles in hospitals, older persons services, hospices and palliative care teams. Social work brings a whole system and relationship focused approach to dying, incorporating family, community and cultural perspectives (Brown and Walter, 2014).

Activity 15.1

Think about the term 'a good death' which is sometimes used in palliative care. What does this term mean to you? Do you think it might mean something different from other people?

Death is an individual experience that it is situated within the individual (intrapersonal) but also happens between the individual and others (interpersonal), including the complexity of relationships individuals live within (such as family, employment or religious relationships) and involves 'physical, psychological, and metaphysical components (e.g., existential, spiritual)' (Holland and Proust, 2021, p669). This holistic description of the experience of death suggests clear alignment with social work's key concern for the multi-dimensional nature of human suffering and wellbeing within complex social systems (Brown and Walter, 2014).

The medicalisation of death often reduces the experience of dying to the management of physiological processes and threatens attention being given to individuals' social and spiritual lives and squeezes out the space occupied by social work (as sociologists argue, death and dying is a social experience with some medical aspects, not the other way round (Howarth, 2007 cited in Taels et al., 2021)). This means that social work must claim its valuable role in death and dying, and this chapter does this by articulating insights from lived experience and the vital contribution of skills and knowledge practitioners bring to palliative and end of life care.

What is palliative care

People ask me whether being a palliative care social worker is depressing, and I reply 'no, it is life affirming'. There are multiple descriptions of palliative care, and I highlight the World Health Organisation (WHO) definition as it acknowledges the multi-dimensional facets of human experience that often become clearer or more acute as someone approaches death (WHO, 2002):

Palliative care is an approach that improves the quality of life of patients and their families facing the problems associated with life-threatening/limiting illness, through the prevention and relief of suffering by means of early identification and impeccable assessment and treatment of pain and other problems, physical, psychosocial and spiritual.

This definition indicates that palliative care is not a one-off intervention, but instead can be a longer-term involvement in an individual's and their family's life. Following diagnosis of a life threatening or life-limiting illness, an individual will be referred for palliative care including, potentially, a treatment plan being put in place. The individual might receive treatment to reduce the extent of the spread or management of the disease, or for pain control and managing symptoms. I often hear from carers at the time of diagnosis saying they have become 'secretaries' and have to keep a diary of all the hospital visits, tests and appointments with clinicians. Good communication between professionals and the individual is vital to explain each role and the complexities of treatment, helping the individual to make sense of what is happening to them.

The key principles of palliative care

The key principles of palliative care are:

- Provide relief from pain and other distressing symptoms
- Integrate the psychological and spiritual aspects of patient care
- Offer a support system to help the individual live as actively as possible until death
- Help family to cope during an individual's illness and in their own bereavement

- Ensure the principles of dignity, respect, involvement, choice and control are at the heart of everything that happens
- Ensure comprehensive, timely, consistent, quality support for anyone who needs it, wherever they are
- Recognition that palliative and end of life care is for families, loved and close ones, as well as the dying person
- Ensure specific support in the last few days

(Adapted from the Association of Palliative Care Social Workers, 2022)

Palliative care is often misunderstood and thought of as exclusively for people with a diagnosis of cancer or that a referral for palliative care means death is imminent. This latter point may be the case in a late diagnosis; however, palliative care is about the treatment, care and support individuals, carers and families receive in situations where there is no curative treatment. Palliative care can start at the beginning of a diagnosis, and some people live with a terminal diagnosis for a number of years. In the United Kingdom, end-of-life care is for people who are likely to die within 12 months (NICE, 2015).

Where and to whom is palliative care provided?

Palliative care social workers argue that high-quality end of life and bereavement care should be an essential feature of respecting human dignity (Association of Palliative Care Social Workers, 2022). Palliative and end of life care can be provided in any clinical or domestic setting, although the unique circumstances of each individual impact on the way care is provided and experienced. Inequality, poverty and social exclusion are an important factor in exploring palliative and end of life care. For example, homelessness and housing instability is often a significant issue when planning palliative care. Accommodation may be temporary or unsuitable for adaptation or equipment such as a hospital bed and, therefore, working with housing providers is key to receiving high-quality care.

To give an example, James moved from rough sleeping into bed and breakfast accommodation so he could easily access pain control medication. To address rough sleeping in some areas, there are buses that have been converted to offer shelter and accommodation to sleep and eat. Providing end of life care in this situation is challenging, especially when licenced medication is required for pain management, and the method of delivery is invasive, therefore requiring safe disposal facilities. To facilitate care in such circumstances, palliative care social workers work across health and social care agencies including District Nurses, G.P.'s and housing providers.

Activity 15.2

Haiku poems are a great way of expressing thoughts and feelings succinctly.

A Haiku Poem is made up of three lines of poetry, line one is five syllables long, line two is seven syllables long, line three is five syllables long. Think for a moment about what dignity in death and dying means to you and then write a Haiku. What led you to that particular focus, and why was this important to you?

Palliative care social work

Practitioners in any role may work with death and bereavement, and to highlight key skills and knowledge for this area of practice, the following section discusses specialist palliative care social work in more detail. These social workers are registered with Social Work England (or respective regulatory body) and work predominantly or exclusively with people living with terminal illnesses. They are employed by a range of services including the NHS, local authority Adult and Children's services, independent hospices and charities, and are often funded with money drawn from several different sources including charitable grants.

Social workers bring to this area of practice their skills in supporting people face sensitive issues without judgement; navigating and mediating complex systems such as medical and welfare benefits; crisis management where people may need support when they are overwhelmed or emotionally 'hijacked'. Life transitions can feel destabilising and make the world seem unfamiliar and unreliable, meaning palliative care social workers need to be skilled in authentic communication, emotional intelligence and committed to the values and ethics that underpin practice (Murty et al., 2015).

Jo

The best description of the social work role in palliative care that I have found is that of being present throughout the entire continuum of care, from diagnosis to hospice and end-of-life care, and finally to family bereavement after death (Cain et al, 2018). Social workers can be introduced anywhere along the palliative pathway and remain involved for the whole journey if the individual, carer or family wish. There will be times when social workers are in the background, or there may be regular and frequent 'check ins' or contact over specific situations. For example, liaising with housing to transfer to more suitable accommodation or assisting with setting up a package of care.

I have worked with people who have found their medical treatment too much, and wanted to stop, but feared what the professionals may say. I have talked through with the individual what they might like to say and then been present when they see their clinician, not necessarily saying anything but giving them moral support. Palliative care social workers are a link between the medical or clinical team, society and the individual and their family. We bridge the gap between medical and societal expectations.

Social workers bring a different perspective to palliative care (which often takes place in a medical setting) seeing dying as a social as well as physiological experience; they 'recognize that the end of life is much more than simply the cessation of bodily function' (Holland and Proust, 2021, p670). They use psychosocial approaches to understand and address the concerns of people who are dying, as well as their families and friends. This might involve information giving, empowering people to make choices and control their care or support and the resolution of ethical dilemmas or family disputes. The social worker ensures that services and interventions take account of the whole person as well as any carer(s) and family (Taels et al., 2021).

Strengths-based practice is core as palliative care social workers assist people to realise their own abilities and resources by:

Providing practical information, help and advice around finances, debt counselling, housing and accessing key services

Advocating on behalf of people whose rights are often missed or unmet such as children and older adults who are dying, their families, carers, friends and communities to ensure that their needs are identified and met

Using legal authority to protect people from harm or abuse

Supporting people to make decisions and remain in control of what happens to them so they live as well as possible, within their personal frame of wellbeing, until they die

Engaging with health and social care systems and structures to achieve effective methods of support

The head, hand and heart model (Orr, 1992) discussed in Chapter 1 offers a useful way to understand palliative care social work:

 Knowledge is essential to ensure individuals are kept at the centre of everything that happens by ensuring they are well informed at every stage of their journey. Initially a person's thoughts will be around medical matters including treatment, prognosis, pain, how the treatment will affect them and how will they die. Once this has been discussed, other areas of a practical nature that need to be addressed will become evident. The palliative care social worker's knowledge and experience of how an illness might progress, and the effect of medication means they can support both the individual and family as the situation changes.

Knowledge of someone's life history can help with supporting people at the end of life. For example, if a partner has no experience of death, they may be frightened of waking up beside their loved one who has died in the night. Or someone may have had a bad experience of a loved one's death, and this may affect how they are now coping.

In addition, knowledge about cultural practices and beliefs about death enable understanding and the ability to provide sensitive and appropriate support.

 Practical skills are needed, for example, people may experience financial worries such as concern about paying bills if an individual is unable to work, or their being able to afford food, heating, mortgage or rent, or even worrying about paying for a funeral. Practical assistance with sourcing financial support such as grants, and benefits, is vital. Other forms of practical support are equally important such as animal charities, who can help with dog walking so an individual can keep their pet who might be the most important relationship for them.

Jo

Palliative and end of life care can sometimes require being creative and changing the way we think things should be. Imagine these scenes:
*   A young family sitting on a blanket on the floor of a hospice room, eating their picnic, listening to a tape of the sea, with the children building sandcastles with sand caried into the room.*

(Continued)

Setting up a video link allowing friends and family to watch a hospice patient get married; the bride too busy and cash strapped to buy a wedding dress, so our charity shops brought in some wedding dresses for her to try to with the help of us she chose her dress. We arranged for the Chaplain to officiate, and our catering team provided a lovely wedding breakfast.

Palliative care social workers use their emotional intelligence to build relationships with individuals, carers and their families and work with them in their understanding of what is happening. This requires sensitivity, compassion and empathy to work alongside people in distress and understand how emotions affect behaviour, beliefs, perceptions, interpretations, thoughts and actions (Howe, 2008).

Working with families and carers

Jo

Recognising the complexity of family and social interactions is important when supporting someone with a life limiting or life-threatening illness. Palliative care supports individuals, carers and families by recognising and being sensitive to the different needs of all. The individual is looking at the end of their life whereas other parties are looking at a future without their loved one. They are having to consider what this will mean for their lives going forward; there may be fear of being alone, or a parent may worry about how much to tell their children. These are complex issues that need time for exploration and may involve working with the different parties separately, for example working with children on their own to be able to talk through their worries to someone outside the family. For family members, telling a child that someone important to them is not expected to live, may be overwhelming, especially when the person is distressed, in shock or grieving themselves. For a parent who is seriously ill, the thought that their children will grow up without them is devastating.

Top tip: this is an informative website and also offers a helpline: When someone is not expected to live – supporting children | Child Bereavement UK

Caring for someone is a significant commitment and involves complexity regardless of how much love and care is present. When a terminal or life-limiting illness is diagnosed, roles within relationships may change due to physical, emotional and psychological effects. It can be distressing and dehumanising for individuals to no longer be able to fulfil established roles within relationships which might give identity and purpose, being cast adrift from the familiar (Howarth, 2007). But it can be equally distressing for the person taking on the role who has to sensitively navigate the physical and emotional needs of the cared for person. Learning new skills at a time of stress and worry may add to anxiety and create tension within the relationship.

> **Jo**
>
> *Frank moved into a nursing home after months of him and Les swinging from trying to cope at home, to finally admitting they could not cope any more. Les said, not knowing how long she was going to have to care for him was hard, if she only knew it would only be a month or so, she may have been able to cope.*

Carers will often have questions about leaving or remaining in work, being able to return to work later, money implications, carers leave and benefits. Carers need someone they can talk to in confidence, knowing they are not being judged. Not all people who find themselves in a caring role are able to do what they may feel society and others expect of them or they may find the demand of their loved one overwhelming and feel they cannot continue. Trying to 'hold on' to 'normality' can become an important driver for all parties, as Jo suggests.

> **Jo**
>
> *Astrid and George had always enjoyed fine dining and good food however, he is now unable to eat very much so does not enjoy going out. This has also meant that she has not been able to enjoy eating out, so she decided to order this special fish box. It arrived that morning, there was all she needed in the box, muscles, lobster, the sauces and vegetables, along with a desert and wine. Whilst she knew her husband would not be able to eat very much, they would enjoy getting ready for dinner and sitting down at the table, with candles lit and enjoy that special time together.*

Activity 15.3

Think about something which you really enjoy doing. Have you ever been told you cannot do it anymore or you have had to change the way you go about doing it? What is/could that be like for you?

> **Jo**
>
> *Callum, who looked after his mother who was living with severe dementia, said to me 'I am worried that when mum dies, people will see just how much weight she has lost and say I have not been feeding her properly'.*

(Continued)

Joyce also expressed her fear of being reported to Social Services as Matt, who had a brain tumour, had no concept of danger and kept falling, causing bruising and other injuries.

Carers may also be fearful of their loved one returning home from hospital but worried that saying so will be seen as uncaring. I have been able to talk through their fears with them and work with them to address the causes. There have been times when I have worked with whole families to discuss future care planning and talk through disputes between siblings. I have also worked in situations where a younger parent is dying, and decisions need to be made about who will become the children's guardian and where they will live. If the children are old enough, they will be asked, and their views heard. These conversations need to take place at the direction and speed of the parent(s), although timely decision making is important to ensure the children and parents can have these conversations together. Sadly, this is not always possible, and the outcome will be taken out or their hands. I am supporting Jasmine and Alex. Up until her illness Jasmine managed the household bills, ran the home, cared for the children, twins, one of whom has Special Educational Needs. Alex is now not able to work as he is trying to manage the household and the children and asked if Jasmine can return home to help him care for the children. Her rapid deterioration has come as a shock to them as they had originally thought she had another few years to help bring up the children to a point where he might be able to manage more easily.

Activity 15.4

Thinking about the scenario of Jasmine and Alex:

1. What worries or concerns might Alex have?
2. What worries or concerns might Jasmine have?

Jo

I supported a daughter who was visiting her father. It was noted how 'distant' she was; she did not show affection and admitted she would not be able to care for her father if he were to return home. I was able to invite her to chat to me over a coffee in confidence; we chatted a while and then she revealed how difficult she finds being with her father as he had physically and sexually abused her as a child. She felt she had to help him, as he was such a well-known person in the area and well regarded.

This is very important when working with carers, who are living with someone and caring for them fulltime, ensuring they take their medication, provide nursing care in some instances, giving injections for pain relief, cleaning and feeding, managing catheter bags and supra pubic catheters, colostomy bags, oxygen, providing the right diet, for example, high calorie, thickened fluids. They are doing all they can to keep the person safe, and when that person dies they are left with a void in their life. No further visits from the care agency, the district nurses, the community nurse specialists, the wider community team or support workers. The changes they have gone through are enormous and must never be underestimated.

The importance of cultural literacy in palliative care

The role of the palliative care social worker is to build relationships with individuals and their families, and by doing so gain insight into their personal and cultural expectations around death and dying. Exercising cultural competence is essential because 'cultural beliefs and attitudes affect how individuals and their families respond and cope during the last stages of life and during post-death grieving and the social worker may be the only individual specifically trained in cultural competency' (Murty et al., 2015).

Understanding cultural practices and beliefs in relation to death and dying enables practitioners to support individuals and families appropriately. All cultures have developed ways to cope with death in a respectful manner and interfering with these practices can disrupt people's ability to cope during the grieving process (Cain et al., 2018; Rine, 2018).

The following are key points to consider with individuals and their network:

- Are there cultural expectations and rituals for the deceased person's body, for example, the body staying in the home until cremation?
- Is there a specific ritual for marking the death, for example, staying with the body until buried, as seen in Chapter 8 regarding the traveller community?
- What are the family's beliefs about what happens after death?
- What does the family consider to be the roles of each family member in managing the death?
- Are certain types of death less acceptable (for example, suicide) and what does this mean for the bereaved?
- Are certain types of death considered especially challenging, for example, the death of a child?

Jo

Social workers advocate for people's wishes in death to be respected: Bess expressed the significance of being able to die outside. It was the middle of winter and very cold and wet and I did not feel comfortable allowing her to be wheeled out of the ward in her bed in the weather waiting to die so a tent-like structure was erected, that shielded her from the weather, and allowed her large family to be with her as she passed on.

Knowledge of mental capacity legislation and guidance is essential for a palliative care social worker when working with an individual to understand how they want their needs to be met. This might include consideration of whether they understand the effects of the medication or the consequences of declining medication or certain procedures or treatments, to ensure that their wishes and beliefs are upheld. No one is able to demand treatment; however, they can refuse it. To ensure people are aware of an individual's wishes, an Advanced Statement or Advanced Decision to refuse treatment can be completed; this is a legal document applicable if the individual lacks the mental capacity to make a decision or becomes unable to express their wishes clearly for whatever reason about care and treatment at the relevant time. An important aspect of this is for an individual to state where they wish to be cared for at the end of life: home, hospital or hospice, who they wish to be part of their care, some families and cultures like to take an active part in the care giving, and this is important for all those involved to know; an individual may wish to donate parts of their body, or even their whole body for science, whether an individual wishes to be buried or cremated, have a religious, humanist or no service, and where they wish to be buried or their ashes scattered.

Chapter summary

This chapter has discussed the important role of social work with individuals, carers and families experiencing death, dying and bereavement. Through the shared experiences Jo has brought to this chapter her knowledge and practice wisdom highlighting the privilege of getting to know and supporting people through this life stage and demonstrating how knowledgeable, culturally aware, emotionally intelligent and reflective practitioners bring value to this field of social work not only for the service user but also for their family and friends.

Death and dying can be hard to think about, let alone discuss and plan, and social workers need to draw upon any resources available to help people navigate through this very difficult time. Whether it is making sense of treatments, attending appointments, signposting to funding, helping to arrange special moments or advocating for some normalcy in everyday life and forward planning such as arranging the funeral, this work is upheld by strengths-based practice.

Jo

I posed the question at the beginning of this chapter that I would ask you to again take time to reflect about what you think Palliative Care means now that you have engaged with this chapter. Can think about how your understanding may have changed and why?

Annotated further reading

Read about the Association of Palliative Care Social Workers at: https://www.apcsw.org.uk/

Cain, C. L., Surbone, A., Elk, R. and Kagawa-Singer, M., 2018. Culture and palliative care: Preferences, communication, meaning, and mutual decision making. *Journal of Pain Symptom Management*, 55 (5), 1408–1419. https://doi.org/10.1016/j.jpainsymman.2018.01.007. This journal article discusses how awareness of culture is important in effective palliative care. Howarth, G., 2007. *Death and Dying: A Sociological Introduction*. Cambridge: Polity Press. This book offers national and international perspectives on how humans understand and approach death and dying.

16

Working with unpaid carers

Loren, George, Louise Oliver and Sally Lee

Learning from experts by experience

This chapter has been co-authored by George (pseudonym) and Loren, who are both carers, and Louise and Sally, who are social workers (with extensive experience of social work with unpaid carers) and academics. George and Loren's stories of lived experience provide layered understanding about the realities of care giving.

Introduction

Most people at some point in their life will experience unpaid care, whether this is care giving, receiving or both. Unpaid carers support their children, siblings, partners, parents, other family members or friends. In the United Kingdom, adults have a 50% chance of becoming an unpaid carer by the age of 50 (NHS England, 2022a). A carer can be anyone of any age and background, in the same way that being born with or developing care and support needs can happen to anyone at any time (NHS England, 2022a). It is important for practitioners to be alert to complexity and avoid categorising people in terms of binary opposites with people either being carers or cared for; care is often a mutual experience, and an individual can have care and support needs **and** be a care giver.

This chapter explores care giving, specifically the unpaid care given to adults with care and support needs by their family and friends. It discusses the meaning of care, the legal and social context in which care giving takes place and the lived experience of carers. This discussion will enable you to understand that unpaid carers are core to the United Kingdom's adult care system and your responsibilities as a practitioner working with carers.

Important authors' note: The chapter comes at the end of the book, not because carers are a final thought but because its contents, although often framed in relation to individuals is relevant to every client group discussed within the book and it, therefore, needs to be read with an appreciation of its overarching applicability.

Defining the concept of care

The experience of being cared for and caring for others is often felt deeply as an expression of human connection and concern (see Banks, 2021 for a discussion about the ethic of care and it focus on the relational nature and ethical dimensions of care). Care is a 'universal experience and need and a valuable endeavour that deserves to be better recognised' (James, 2016, p495). Giving and receiving care are intimate experiences that create attachments such as those felt between parent and child or between partners.

Care is connected to human (and professional social work) values and motivations – think back to Chapter 1 and the interviewees wanting to become social workers to care for others. The concept of care resonates on a personal level as it supports human dignity and wellbeing and expresses attachment; it resonates on a cultural level as a shared human value that underpins a compassionate culture, and resonates on a social level as care is a means of expressing solidarity in recognition of the shared experience of being human: it is about treating others as we wish to be treated ourselves.

Care giving involves a broad range of activities, for example, 'emotional support, personal care, managing medication and help with eating, drinking, getting dressed, preparing meals, doing shopping and household cleaning' (Chan et al., 2020, p683). This list of activities highlights the relational nature of care; it is done by people to/for/with people.

The title 'carer' can be challenging for some people to identify with. You will often work with individuals who perceive that the care they provide is a natural aspect of their relationship, for example, a parent providing personal care to their young child or a partner assisting their loved one. The difference between someone **caring** for another person and being their **carer** is personal to each individual and, therefore, practitioners need to communicate sensitively to avoid challenging carers' capabilities and identity. It can be difficult for unpaid carers who find themselves to have become a carer by extension of a pre-existing personal attachment, such as parent or spouse, to recognise that their care giving is perhaps more than might be expected as part of the relationship. For example, parents expect to provide personal care to their children for a limited time, because, as their child develops, they manage an increasing range of tasks independently. However, if their child is disabled or unwell, they may not develop the capacity to manage some or all those tasks and require ongoing personal care and support. Carers usually want the best care for their loved one and, for many, that means providing it themselves and, therefore, sensitive and skilful help can be required to enable unpaid carers to recognise and acknowledge their own needs and accept support.

Many unpaid carers find profound personal meaning through care giving, and this sense of meaning is a source of motivation enabling them to navigate the 'physiological, psychological and financial strains associated with providing care to another person' (Chan et al., 2020, p692). As such, practitioners can support the unpaid carers they work with to identify and sustain their individual sense of meaning.

The power dynamics of care

Giving and receiving of care are deeply felt experiences, the acceptance of which can be an acknowledgement of need, perhaps signalling a change in a person's life or the relinquishing of established roles. Equally, carers may be taking on new responsibilities and feel uncertain and unsupported (Woolham et al., 2018), and such periods of transition and accepting change can be challenging or distressing. To appreciate the experience of unpaid care giving, social workers need to be alert to power dynamics within relationships as care can involve the exercise of power of one person over another. Carers occupy positions of power in relation to the care receiver because they meet needs the cared for person cannot meet themselves; this reliance on others creates risk of harm (this point is made by Safeguarding Adult Boards safeguarding policy and information, for example, BCP Council: https://www.bcpsafeguardingadultsboard.com/what-is-safeguarding.html). For example, a carer might neglect an individual's dietary needs or deliberately harm them. However, practitioners must not infantilise individuals who have care and support needs by only considering risks they may face based on assumptions that an individual with care and support needs cannot exercise power over care givers. Michael's lived experience shared in Chapter 9 illustrates how people with significant care and support needs can abuse their care giver; in his case, this was through his father's coercion and control of his mother even when his father had significant care needs himself. Acknowledging the complexity of individuals, that they can be both vulnerable to harm and put others at risk, is essential to effective practice.

The social context of unpaid care giving: who cares for carers?

Carers UK report (2020), that 'For a full year...we estimate the value of carers' unpaid support to be £193 billion of care a year' (2020, p4). They report that 'no doubt the NHS and social care system would collapse without this support' (2020, p6). This information indicates the significant contribution unpaid carers make to society and the importance of unpaid care to all citizens. As has been stated, many people in the United Kingdom will become unpaid carers during their lives. Petrillo et al. (2022) report that between 2010 and 2020 on average, nearly 7% of the adults in the United Kingdom (4.3. million people) became unpaid carers each year, and approximately 6% of people left their unpaid care roles each year. DWP (2022, no page) also report in their annual Resources Survey 2020–2021 that although figures fluctuate:

- Around 60% off carers are women and 40% are men.
- 16% of adult unpaid carers provide 50 or more hours care per week and 36% reported providing informal care for 35 or more hours per week.

The information above demonstrates that giving and receiving unpaid care is a widespread human experience and one that, for many carers, is profoundly meaningful (Chan et al., 2020). Unpaid carers contribute to the personal wellbeing of their loved ones, but also wider societal wellbeing. The following activities ask you to reflect on the information you have read so far.

Activity 16.1

Which of the statistics above jumped out at you most? Did any statistic surprise you and if so, why do you think this is?

Unpaid care is often perceived in terms of gender (Chan et al., 2020), and the statistics above demonstrate that female unpaid carers outnumber males. However, many men, including some into their older years, also provide unpaid care and often their voices are unheard as explained in the following activity.

Activity 16.2

Watch the short film made by Bournemouth University Public Involvement in Education and Research (PIER) network entitled Chief Cook and Bottle Washer at:

https://www.youtube.com/watch?v=VWgEaUHs97s

The film features stories from older male network members, each of whom cared for their partners. Does anything in the film surprise you? Do you know any older people caring for a partner? If you do, ask them to tell you about their experiences.

The stories in the film illustrate how carers are often expected to fulfil technical, even medical tasks while often inadequately supported to take on the level of responsibility of care giving that they provide (Woolham et al., 2018). Carers may accept this situation because they feel obliged, or to ensure their loved one receives good quality care.

In the United Kingdom and elsewhere, carers face significant challenges, and this chapter is co-written by two carers to help you explore and critically consider what it is like being a carer and the ways in which practitioners can enhance carers' wellbeing. We will now introduce you to George and Loren.

George

I became a carer for my wife after she was initially diagnosed with post-natal depression after the birth of our daughter in 1990. This initial diagnosis was changed to depression and then some years later borderline personality disorder. I have witnessed her being sectioned (detained under the Mental Health Act 1983) *by both her social worker working with her GP and the police on 12–15 occasions and referred to an Acute Mental Health Hospital and supported accommodation as well as coming home. She has self-harmed and threatened suicide on numerous occasions.*

Loren

From the age of 15 Justin was diagnosed with a muscle-wasting disease. He was actually able-bodied until he was 15. So, that was a bit... You know what I mean? It was, well, your whole world's turned upside down. I think as a mother when you have a child, the first thing you ask is, is the child okay? When they say, yes, you just think, well, that's it, it's wonderful, don't you, because that's the first thing that you ask.

(Continued)

(Continued)

And I suppose being told at 15 that he's got a muscle-wasting disease that he would always have because it's genetic. It takes time to come through the real hard-hitting bit. So, from the age of 15, Justin's now 33, I did all the caring part and everything myself. He went into a wheelchair when he was 18 and where we are now, Justin is hoisted. He cannot stand, he can't do anything, so he's totally reliant on a hoist to move onto the commode to go to the toilet, hoisted into bed, hoisted into shower chairs.

Then six years ago he was still.... Even though he was in the wheelchair, he was still getting himself around. He was in a manual wheelchair, propelling himself and he used to go to rock festivals and then overnight he went blind. He had another genetic condition that we didn't know about. Literally blind overnight. And then he was diagnosed with Multiple Sclerosis as well.

So he's got three major conditions. His illnesses have just got progressively worse. We've had to deal with the Friedreich's ataxia, the muscle-wasting disease, then we had to deal with the MS, then we've had to deal with the blindness as well. So it's just gone from one thing to another.

We hope these introductions to George and Loren have prompted you to think about their experiences and how you might respond in such circumstances. As discussed, the role and responsibilities of carers varies from one person to the next; for Loren, her responsibilities are both physical, such as hoisting Justin in and out of bed, and emotional in terms of the support she gives as they navigate their lives together. For George, the care he provides is focused on maintain his wife's emotional wellbeing.

So let's now take a look at legislation and how it supports Carers needs.

How social work law recognises carers

The Care Act 2014 recognises carers as service users, and their right to an assessment and potential support is not dependent on the cared for person having eligible needs (Mandelstam, 2017). The extent of care provided by a carer is no longer relevant because eligibility concerns the impact of their caring role on their well-being and Local Authorities have a duty to meet eligible needs (Deville et al., 2019) and to provide appropriate and relevant information to help meet carers' needs and signposting to other agencies as necessary (Mitchell and Glendinning, 2017; Deville et al., 2019).

The Care Act 2014 (s.10) states that a carer's assessment must be completed:

(1) Where it appears to a local authority that a carer may have needs for support (whether currently or in the future), the authority must assess—

(a) whether the carer does have needs for support (or is likely to do so in the future), and

(b) if the carer does, what those needs are (or are likely to be in the future).

The definition of carer used in adult social care excludes anyone providing care through a contract or voluntary work but may include someone who provides more care than they are paid for, for example, a spouse receiving a direct payment who provides additional unpaid care. This applies to carers aged 18 and over, and young carers when they transition into adulthood (Mandelstam, 2017).

Carer's assessments consider the individual's caring responsibilities and any impact those responsibilities may have on their physical and mental health as well as how their other relationships, leisure time and employment may be affected (NHS, 2022b). The assessment will determine whether the unpaid carer is able to achieve their identified outcomes (Manthorpe et al., 2020). Undertaking a carer's assessment is a personal exploration of an individual's role and relationship, and for many carers, this can provide an opportunity to reflect on their situation and identify ways of making positive changes. Or, conversely, it can reinforce negative feelings, and sensitivity is required from practitioners to be supportive while also managing expectations about available services. The experience of assessment will be different for each person depending on their circumstances, and the practitioner's approach is an important factor in the carer's experience (Sue and Spicer, 2019). It is, therefore, important for practitioners to learn from experts by experience, and here George shares his experience of completing his first carers assessment.

George

When you have your carers assessment for the first time it can be a very bewildering experience especially if the person you care for has just been sectioned (detained) *and put into an Acute Mental Health hospital, some of the thoughts that went through my head were as follows:*

- *What do I tell our children about where Mum is?*
- *How do I sleep with all this going on?*
- *How supportive will work be to me and my family, will I have to give up work?*
- *How do I let the in laws know what is happening?*
- *What the hell is unmet need !!!!!*
- *What the hell is a key worker !!!!!*
- *Why do I have to repeat my story to each new duty Social Worker?*

Loren shares a notable experience of assessment that left her feeling angry and undervalued.

Loren

I was actually told after we had an assessment, and each time that I've had an assessment, I think the most patronising thing that I was ever told by the person that was doing the assessment was to 'give yourself a gold star for being such a wonderful mother that you don't need a social worker. There's no drug issues, there's no alcohol issues and your son's being well looked after.

The following activity asks you to use George and Loren's experiences to inform your practice.

Activity 16.2

When conducting a carer's assessment, how would you initially approach this very important and sensitive situation? And why? How would you explore the carer's relationship with their loved one?

Top tips in engaging successfully with carers

For both Loren and George, engaging with professionals and accessing support area demanding aspects of being a carer and building on the insights from lived experience and Activity 16.2, George suggests some helpful methods for engaging an unpaid carer in their assessment.

George

- *It is crucial to do the assessment at the right stage for the carer not after an initial shock of sectioning*
- *Arrange when and where the assessment will be completed with the cooperation of the carer (don't force a time or venue on them that is comfortable for you and not them)*
- *If there are children involved as carers as well, think about their needs to*
- *Be very honest and truthful with the carer as this will enable a strong bond to build between you both*
- *Say what you can and can't do*
- *What is the most comfortable means of communication for the carer?*

Activity 16.3

Having read George's top tips for engaging in a carers assessment return to Activity 16.2, would you now approach an assessment differently than previously thought, and if so why and in what way(s)?

Carers support

Following an assessment, the carer may receive support such as:

- Information about services such as carers support groups

- Respite and short breaks services
- Support provided directly to the carer, for example, relaxation classes, gym or leisure centre membership, adult learning, development of new work skills or refreshing existing skills (so they might be able to stay in, take up or return to paid employment alongside caring)
- Pursuit of hobbies and leisure activities
- Purchase of equipment to enhance wellbeing, for example, a computer/tablet for keeping in touch with supportive networks
- A personal budget from the Local Authority to meet assessed needs – this may be a one off or ongoing payment

---

George

It is very important to record the unmet needs of the carer in their assessment as these can be looked at overall by the social work team, to highlight generic problems for carers in the local area that can be acted on so as to improve services.

Offering a variety of respite opportunities for both Adult and Child Carers is important as one size does not fit all. This will enable the carers to recharge their batteries which is vital for them as well as in some instances talk to other carers and get useful tips from them.

Loren explains how she uses her personal budget:

Loren

Yeah. So, they've also given.... So, we have the hour sit, which is this afternoon, but he's brilliant, his carer. He will do a bit of washing up for me or he sits with him while I go shopping. There's not enough time, I would say, for the carer. You know what I mean? It's actually two hours a week, actually, I give but I only use the hour. And then, when I go to Compton Acres next week, I've got one of them doing a five-hour sit. So, I can go and do a little bit of shopping as well.

Activity 16.4

Imagine you are working with a carer who is isolated, struggling to pay the bills and would like to get a job.

Spend 30 minutes looking to see what is available for carers – look on the council websites, look on local services websites and find an account of lived experience.

Make a plan of how you will support the carer.

Carer's support plans are periodically reviewed to reflect any changes in circumstances, for example, the respite care needs of someone supporting an individual living with Alzheimer's will change over time as the disease progresses (Caulfield et al., 2022). Chapter 2 discussed the labour and anxiety often experienced by service users by the assessment process; this is equally relevant for unpaid carers. Practitioners demonstrate their professional values approaching carers with respect and developing positive relationships.

The experience of carers

Wellbeing, and the impact of care giving on wellbeing, is the primary focus of social work practice with carers (Madelstam, 2017). Carers report experiencing stress, exhaustion and feelings of anxiety (Sue and Spicer, 2019; Manthorpe et al., 2020). Loren expresses this herself:

Loren

I'm with a carers group and, you know what I mean, everyone just feels forgotten, and you're continuously caring. It's like sometimes I get up five, six times in the night, so I have no sleep whatsoever, but you've still got to keep going the next day, and you've still got to try to keep your spirits up for the person that you're caring for. And you've even, like with my son, being blind, he will pick up on a sigh. You've got to be so careful that you're impacting how you're feeling on the person that you're caring for as well.

Carers often feel isolated, many are unable to work, socialise or pursuit leisure activities due to their caring responsibilities. Research by Carers UK (2022, p6) indicates that:

- Carers are a particularly vulnerable group to the effects of the cost-of-living crisis, due to their limited ability to earn an income and the extra costs they incur as a result of caring.
- One in six (16%) unpaid carers are in debt as a result of their caring role and their financial situation, increasing to two in five (40%) for unpaid carers in receipt of Carer's Allowance.
- The proportion of carers unable to afford their utility bills has more than doubled since last year – from 6% in 2021 to 14% in 2022.
- 77% of carers said that the rising cost of living was one of the main challenges they would face over the coming year.
- More than a third of carers are spending a significant amount of their income on energy costs: 35% of carers said that over 20% of their income went towards their gas and electricity bills.

Many carers give up employment to provide care for a loved one (Pickard et al., 2018), which impacts on the wider economy through the loss of skilled and experienced employees and for individuals whose current and future income are reduced (Carers

UK, 2019). While legislation enables flexible working for carers, nonetheless, the impact of juggling care giving and work can be stressful.

Undervaluing unpaid carers

Unpaid carers fulfil vital roles, and yet they may be unacknowledged in health and social care practice (Parker, 2021) and while policy, such as the Care Act 2014, promotes carer's rights, the reality of available support suggests unpaid care is undervalued (Sue and Spicer, 2019). For example, the limited availability of respite services and the high cost of purchasing replacement care can mean that unpaid carers provide care for extended periods without breaks (Sue and Spicer, 2019). To gain further understanding of the hidden nature of unpaid care listen to the King's Fund podcast entitled the hidden value of unpaid carers: a conversation with Fatima Khan-Shah at https://www.kingsfund.org.uk/audio-video/podcast/value-unpaid-carers-fatima-khan-shah. Loren also highlights the unacknowledged work unpaid carers do:

> **Loren**
>
> *'It's just a very.... I don't know. It's just forgotten. You just get on and you just do it and you're just expected to go along. I suppose being like a robot but you're actually a human being. You get tired but there just doesn't seem to be any sort of give up or let offs at times when, you know what I mean, I could just flop on the bed and just want to go to sleep. You can't actually do that because you've got somebody calling you continuously. So, that's what it feels like for me'.*

When care breaks down

The chapter has discussed the ways in which care can enhance wellbeing both for the receiver and giver, but it has also brought attention to the challenges unpaid carers face including significant demands on their time, energy and personal resources that can lead to fatigue, stress and ill health. In such circumstances, care and support from unpaid carers may break down with little or no notice requiring alternative provision to be arranged as a matter of urgency. Social workers may be involved to undertake rapid assessment and source appropriate support services.

Part of the purpose of a carers assessment is to prevent deterioration and support carers in their caring role to avoid breakdown. An assessment should work with carers to identify their strengths as well as their own care and support needs and thereby prevent breakdown by ensuring appropriate support is available and plans in place for emergency situations. In addition, practitioners can develop trusting relationships in which carers can openly express their needs and develop protective strategies. George has extensive experience of the challenges of unpaid care and shares some key points that he has learnt over the years about how to promote his wellbeing and enable him to continue in his caring role.

> ### George
>
> - *It is useful to accept the help of a key worker who can help you source the respite breaks you need as well as for your children and identifying other areas of support like Carer Support group's run by local charities.*
> - *Link up with Multi-Disciplinary Teams; this saves you having to make loads of phone calls.*
> - *Men are less likely to ask for help when they need it.*
> - *Spending short periods of time on your own with nature is incredibly beneficial; my escape was going fishing and walking in the countryside.*
> - *We all have different ways of de-stressing; it's important to find yours.*

George's experience provides guidance for practitioners in ways they can work effectively with carers through preparation, openness, flexibility, clear communication and the full range of skills discussed throughout the book. As stated at the start of this chapter, carers are an integral part of social work practice with adults and, therefore, practitioners need to acknowledge the work they do and work in positive ways to enhance carer's wellbeing.

Chapter summary

This chapter has provided insights from experts by experience into unpaid care giving and how practitioners can work with carers to support them in their roles. It has discussed how legislation and policy promotes the rights of carers but does not adequately meet the real-life complexity of care giving. Unpaid carers continue to be undervalued, especially when this is understood in the context of the vital role they play both in caring for others but also their significant contribution to the wider UK economy.

Annotated further reading

Sue and Spicer, E., 2019. I had a carer's assessment. *In*: Hughes, M., ed. *A Guide to Statutory Social Work Interventions: The Lived Experience*. London: Red Globe.
  This chapter, written by Sue, an unpaid carer and Emma Spicer, a social worker, highlights the joys and challenges of being a care giver alongside information and insights for professional social work practice.

Useful websites

Carers UK provide advice, information and support regarding care. They also conduct research focusing upon care giving:

https://www.carersuk.org
 Carers Trust work to transform the lives of unpaid carers through collaboration, influence, evidence and innovation. The provide support, publish research and help carers make links with their community:

https://carers.org/

Conclusion

Sally Lee and Louise Oliver

This book was created in the spirit of co-production. It is, therefore, co-written with adults who access services, carers and practitioners to express their experience in their own words, rather than writing on their behalf or simply writing about them. This is done in order to learn from experts by experience and gain knowledge and under-standing of a life like or unlike your own (Hughes, 2019). A recognised need in social work education is to make the links between theory and practice; therefore, learning through the voice of those who access services seems paramount.

This book supports you to develop the knowledge and skills required that enable you to practice social work ethically and effectively in diverse settings with a variety of adults. It considers the legislative and social policy context of social work with adults and addresses core professional standards of practice identified by the UK social work regulatory bodies. The book also explores social work values and ethics, and how these can be applied to working with complexity in adult social work practice.

The breadth and diversity of social work practice with adults is a focus of the book which draws on unique perspectives, insights and knowledge from individuals accessing social work services, carers and practitioners to explore this diversity: what it looks like, feels like, who 'does' it and with whom. When considering the value of learning from lived experience, Hughes (2019) notes that engaging with the voice of service users not only deepens knowledge and understanding but also supports a change in perceptions and thinking regarding practice and also their world view. This book, therefore, aims to enable readers to develop a critical understanding of professional social work through the lens of those who access social services/carers and practitioners.

This final chapter highlights four key learning points which have been identified within this book. Each learning point is based upon anti-oppressive and anti-discriminatory practice and builds on the principles of person-centred practice.

Key learning points

1. *People who access services are the experts of their lives and the commitment to uphold the rights of the individual should remain at the heart of social work practice.*

   Human rights are key to practice and part of the social work role is to ensure rights are upheld. The Care Act 2014 notes six principles, empowerment, protection, prevention, proportionality, partnership and accountability. These principles promote a person-centred approach, keeping the individual at the centre of decision making and above all, promoting autonomy and self-empowerment for the individual and, therefore, upholding human rights. The Mental Capacity Act 2005 legislates that professional's must do all that they can to support individuals to make their own decisions, and if this is not possible (time and decision specific), then the best interests of that person must be taken into account.

   The significance of working in partnership with people who access services has recently been included in a report providing evidence to the House of Lords Adult Social Care Committee, the report notes: 'It is vital that social care practice and research work in partnership with individuals and communities to achieve best outcomes for those who require social care support' (House of Lords, 2022, p79). This shows the vital nature of partnership working, as it respects those we work with and their expertise, therefore, stepping away from ageist, disablist discourses and fights against parentification. This way of working is also written within Social Work England's professional standards (2019):

   As a social worker, I will:

   1.1 *Value each person as an individual, recognising their strengths and abilities.*
   1.2 *Respect and promote the human rights, views, wishes and feelings of the people I work with, balancing rights and risks and enabling access to advice, advocacy, support and services.*
   1.3 *Work in partnership with people to promote their wellbeing and achieve best outcomes, recognising them as experts in their own lives.*

   This is, therefore, core to social work values and standards to professionalism. However, consideration of personal bias may influence how we work with individuals and can affect decision making including positive risk taking. Professionals, therefore, need to remain critically reflective, especially when working with marginalised and seldom heard people.

2. *Anti-oppressive and anti-discriminatory practice which promotes social justice as well as individual dignity, choice and control underpins effective practice and is supported through legislation and case law.*

The ways in which society is structured and organised place barriers to equality and justice, including disparity in access to health and social care services. It is the role of social work to challenge and push back at these barriers. Practitioners do this in relation to micro level practice with individuals and communities and macro level work engaging with policy making. This can be achieved through being mindful about their use of language, whether they reinforce disempowering systems, being politically aware and challenging oppressive discourses.

It is important to note that the secularised and philosophical rationales for descriptions of 'good' conduct, professionalism, ethical approaches and accountability have led to the creation of social work codes of ethics and standards as well as regulation and registration which have anti-oppressive and anti-discriminatory practice running through them all.

3. *Effective communication is a fundamental skill enabling social workers to engage with diverse individuals and meet the uniqueness of each person.*

A theme that recurs within this book is the necessity of effective communication as an essential social work skill. Listening to the wishes, thoughts, feelings and needs of the person is paramount in social work practice, and partnership working is not possible without good communication. If the social worker is not able to effectively communicate with someone, then it is important that the worker takes time to develop the required communication skill or access specialist then communication support, for example, an interpreter.

Individuals accessing services and carers need to be able to engage with and understand the information being shared with them so that they can process what is being communicated. The kind of information being shared could be about available resources, case notes and assessments. For example, when conducting a Mental Capacity Assessment, the person taking the lead needs to make sure that the individual having the assessment can understand the information being presented to them about the specific decision and be able to weigh it up and communicate this back. Therefore, good communication skills are essential to conduct this assessment.

The social worker must not make any assumptions about the ability of the individual to express their thoughts and views. Social workers need to engage with reflective practice about any pre-judgements they may have about the communication abilities of the individual to sustain anti-oppressive and anti-discriminatory practice. Especially as communication techniques and skills can be either a gateway or a barrier to engagement and relationship building.

4. *Relationship building is a fundamental element to partnership working and requires the practitioner to be reflective so that they are aware of the use of self and any potential bias which could affect the relationship.*

Person-centred approaches put the individual at the centre of decision making, respecting their personhood and enabling decision making to be personalised. Taking time to get to know the person and engage with them without judgement is a part of this work. The Health Foundation (2014) and quoted by BASW (2014) describe person-centred care as care that:

supports people to develop the knowledge, skills and confidence they need to more effectively manage and make informed decisions about their own health and health care. It is coordinated and tailored to the needs of the individual. And, crucially, it ensures that people are always treated with dignity, compassion and respect.

(2014, p3)

The skills to do this are centred around being a reflective practitioner who is aware of their use of self, the language used, including non-verbal ques, being open, honest and transparent and doing what they say they are going to do. In addition to this, it includes making sure that the individual's voice is prioritised, that they are involved in every step of decision making, giving autonomy and control wherever possible.

A last word

Overall, this book provides readers with key information about the knowledge and skills required for effective social work with adults. A diverse range of people who use social work services, carers and practitioners contributed their knowledge and experience to inform readers about the lived experience of both receiving and providing social work services. Learning from lived experience is a vital part of anti-discriminatory and anti-oppressive practice as it is through insight from experts by experience that practice progresses.

We hope this book has helped you to further understand your own approach to practice and how this can be developed to keep those we work with at the centre of practice.

Appendix 1

Professional capabilities framework

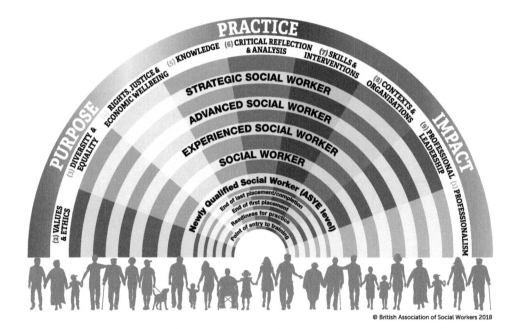

© British Association of Social Workers 2018

The 9 domains

1. PROFESSIONALISM – Identify and behave as a professional social worker, committed to professional development.
2. VALUES AND ETHICS – Apply social work ethical principles and value to guide professional practices.
3. DIVERSITY AND EQUALITY – Recognise diversity and apply anti-discriminatory and anti-oppressive principles in practice.
4. RIGHTS, JUSTICE AND ECONOMIC WELLBEING – Advance human rights and promote social justice and economic wellbeing.
5. KNOWLEDGE – Develop and apply relevant knowledge from social work practice and research, social sciences, law, other professional and relevant fields, and from the experience of people who use services.

6. CRITICAL REFLECTION AND ANALYSIS – Apply critical reflection and analysis to inform and provide a rationale for professional decision making.
7. SKILLS AND INTERVENTIONS – Use judgement, knowledge and authority to intervene with individuals, families and communities to promote independence, provide support, prevent harm and enable progress.
8. CONTEXTS AND ORGANISATIONS – Engage with, inform and adapt to changing organisational contexts, and the social and policy environments, that shape practice. Operate effectively within and contribute to the development of organisations and services, including multi-agency and inter-professional settings.
9. PROFESSIONAL LEADERSHIP – Promote the profession and good social work practice. Take responsibility for the professional learning and development of others. Develop personal influence and be part of the collective leadership and impact of the profession.

Published with kind permission of BASW – www.basw.co.uk.

Appendix 2

Subject benchmark for social work

5 Knowledge, understanding and skills

Subject knowledge and understanding

5.1   During their qualifying degree studies in social work, students acquire, critically evaluate, apply and integrate knowledge and understanding in the following five core areas of study.

5.2   Social work theory, which includes:

    i.   critical explanations from social work theory and other subjects which contribute to the knowledge base of social work

    ii.   an understanding of social work's rich and contested history from both a U.K. and comparative perspective

    iii.   the relevance of sociological and applied psychological perspectives to understanding societal and structural influences on human behaviour at individual, group and community levels, and the relevance of sociological theorisation to a deeper understanding of adaptation and change

    iv.   the relevance of psychological, physical and physiological perspectives to understanding human, personal and social development, wellbeing and risk

    v.   social science theories explaining and exploring group and organisational behaviour

    vi.   the range of theories and research-informed evidence that informs understanding of the child, adult, family or community and of the range of assessment and interventions which can be used

    vii.   the theory, models and methods of assessment, factors underpinning the selection and testing of relevant information, knowledge and critical appraisal of relevant social science and other research and evaluation methodologies, and the evidence base for social work

    viii.   the nature of analysis and professional judgement and the processes of risk assessment and decision-making, including the theory of risk-informed decisions and the balance of choice and control, rights and protection in decision-making

    ix.   approaches, methods and theories of intervention in working with a diverse population within a wide range of settings, including factors guiding the choice and critical evaluation of these, and user-led perspectives.

5.3   Values and ethics, which include:

    i.   the nature, historical evolution, political context and application of professional social work values, informed by national and international definitions and ethical statements, and their relation to personal values, identities, influences and ideologies

    ii.   the ethical concepts of rights, responsibility, freedom, authority and power inherent in the practice of social workers as agents with statutory powers in different situations

    iii.   aspects of philosophical ethics relevant to the understanding and resolution of value dilemmas and conflicts in both interpersonal and professional context

    iv.   understanding of, and adherence to, the ethical foundations of empirical and conceptual research, as both consumers and producers of social science research

    v.   the relationship between human rights enshrined in law and the moral and ethical rights determined theoretically, philosophically and by contemporary society

    vi.   the complex relationships between justice, care and control in social welfare and the practical and ethical implications of these, including their expression in roles as statutory agents in diverse practice settings and in upholding the law in respect of challenging discrimination and inequalities

    vii.   the conceptual links between codes defining ethical practice and the regulation of professional conduct

    viii.   the professional and ethical management of potential conflicts generated by codes of practice held by different professional groups

    ix.   the ethical management of professional dilemmas and conflicts in balancing the perspectives of individuals who need care and support and professional decision-making at points of risk, care and protection

    x.   the constructive challenging of individuals and organisations where there may be conflicts with social work values, ethics and codes of practice

    xi.   the professional responsibility to be open and honest if things go wrong (the duty of candour about own practice) and to act on concerns about poor or unlawful practice by any person or organisation

    xii.   continuous professional development as a reflective, informed and skilled practitioner, including the constructive use of professional supervision

5.4   Service users and carers, which include:

    i.   the factors which contribute to the health and well-being of individuals, families and communities, including promoting dignity, choice and independence for people who need care and support

    ii.   the underpinning perspectives that determine explanations of the characteristics and circumstances of people who need care and support, with critical evaluation drawing on research, practice experience and the experience and expertise of people who use services

    iii.   the social and psychological processes associated with, for example, poverty, migration, unemployment, trauma, poor health, disability, lack of education and other sources of disadvantage and how they affect wellbeing, how they interact and may lead to marginalisation, isolation and exclusion, and demand for social work services

    iv.   explanations of the links between the factors contributing to social differences and identities (for example, social class, gender, ethnic differences, age, sexuality and religious belief) and the structural consequences of inequality and differential need faced by service users

v.   the nature and function of social work in a diverse and increasingly global society (with particular reference to prejudice, interpersonal relations, discrimination, empowerment and anti-discriminatory practices)

5.5   The nature of social work practice, in the United Kingdom and more widely, which includes:

i.   the place of theoretical perspectives and evidence from European and international research in assessment and decision-making processes

ii.   the integration of theoretical perspectives and evidence from European and international research into the design and implementation of effective social work intervention with a wide range of service users, carers and communities

iii.   the knowledge and skills which underpin effective practice, with a range of service users and in a variety of settings

iv.   the processes that facilitate and support service user and citizen rights, choice, co-production, self-governance, wellbeing and independence

v.   the importance of interventions that promote social justice, human rights, social cohesion, collective responsibility and respect for diversity and that tackle inequalities

vi.   its delivery in a range of community-based and organisational settings spanning the statutory, voluntary and private sectors, and the changing nature of these service contexts

vii.   the factors and processes that facilitate effective interdisciplinary, interprofessional and interagency collaboration and partnership across a plurality of settings and disciplines

viii.   the importance of social work's contribution to intervention across service user groups, settings and levels in terms of the profession's focus on social justice, human rights, social cohesion, collective responsibility and respect for diversities

ix.   the processes of reflection and reflexivity as well as approaches for evaluating service and welfare outcomes for vulnerable people, and their significance for the development of practice and the practitioner

5.6   The leadership, organisation and delivery of social work services, which includes:

i.   the location of contemporary social work within historical, comparative and global perspectives, including in the devolved nations of the United Kingdom and wider European and international contexts

ii.   how the service delivery context is portrayed to service users, carers, families and communities

iii.   the changing demography and cultures of communities, including European and international contexts, in which social workers practise

iv.   the complex relationships between public, private, social and political philosophies, policies and priorities and the organisation and practice of social work, including the contested nature of these

v.   the issues and trends in modern public and social policy and their relationship to contemporary practice, service delivery and leadership in social work

vi.   the significance of legislative and legal frameworks and service delivery standards, including on core social work values and ethics in the delivery of services which support, enable and empower

vii.   the current range and appropriateness of statutory, voluntary and private agencies providing services and the organisational systems inherent within these

viii.   development of new ways of working and delivery, for example, the development of social enterprises, integrated multi-professional teams and independent social work provision

ix.   the significance of professional and organisational relationships with other related services, including housing, health, education, police, employment, fire, income maintenance and criminal justice

x.   the importance and complexities of the way agencies work together to provide care, the relationships between agency policies, legal requirements and professional boundaries in shaping the nature of services provided in integrated and interdisciplinary contexts

xi.   the contribution of different approaches to management and leadership within different settings, and the impact on professional practice and on quality of care management and leadership in public and human services

xii.   the development of person-centred services, personalised care, individual budgets and direct payments all focusing upon the human and legal rights of the service user for control, power and self-determination

xiii.   the implications of modern information and communications technology for both the provision and receipt of services, use of technologically enabled support and the use of social media as a process and forum for vulnerable people, families and communities, and communities of professional practice.

Subject-specific skills and other skills

5.7   The range of skills required by a qualified social worker reflects the complex and demanding context in which they work. Many of these skills may be of value in many situations, for example, analytical thinking, building relationships, working as a member of an organisation, intervention, evaluation and reflection. What defines the specific nature of these skills as developed by social work students is:

i.   the context in which they are applied and assessed (for example, communication skills in practice with people with sensory impairments or assessment skills in an interprofessional setting)

ii.   the relative weighting given to such skills within social work practice (for example, the central importance of problem-solving skills within complex human situations)

iii.   the specific purpose of skill development (for example, the acquisition of research skills in order to build a repertoire of research-based practice)

iv.   a requirement to integrate a range of skills (that is, not simply to demonstrate these in an isolated and incremental manner).

5.8   All social work graduates demonstrate the ability to reflect on and learn from the exercise of their skills, in order to build their professional identity. They understand the significance of the concepts of continuing professional development and lifelong learning, and accept responsibility for their own continuing development.

5.9   Social work students acquire and integrate skills in the following five core areas.

Problem-solving skills

5.10   These are subdivided into four areas.

5.11   Managing problem-solving activities: graduates in social work are able to:

    i.   think logically, systematically, creatively, critically and reflectively, in order to carry out a holistic assessment

    ii.   apply ethical principles and practices critically in planning problem-solving activities

    iii.   plan a sequence of actions to achieve specified objectives, making use of research, theory and other forms of evidence

    iv.   manage processes of change, drawing on research, theory and other forms of evidence.

5.12   Gathering information: graduates in social work are able to:

    i.   demonstrate persistence in gathering information from a wide range of sources and using a variety of methods, for a range of purposes. These methods include electronic searches, reviews of relevant literature, policy and procedures, face-to-face interviews, and written and telephone contact with individuals and groups

    ii.   take into account differences of viewpoint in gathering information and critically assess the reliability and relevance of the information gathered

    iii.   assimilate and disseminate relevant information in reports and case records

5.13   Analysis and synthesis: graduates in social work are able to analyse and synthesise knowledge gathered for problem-solving purposes, in order to:

    i.   assess human situations, taking into account a variety of factors (including the views of participants, theoretical concepts, research evidence, legislation and organisational policies and procedures)

    ii.   analyse and synthesise information gathered, weighing competing evidence and modifying their viewpoint in the light of new information, then relate this information to a particular task, situation or problem

    iii.   balance specific factors relevant to social work practice (such as risk, rights, cultural differences and language needs and preferences, responsibilities to protect vulnerable individuals and legal obligations)

    iv.   assess the merits of contrasting theories, explanations, research, policies and procedures and use the information to develop and sustain reasoned arguments

    v.   employ a critical understanding of factors that support or inhibit problem solving, including societal, organisational and community issues as well as individual relationships

    vi.   critically analyse and take account of the impact of inequality and discrimination in working with people who use social work services.

5.14   Intervention and evaluation: graduates in social work are able to use their knowledge of a range of interventions and evaluation processes creatively and selectively to:

    i.   build and sustain purposeful relationships with people and organisations in communities and interprofessional contexts

    ii.   make decisions based on evidence, set goals and construct specific plans to achieve outcomes, taking into account relevant information, including ethical guidelines

    iii.   negotiate goals and plans with others, analysing and addressing in a creative and flexible manner individual, cultural and structural impediments to change

    iv.   implement plans through a variety of systematic processes that include working in partnership

    v.   practice in a manner that promotes wellbeing, protects safety and resolves conflict

    vi. act as a navigator, advocate and support to assist people who need care and support to take decisions and access services

    vii. manage the complex dynamics of dependency and, in some settings, provide direct care and personal support to assist people in their everyday lives

    viii. meet deadlines and comply with external requirements of a task

    ix. plan, implement and critically monitor and review processes and outcomes

    x. bring work to an effective conclusion, taking into account the implications for all involved

    xi. use and evaluate methods of intervention critically and reflectively

Communication skills

5.15 Graduates in social work are able to communicate clearly, sensitively and effectively (using appropriate methods which may include working with interpreters) with individuals and groups of different ages and abilities in a range of formal and informal situations, in order to:

    i. engage individuals and organisations, who may be unwilling, by verbal, paper-based and electronic means to achieve a range of objectives, including changing behaviour

    ii. use verbal and non-verbal cues to guide and inform conversations and interpretation of information

    iii. negotiate and, where necessary, redefine the purpose of interactions with individuals and organisations and the boundaries of their involvement

    iv. listen actively and empathetically to others, taking into account their specific needs and life experiences

    v. engage appropriately with the life experiences of service users, to understand accurately their viewpoint, overcome personal prejudices and respond appropriately to a range of complex personal and interpersonal situations

    vi. make evidence-informed arguments drawing from theory, research and practice wisdom, including the viewpoints of service users and/or others

    vii. write accurately and clearly in styles adapted to the audience, purpose and context of the communication

    viii. use advocacy skills to promote others' rights, interests and needs

    ix. present conclusions verbally and on paper, in a structured form, appropriate to the audience for which these have been prepared

    x. make effective preparation for, and lead, meetings in a productive way.

Skills in working with others

5.15 Graduates in social work are able to build relationships and work effectively with others, in order to:

    i. involve users of social work services in ways that increase their resources, capacity and power to influence factors affecting their lives

    ii. engage service users and carers and wider community networks in active consultation

    iii. respect and manage differences such as organisational and professional boundaries and differences of identity and/or language

    iv.   develop effective helping relationships and partnerships that facilitate change for individuals, groups and organisations while maintaining appropriate personal and professional boundaries

    v.   demonstrate interpersonal skills and emotional intelligence that creates and develops relationships based on openness, transparency and empathy

    vi.   increase social justice by identifying and responding to prejudice, institutional discrimination and structural inequality

    vii.   operate within a framework of multiple accountability (for example, to agencies, the public, service users, carers and others)

    viii.   observe the limits of professional and organisational responsibility, using supervision appropriately and referring to others when required

    ix.   provide reasoned, informed arguments to challenge others as necessary, in ways that are most likely to produce positive outcomes

Skills in personal and professional development

5.17 Graduates in social work are able to:

    i.   work at all times in accordance with codes of professional conduct and ethics

    ii.   advance their own learning and understanding with a degree of independence and use supervision as a tool to aid professional development

    iii.   develop their professional identity, recognise their own professional limitations and accountability and know how and when to seek advice from a range of sources, including professional supervision

    iv.   use support networks and professional supervision to manage uncertainty, change and stress in work situations while maintaining resilience in self and others

    v.   handle conflict between others and internally when personal views may conflict with a course of action necessitated by the social work role

    vi.   provide reasoned, informed arguments to challenge unacceptable practices in a responsible manner and raise concerns about wrongdoing in the workplace

    vii.   be open and honest with people if things go wrong

    viii.   understand the difference between theory, research, evidence and expertise and the role of professional judgement.

Use of technology and numerical skills

5.18 Graduates in social work are able to use information and communication technology effectively and appropriately for:

    i.   professional communication, data storage and retrieval and information searching

    ii.   accessing and assimilating information to inform working with people who use services

    iii.   data analysis to enable effective use of research in practice

    iv.   enhancing skills in problem solving

    v.   applying numerical skills to financial and budgetary responsibilities

    vi.   understanding the social impact of technology, including the constraints of confidentiality and an awareness of the impact of the 'digital divide'.

References

A Local Authority v JB [2021] UKSC 52.

A Local Authority v RS [2020] EWCOP 29.

Abreu, L., 2022. *The UN Convention on the Rights of Persons with Disabilities: UK Implementation House of Commons Library.* Available from: https://researchbriefings.files.parliament.uk/documents/CBP-7367/CBP-7367.pdf.

Acciarini, C., Brunetta, F. and Boccardelli, P., 2020. Cognitive biases and decision-making strategies in times of change: A systematic literature review. *Management Decision,* 59(3), 638–652.

Ackoff, R. L., 1978. *The Art of Problem Solving* [online]. New York: Wiley.

Adams, R., 2003. *Social Work and Empowerment.* London: Palgrave.

ADASS and LGA, 2015. *Adult Safeguarding and Domestic Abuse: A Guide to Support Practitioners and Managers* (2nd ed). Available from: Adult-Safeguarding-and-do-cfe.Pdf. local.gov.uk [Accessed 13 Dec 2021].

Age UK, 2022a. *Carer's Assessment.* Available from: https://www.ageuk.org.uk/information-advice/care/helping-a-loved-one/getting-a-carers-assessment/.

Age UK, 2022b. *Care in Crisis* [online]. Age UK. Available from: https://www.ageuk.org.uk/our-impact/campaigning/care-in-crisis/ [Accessed 11 Jun 2022].

Aintree University Hospitals NHS Foundation Trust v James [2013] UKSC 67).

Aked, J., Marks, N., Cordon, C., and Thompson, S., 2008. *Five Ways to Wellbeing.* New Economics Foundation. Available from: https://neweconomics.org/2008/10/five-ways-to-wellbeing.

Aliev, R. A. and Huseynov, O. H., 2014. *Decision Theory with Imperfect Information* [online]. Hackensack.

Allen, D. and Riding, S., 2018. *The Fragility of Professional Competence: A Preliminary Account of Child Protection Practice with Romani and Traveller Children.* Budapest: European Roma Rights Centre.

Allen, D. and Hulmes, A., 2021. Aversive racism and child protection practice with gypsy, Roma and traveller children and families. *Seen and Heard,* 31(2).

Alzheimer's Research UK, 2015. *Dementia in the Family: The Impact on Carers – Alzheimer's Research UK* [online]. Alzheimer's Research UK. Available from: https://www.alzheimersresearchuk.org/about-us/our-influence/policy-work/reports/carers-report/ [Accessed 12 Jun 2022].

Alzheimer's Research UK, 2022a. *Prevalence – Dementia Statistics Hub* [online]. Dementia Statistics Hub. Available from: https://www.dementiastatistics.org/statistics-about-dementia/prevalence-2/ [Accessed 12 Jun 2022].

Alzheimer's Research UK, 2022b. *Types of Dementia – Alzheimer's Research UK* [online]. Alzheimer's Research UK. Available from: https://www.alzheimersresearchuk.org/dementia-information/types-of-dementia/ [Accessed 10 Jun 2022].

Alzheimer's Society, 2022a. *Dementia and Language* [online]. Alzheimer's Society. Available from: https://www.alzheimers.org.uk/about-dementia/symptoms-and-diagnosis/symptoms/dementia-and-language [Accessed 12 Jun 2022].

Alzheimer's Society, 2022b. *How Technology Can Help* [online]. Alzheimer's Society. Available from: https://www.alzheimers.org.uk/get-support/staying-independent/how-technology-can-help [Accessed 11 Jun 2022].

Ambady, N. and Rosenthal, R., 1992. Thin slices of expressive behavior as predictors of interpersonal consequences: A meta-analysis. *Psychological Bulletin, 111*(2), 256–274.

Ambady, N. and Rosenthal, R., 1993. Half a minute: Predicting teacher evaluations from thin slices of nonverbal behavior and physical attractiveness. *Journal of Personality and Social Psychology, 64*(3), 431–441.

American Psychiatric Association (APA), 2013. *Diagnostic and Statistical Manual of Mental Disorders* (5th ed). Arlington: American Psychiatric Publishing.

An NHS Trust and others v Y (by his litigation friend, the Official Solicitor) and another [2018] UKSC 46.

Andree, C., 2021. Sex, love and disability on screen. *In*: Shuttleworth, R. and Mona, L., eds. *The Routledge Handbook of Disability and Sexuality*. Abingdon: Routledge, 249–261.

Anyikwa, V. A., 2016. Trauma informed approach to survivors of intimate partner violence. *Journal of Evidence Informed Social Work, 13*(5), 484–491.

Arnstein, S., 1969. A ladder of citizen participation. *Journal of the American Planning Association, 35*, 216–224.

Association of Palliative Care Social Workers, 2022. Available from: https://www.apcsw.org.uk/social-worker-role/.

Baines, D., ed., 2017. *Doing Anti-oppressive Practice* (3rd ed). Nova Scotia: Fernwood Publishing.

Baird, S. L., Alaggia, R. and Jenney, A., 2021. Like opening up old wounds: Conceptualizing intersectional trauma among survivors of intimate partner violence. *Journal of Interpersonal Violence, 36*(17–18), 8118–8141.

Bancroft, L., 2002. *Why Does He Do that? Inside the Minds of Angry and Controlling Men*. New York, NY: The Penguin Group.

Banks, S. and Rutter, N., 2021. Pandemic ethics: Rethinking rights, responsibilities and roles in social work. *British Journal of Social Work, 2022*(52), 3460–3479. doi:10.1093/bjsw/bcab253.

Banks, S., 2020. *Ethics and Values in Social Work* (5th ed). Basingstoke: Palgrave Macmillan.

Banks, S., 2021. *Ethic and Values in Social Work* (5th ed). London: Red Globe Press.

Barajas-Gonzalez, R. G., Ayón, C., Brabeck, K., Rojas-Flores, L. and Valdez, C. R., 2021. An ecological expansion of the adverse childhood experiences (ACEs) framework to include threat and deprivation associated with U.S. immigration policies and enforcement practices: An examination of the Latinx immigrant experience. *Social Science and Medicine, 282*.

Barnard, A., 2008. Values, ethics and professionalization: A social work history. *In*: Barnard, A., Horner, N. and Wild, J., eds. *The Value Base of Social Work and Social Care*. Maidenhead: Open University Press.

Baron, J., 2000. *Thinking and Deciding*. Cambridge University Press.

BASW, 2018. *Capabilities Statement for Social Workers in England Who Work with Older People*. Available at: https://www.basw.co.uk/resources/capabilities-statement-social-workers-england-who-work-older-people.

BASW, 2018. *Professional Capabilities Framework (PCF)* [online]. BASW. www.basw.co.uk [Accessed 7 Feb 2023].

BASW (British Association of Social Workers), 2012. *Code of Ethics for Social Workers*. Birmingham: BASW.

BASW and DOH, 2018. *Capabilities Statement for Social Workers in England Who Work with Older People*. Birmingham: BASW.

Bauman, D. J., Fluke, J. D., Dalgleish, L. and Kern, H., 2014. The decision-making ecology. *In*: Shlonsky, A. and Benbenishty, R., eds. *From Evidence to Outcomes in Child Welfare. An International Reader*. Oxford: Oxford University Press, 24–38.

Bazerman, M. H., 1984. The relevance of Kahneman and Tversky's concept of framing to organizational behaviour. *Journal of Management, 10*(3), 333–343.

BBC news report, 2022. *How Many Ukrainian Refugees Are There and Where Have They Gone?*. Available from: https://www.bbc.co.uk/news/world-60555472.

Beckett, C. and Maynard, A., 2017. *Values and Ethics in Social Work* (3rd ed). London: SAGE Publications Ltd.

Belton, B., 2005. *Gypsy and Traveller Ethnicity: The Social Generation of an Ethnic Phenomenon.* Abingdon: Routledge.

Bent-Goodley, T., 2019. The necessity of trauma-informed practice in contemporary social work. *Social Work*, 64(1), 5–8.

Bhopal, K. and Myers, M., 2008. *Insiders, Outsiders and Others: Gypsies and Identity.* Hatfield: University of Hertfordshire Press.

Biggs, S., 1993. *Understanding Ageing.* Buckingham: Open University Press.

Bonnick, H., 2019. *Child to Parent Violence and Abuse: A Practitioner's Guide to Working with Families.* West Sussex: Pavilion Publishing and Media Ltd.

Bonnick, H. and Oliver, L., 2018. Child to parent violence and sexually inappropriate behaviour. *Holes in the Wall.* Available from: holesinthewall.co.uk/tag/louise-oliver/.

Bows, H., 2020. Violence and abuse of older people: A review of current proposals for criminalisation. *Criminal Law Review*, 10, 877–894.

Brammer and Pritchard-Jones, 2019. *Safeguarding Adults* (2nd ed). London: Red Globe.

Brandt, S. and Rudden, M., 2020. A psychoanalytic perspective on victims of domestic abuse and coercive control. *International Journal of Applied Psychoanalytical Studies*, 17, 215–213.

Braye, S., Orr, D. and Preston-Shoot, M., 2020. *Working with People Who Self-Neglect.* Totnes: Research in Practice.

Brian, Social Care Institute for Excellence, 2020. *What Other People Can Due to Help Me Live Well – Dementia* [online]. SCIE. Scie.org.uk. Available from: https://www.scie.org.uk/dementia/after-diagnosis/knowing-the-person/help-me-live-well.asp [Accessed 15 Jun 2022].

British Association of Social Work, 2018. *Professional Capabilities Framework.* Available from: https://www.basw.co.uk/pcf/.

British Association of Social Workers (BASW), 2014. *The Code of Ethics for Social Work.* Birmingham: British Association of Social Workers (BASW).

British Association of Social Work (BASW), 2018. *Professional Capabilities Framework.* Available from: https://www.basw.co.uk/pcf/.

British Association of Social Workers (BASW) and Child Welfare Inequalities Project (CWIP), 2019. *Anti-poverty Practice Guide for Social Work.* Available via: https://www.basw.co.uk/resources/anti-poverty-practice-guide-social-work.

British Association of Social Workers (BASW), 2022. *The Capabilities for Social Work with Adults Who Have Learning Disability.* Available from: www.basw.co.uk/capabilities-social-work-adults-who-have-learning-disability [Accessed 04 Oct 2022].

British Association of Social Workers and Child Welfare Inequalities Project, 2019. *Anti-poverty Practice Guide for Social Work.* Available from: https://www.basw.co.uk/resources/anti-poverty-practice-guide-social-work.

British Association of Social Workers, 2014. *Code of Ethics for Social Workers.* Available from: www.basw.co.uk/about-basw/code-ethics.

British Association of Social Workers, 2021. *Code of Ethics (Refreshed Version).* Available from: https://www.basw.co.uk/system/files/resources/basw_code_of_ethics_-_2021.pdf.

Brodie, S. and Swan, C., 2018. Human growth and development. *In*: Lishman, J., Yuill, C., Brannan, J. and Gibson, A., eds. *Social Work an Introduction.* London: SAGE, 110–123.

Bronfenbrenner, U., 1979. *The Ecology of Human Development: Experiments by Mature and Design.* Cambridge, MA: Harvard University Press.

Brown, L. and Walter, T., 2014. Towards a social model of end-of-life care. *The British Journal of Social Work*, 44(8), 2375–2390.

Bryant, R. A., 2016. *Acute Stress Disorder: What It Is and How to Treat It*. The Guilford Press.

Buckley, S. and Lee, S., 2019. I was assessed under the Care Act to enable me to live independently. *In*: Hughes, M., ed. *A Guide to Statutory Social Work Interventions*. London: Red Globe.

Burke- Harris, N., 2018. *The Deepest Well: Healing the Long-Term Effects of Childhood Adversity*. Monument, Colorado: Bluebird Publishers.

Burt, M., 2020. *A History of the Roles and Responsibilities of Social Workers*. London: Routledge.

Butler, R., 1969. Age-ism: Another form of bigotry. *The Gerontologist*, 9, 243–246.

Bytheway, B., 1994. *Ageism*. Buckingham: Open University Press.

Cain, C. L., Surbone, A., Elk, R. and Kagawa-Singer, M., 2018. Culture and palliative care: Preferences, communication, meaning, and mutual decision making. *Journal of Pain and Symptom Management*, 55(5), 1408–1419. doi:10.1016/j.jpainsymman.2018.01.007.

Calvete, E., Orue, I., Bertino, L., Gonzalez, Z., Montes, Y., Padilla, P. and Pereira, R., 2014. Child-to-parent violence in adolescents: The perspectives of the parents, children and professionals in a sample of Spanish focus group participants. *Journal of Family Violence*, 29(3), 343–352.

Care Act 2014. Care and Support (Eligibility Criteria) Regulations 2015.

Care Quality Commission, 2016. *Gypsies and Travellers – A Different Ending: Addressing Inequalities in End of Life Care*. Newcastle upon Tyne: Care Quality Commission. 20160505. Available from: CQC_EOLC_Gypsies_FINAL_2.pdf [Accessed 29 Aug 2022].

Carers UK, 2022a. *State of Caring 2022*. Available from: https://www.carersuk.org/images/Research/CUK_State_of_Caring_2022_report.pdf.

Carers UK, 2019. *Juggling Work and Unpaid Care: A Growing Issue*. Available from: https://www.carersuk.org/help-and-advice/work-and-career.

Carers UK, 2020. *Unseen and Underpaid: The Value of Unpaid Care Provided to Date during the Covid-19 Pandemic*. Available from: https://www.carersuk.org/images/News_and_campaigns/Unseen_and_undervalued.pdf.

Carers UK, 2022b. *Heading for Crisis: Caught between Caring and Rising Costs*. Available from: https://www.carersuk.org/images/Research/Heading_for_crisis_report.pdf.

Carney, G. M. and Nash, P., 2020. *Critical Questions for Ageing Societies*. Bristol: Policy Press.

Carrie., 2013. [Film, DVD]. Directed by Peirce, K.USA: Misher Films.

Caton, S., Thackray, D., Carr, N., 2021. *An Evaluation of the 'Us Too' Project: People with Learning Disabilities Speaking Up on Domestic Abuse*. Manchester: Manchester Met University. Available from: https://arcengland.org.uk/wp-content/uploads/2021/07/Us-Too-Evaluation-report-by-MMU-June-2021.pdf [Accessed 1 Nov 2021].

Caulfield, M., Seddon, D., Williams, S. and Hedd Jones, C., 2022. Understanding break needs, break experiences and break outcomes over the care-giving career: A narrative approach. *The British Journal of Social Work*, bcac178. doi:10.1093/bjsw/bcac178.

CC v KK and STCC [2012] EWCOP 2136 (COP).

Cemlyn, S., 2000. *Policy and Provision by Social Services for Traveller Children and Families: A Research Study*. Bristol: University of Bristol, School for Policy Studies.

Cemlyn, S., 2008. Human rights and gypsies and travellers: An exploration of the application of a human rights perspective to social work with a minority community in Britain. *British Journal of Social Work*, 38(1), 153–173.

Cemlyn, S., Greenfields, M., Burnett, S., Matthews, Z. and Whitwell, C., 2009. *Inequalities Experienced by Gypsy and Traveller Communities: A Review*. Manchester: Equality and Human Rights Commission.

Centers for Disease Control and Prevention, 2022. *About the CDC-Kaiser ACE Study*. Available from: https://www.cdc.gov/violenceprevention/aces/about.html.

CH v A Metropolitan Council [2017] EWCOP 12 (28 July 2017). Available from: www.bailii.org/ew/cases/EWCOP/2017/12.html [Accessed 10 Apr 2022].

Chan, C., Vickers, T. and Barnard, A., 2020. Meaning through caregiving: A qualitative study of the experiences of informal carers. *The British Journal of Social Work*, *50*(3), 682–700. doi: 10.1093/bjsw/bcz039.

Cheung, J. C. S., 2017. Practice wisdom in social work: An uncommon sense in the intersubjective encounter. *European Journal of Social Work*, *20*(5), 619–629.

Chow, A., 2013. Developing emotional competence of social workers of end-of-life and bereavement care. *The British Journal of Social Work*, *43*(2), 373–393.

Churchman, C. W., 1968. *Challenge to Reason [by] C. West Churchman*. [online]. New York: McGraw-Hill [1968].

Clark, C. and Greenfields, M., 2006. *Here to Stay: The Gypsies and Travellers of Britain*. Hatfield: University of Hertfordshire Press.

Clark, C., 2006. Who are the gypsies and travellers of Britain?. *In*: Clark, C. and Greenfields, M., eds. *Here to Stay: The Gypsies and Travellers of Britain*. Hatfield: University of Hertfordshire Press, 10–27.

Clarke, K., Holt, A., Norris, C. and Nel, P. E., 2017. Adolescent-to-parent violence and abuse: Parents' management of tension and ambiguity – An interpretative phenomenological analysis. *Child and Family Social Work*, 1–8.

Classen, C. C. and Clark, C. S., 2017. Trauma-informed care. *APA Handbook of Trauma Psychology: Trauma Practice*. American Psychological Association, *Vol. 2*, 515–541.

Commission on Race and Ethnic Disparities, 2021. Available from: https://www.gov.uk/government/publications/the-report-of-the-commission-on-race-and-ethnic-disparities [Accessed 29 Aug 2022].

Condry, R. and Miles, C., 2014. Adolescent to parent violence: Framing and mapping a hidden problem. *Criminology and Criminal Justice*, 1–19.

Condry, R., Miles, C., Brunton-Douglas, T. and Oladapo, A., 2020. *Experiences of Child and Adolescent to Parent Violence in the Covid-19 Pandemic*. Oxford: University of Oxford.

Cook, L. L., 2017. Making sense of the initial home visit: The role of intuition in child and family social workers' assessments of risk. *Journal of Social Work Practice*, *31*(4, SI), 431–444.

Cook, L. L., 2020. The home visit in child protection social work: Emotion as resource and risk for professional judgement and practice. *Child & Family Social Work*, *25*(1), 18–26.

Corradi, L., 2018. *Gypsy Feminism: Intersectional Politics, Alliances, Gender and Queer Activism*. Abingdon: Routledge.

Cottrell, B., 2003. *Parent Abuse: The Abuse of Parents by Their Teenage Children*. National Clearing House, 1–9. Government of Canada. Available from: https://canadiancrc.com/PDFs/Parent_Abuse-Abuse_of_Parents_by_Their_Teenage_Children_2001.pdf

Council of Europe, European Convention for the Protection of Human Rights and Fundamental Freedoms, as amended by Protocols Nos. 11 and 14, 4 November 1950, ETS 5. Available from: https://www.refworld.org/docid/3ae6b3b04.html [Accessed 21 March 2023].

Court of Protection, 2020. *Practice Direction 9E-Serious Medical Treatment*. Available from: https://www.judiciary.uk/wp-content/uploads/2020/01/SMT-Guidance-draft.pdf [Accessed 23 May 2022].

Crandall, B., Klein, G. and Hoffman, R., 2006. *Working Minds: A Practitioner's Guide to Cognitive Task Analysis* [online]. The MIT Press.

Crenshaw, K., 1989. *Demarginalizing the Intersection of Race and Sex: A Black Feminist Critique of Antidiscrimination Doctrine, Feminist Theory and Antiracist Politics*. Chicago: University of Chicago Legal Forum, 138–167.

Cumming, E. and Henry, W., 1961. *Growing Old: The Process of Disengagement*. New York: Basic Books.

Cunningham, J. and Cunningham, S., 2017. *Social Policy and Social Work* (2nd ed). Exeter: Learning Matters.

Davies, K. and Jones, R., 2016. *Skills for Social Work Practice*. London: Palgrave.

de Bellis, M. D. and Zisk, A., 2014, April. The biological effects of childhood trauma. *Child and Adolescent Psychiatric Clinics of North America, 23*(2), 185–222.

Department for Constitutional Affairs, 2007. *Mental Capacity Act 2005 Code of Practice.* London: TSO.

Department for Education (DfE), 2015. *Education Select Committee Memorandum: Social Work Reform* [online]. Available from: https://www.gov.uk/government/groups/serious-case-review-.

Department for Work and Pensions, 2022. *National Statistics Family Resources Survey: Financial Year 2020 to 2021.* Available from: https://www.gov.uk/government/statistics/family-resources-survey-financial-year-2020-to-2021/family-resources-survey-financial-year-2020-to-2021#care-1.

Department of Health, 2000. *No Secrets.* Available from: No_secrets__guidance_on_developing_and_implementing_multi-agency_policies_and_procedures_to_protect_vulnerable_adults_from_abuse.pdfpublishing.service.gov.uk.

Department of Health. 2014. *Transforming Care: A National Response to Winterbourne View Hospital.* Available from: https://assets.publishing.service.gov.uk/government/uploads/system/uploads/attachment_data/file/213215/final-report.pdf [Accessed 31 Oct 2022].

Department of Health, 2009. *Good Learning Disability Partnership Boards: Making It Happen for Everyone.* A Guide about What a Good Learning Disability Partnership Board Should Be like. Available from: www.choiceforum.org/docs/pbguide.pdf [Accessed 04 Dec 2022].

Department of Health, 2011. *Positive Practice Positive Outcomes: A Handbook for Professionals in the Criminal Justice System Working with Offenders with Learning Disabilities.* Available from: assets.publishing.service.gov.uk/government/uploads/system/uploads/attachment_data/file/216318/dh_124744.pdf [Accessed 04 Dec 2022].

Department of Health. 2012. *Transforming Care: A National Response to Winterbourne View Hospital.* https://assets.publishing.service.gov.uk/government/uploads/system/uploads/attachment_data/file/213215/final-report.pdf [Accessed 31 Oct 22].

Department of Health, 2015. *Knowledge and Skills Statement for Social Workers in Adult Services.* Available from: https://assets.publishing.service.gov.uk/government/uploads/system/uploads/attachment_data/file/411957/KSS.pdf.

Department of Health, 2017. *Strengths Based Social Work Practice with Adults.* London Online. Available from: publishing.service.gov.uk [Accessed 8 Apr 2022].

Department of Health, 2022. *Care and Support Statutory Guidance: Issued under the Care Act 2014.* London: Department of Health.

Department of Health and Social Care, 2022a. *Care and Support Statutory Guidance – GOV.UK (www.gov.uk).* Available from: https://www.gov.uk/government/publications/care-act-statutory-guidance/care-and-support-statutory-guidance [Accessed 10 Feb 2022].

Department of Health and Social Care, 2022b. *Care and Support Statutory Guidance.* Available from: www.gov.uk/government/publications/care-act-statutory-guidance/care-and-support-statutory-guidance#safeguarding-1 [Accessed 10 Apr 2022].

Department of Health and Social Care, Care Act Statutory Guidance online: Care and Support Statutory Guidance. GOV.UK. Available from: https://www.gov.uk/government/publications/care-act-statutory-guidance/care-and-support-statutory-guidance [Accessed 5 Nov 2021].

Department of Health and Social Care, 2022c. *Care and Support Statutory Guidance (Updated Quarterly).* Available from: https://www.gov.uk/government/publications/care-act-statutory-guidance/care-and-support-statutory-guidance.

Department of Health and Social Care, 2015. *Knowledge and Skills Statement for Social Workers in Adult Services.* Available from: https://www.gov.uk/government/uploads/system/uploads/attachment_data/file/411957/KSS.pdf.

Deville, J., Davies, H., Kane, R., Nelson, D. and Mansfield, P., 2019. Planning for the future: Exploring the experiences of older carers of adult children with a learning disability. *British*

Journal of Learning Disabilities, *47*(3), 208–214. Available from: https://search.ebscohost.com/login.aspx?direct=true&db=eric&AN=EJ1224350&site=ehost-live [Accessed 25 Nov 2022].

DHSC, 2022. *Care and Support Guidance*. Available from: https://www.gov.uk/government/publications/care-act-statutory-guidance/care-and-support-statutory-guidance#annexes.

Domestic Abuse Act 2021. Available from: https://www.legislation.gov.uk/ukpga/2021/17/contents/enacted [Accessed 2 Dec 2021].

Donnelly, S., Begley, E. and O'Brien, M., 2018. How are people with dementia involved in care-planning and decision-making? An Irish social work perspective. *Dementia*, *18*(7–8), 2985–3003. Available from: https://journals.sagepub.com/doi/full/10.1177/1471301218763180?casa_token=bGu5qzVld8kAAAAA%3AYQxRtvHTocGblTLP_5Pbd1kP1TGlJDn2qLtHD4LN1idiHk6B0SkzyIjHbmTSUUhwD0by-AKiQm0 [Accessed 11 Jun 2022].

Dreyfus, H. L., Dreyfus, S. E. and Athanasiou, T., 1986. *Mind over Machine: The Power of Human Intuition and Expertise in the Era of the Computer.* [online]. Oxford: Blackwell.

Dyke, C., 2019. *Writing Analytical Assessments in Social Work*. ST Albans: Critical Publishing.

Easy Read UK, 2022. Available from: www.easyreaduk.co.uk/about-easy-read/ [Accessed 04 Dec 2022].

Equality Act 2010. [online]. Available from: https://www.legislation.gov.uk/ukpga/2010/15/contents.

Evandrou, M., Falkingham, J., Qin, M. and Vlachantoni, A., 2020. Available from: https://www.understandingsociety.ac.uk/blog/2020/09/30/changing-living-arrangements-and-stress-in-lockdown [Accessed 11 Feb 2022].

Evans, E. and Lee, S., 2020. Social work and learning disabilities (children, young people and adults). *In:* Parker, J., ed. *Introducing Social Work*. London: Learning Matters, 265–275.

Ezell, J. M., et al., 2021. Stigmatize the use, not the user? Attitudes on opioid use, drug injection, treatment, and overdose prevention in rural communities. *Social Science & Medicine*, *268*. doi: 10.1016/J.SOCSCIMED.2020.113470.

Farmer, T., 2017. *Grandpa on a Skateboard* (2nd ed). Norwich: Rethink Press.

Farmer, Y., 2015. Using vNM expected utility theory to facilitate the decision-making in social ethics. *Journal of Risk Research*, *18*(10), 1307–1319.

Faulkner, A., 2012. *The Right to Take Risks: Service Users' Views of Risk in Adult Social Care*. York: Joseph Rowntree Foundation. Available from: https://www.jrf.org.uk/sites/default/files/jrf/migrated/files/right-to-take-risks-faulkner.pdf.

Fazio, S., Pace, D., Flinner, J. and Kallmyer, B., 2018. The fundamentals of person-centered care for individuals with dementia. *The Gerontologist*, *58*(suppl_1), S10–S19. Available from: https://academic.oup.com/gerontologist/article/58/suppl_1/S10/4816735?login=false [Accessed 12 Jun 2022].

Felitti, V. J., Anda, R. F., Nordenberg, D., Williamson, D. F., Spitz, A. M., Edwards, V., Koss, M. P. and Marks, J. S., 1998. Relationship of childhood abuse and household dysfunction to many of the leading causes of death in adults: The adverse childhood experiences (ACE) study. *American Journal of Preventive Medicine*, *14*(4), 245–258.

Fishburn, P. C., 1964. *Decision and Value Theory* [online]. New York: Wiley [1964].

Fitzgerald, E., Hor, K. and Drake, A. J., 2020. Maternal influences on fetal brain development: The role of nutrition, infection and stress, and the potential for intergenerational consequences. *Early Human Development*, *150*.

Foley, N., Powell, A., Clark Brione, P., Kennedy, S., Powell, T., Roberts, N., Harker, R., Francis-Devine, B. and Foster, D., 2022. *Informal Carers Research Briefing*. House of Commons Library. Available from: https://researchbriefings.files.parliament.uk/documents/CBP-7756/CBP-7756.pdf.

Fook, J., 2016. *Social Work. A Critical Approach to Practice*. London: SAGE.

Foundation for People with Learning Disabilities, 2021. Available from: www.learningdisabilities.org.uk/learning-disabilities/a-to-z/l/learning-difficulties [Accessed 4 Oct 2022].

Foundation for People with Learning Disabilities, 2022. *Hearing Loss*. Available from: www. learningdisabilities.org.uk/learning-disabilities/a-to-z/h/hearing-loss [Accessed 4 Oct 2022].

Fox, M., McIlveen, J. and Murphy, E., 2021. Death, dying and bereavement care during COVID-19: Creativity in hospital social work practice. *Qualitative Social Work*, 20(1–2), 131–137.

Freire, P., 1972. *Pedagogy of the Oppressed*. Harmondsworth: Penguin.

G v E (Deputyship and Litigation Friend) [2010] EWCOP 2512.

Gallagher, E., 2018. *Who's in Charge?: Why Children Abuse Parents, and What You Can Do About It*. London; Cambridge; New York and Sharjah: Austin Macauley Publishers.

Galvani, S., 2015a. *Alcohol and Other Drug Use: The Roles and Capabilities of Social Workers, Manchester Metropolitan University*. Manchester: Manchester Metropolitan University. Available from: http://cdn.basw.co.uk/upload/basw_25925-3.pdf (Accessed 2 Feb 2017).

Galvani, S., 2015b. "Drugs and relationships don't work": Children's and young people's views of substance use and intimate relationships. *Child Abuse Review*, 24(6), 440–451. doi: 10.1080/02615479.2010.504981.

Galvani, S. and Forrester, D., 2011. How well prepared are newly qualified social workers for working with substance use issues? Findings from a national survey in England. *Social Work Education*, 30(4), 422–439. doi:10.1080/02615479.2010.504981.

Galvin and Todres, 2013. *Caring and Well-Being A Lifeworld Approach*. London: Routledge.

George, M. and Gilbert, S., 2018. Mental Capacity Act (2005) assessments: Why everyone needs to know about the frontal lobe paradox. *The Neuropsychologist*, 5, 59–66. Available from: https://shop. bps.org.uk/publications/publications-by-subject/neuropsychology/the-neuropsychologist-issue-5-may-2018.html [Accessed 19 Apr 2022].

Gerassi, L. B. and Nichols, A. J., 2018. *Sex Trafficking and Commercial Sexual Exploitation: Prevention, Advocacy, and Trauma-Informed Practice*. Springer Publishing Company.

Ghesquiere, A., et al., 2011. Risks for complicated grief in family caregivers. *Journal of Social Work in End-of-Life & Palliative Care*, 7, 216–240.

Gigerenzer, G. and Gaissmaier, W., 2011. Heuristic decision making. *Annual review of psychology*, 62, 451–482.

Gilchrist, A., 2019. *The Well-Connected Community: A Networking Approach to Community Development*. Bristol: Policy Press.

Gilleard, C. and Higgs, P., 2000. *Cultures of Ageing: Self, Citizen and the Body*. London: Routledge.

Goergen, M., 2010. *Corporate Governance and Complexity Theory*. [electronic resource] [online]. Cheltenham, UK; Northhampton, MA: Edward Elgar, c2010.

Goethals, T., De Schauwer, E. and Van Hove, G., 2015. Weaving intersectionality into disability studies research: Inclusion, reflexivity and anti-essentialism. DiGeSt. *Journal of Diversity and Gender Studies*, 2(1–2), 75–94.

Gomez-Jimenez, M.-L. and Parker, J., eds., 2014. *Active Ageing? Perspectives from Europe on a Vaunted Topic*. London: Whiting and Birch.

Gonzales, R., Sigona, N., Franco, M. and Papoutsi, A., 2019. *Undocumented Migration*. Cambridge: Polity Press.

Gove, M., 2013. *Getting it Right for Children in Need* [online]. Available from: https://www.gov. uk/government/speeches/getting-it-right-for-children-in-need-speech-to-the-nspcc [Accessed 10 Oct 2022].

Gravell, C., 2012. *Loneliness and Cruelty: People with Intellectual Disabilities and Their Experiences of Harassment, Abuse and Related Crime in the Community*. London: Lemos and Crane.

Greenfields, M., Cemlyn, S. and Berlin, J., 2014. *Gypsy, Traveller and Roma Health and Social Work Engagement: Thematic Meeting Report and Policy Guidance from a Council of Europe/ European Academic Network on Romani Studies Funded International Seminar*. Buckingham: Council of Europe Buckinghamshire New University.

Grenier, A., Lloyd, L. and Phillipson, C., 2017. Precarity in late life: Rethinking dementia as 'frailed' old age. *Sociology of Health and Illness*, 39(2), 318–30.

Grootegoed, E. and Smith, M., 2018. The emotional labour of austerity: How social workers reflect and work on their feelings towards reducing support to needy children and families. *The British Journal of Social Work*, 48(7), 1929–1947. doi:10.1093/bjsw/bcx151.

Gubrium, J. and Holstein, J. A., 2003. *Ways of Aging*. London: Wiley.

Guidance Liberty Protection Safeguards: what they are. 2021. Department of Health and Social care. Available from: https://www.gov.uk/government/publications/liberty-protection-safeguards-factsheets/liberty-protection-safeguards-what-they-are.

Gunaratnam, Y., 2011. Cultural vulnerability and professional narratives. *Journal of Social Work in End-of-Life & Palliative Care*, 7, 338–349.

Hancock, I., 2007. On the interpretation of a word: "Porrajmos" as Holocaust. *In*: Hayes, M. and Acton, T., eds. *Travellers, Gypsies, Roma: The Demonisation of Difference*. Newcastle: Cambridge Scholars Publishing, 53–57.

Harrison, K. and Ruch, G., 2007. Social work and the use of self: On becoming and being a social worker. *Social Work: A Companion to Learning*, 40–50. doi:10.4135/9781446247167.n4.

Havighurst, R. and Albrecht, R., 1953. *Older People*. London: Longman.

Headway. 2022. *Executive Dysfunction after Brain Injury*. Available from: https://www.headway.org.uk/about-brain-injury/individuals/effects-of-brain-injury/executive-dysfunction/#:~:text=You%20may%20hear%20different%20names,the%20symptoms%20usually%20occur%20together [Accessed 1 Apr 2022].

Health and Social Care Act 2012.

Heanue, K. and Lawton, C., 2012. *Working with Substance Users*. Maidenhead: McGraw-Hill/Open University Press.

Hepple, J., 2016. *If You're a Disabled, Gay Twentysomething, Grindr Is a Godsend*. Available from: https://www.theguardian.com/commentisfree/2016/dec/01/disabled-gay-twentysomething-grindr-cerebral-palsy.

Herbert, J., 2020. *Accompaniment, Community and Nature: Overcoming Isolation, Marginalisation and Alienation through Meaningful Connection*. London: Jessica Kingsley Publishers.

Heslop, P. and Meredith, C., 2019. *Social Work from Assessment to Intervention*. London: SAGE.

Hine, B., 2019. It can't be that bad, I mean he's a guy': Exploring judgements towards domestic violence scenarios varying on perpetrator and victim gender, and abuse type. *In*: Bates, E. A. and Taylor, J. C., eds. *Intimate Partner Violence: New Perspectives in Research and Practice*. Oxon: Routledge.

HM Government, 2009. *Valuing People Now: A New Three-Year Strategy for People with Learning Disabilities. 'Making it Happen for Everyone'*. Available from: https://www.base-uk.org/sites/default/files/%5Buser-raw%5D/11-06/valuing_people_now_executive_summary.pdf [Accessed 11 Feb 2022].

HM Government, 2001. *Valuing People: A New Strategy for Learning Disability for the 21st Century*. A White Paper. Department of Health. Available from: assets.publishing.service.gov.uk/government/uploads/system/uploads/attachment_data/file/250877/5086.pdf [Accessed 04 Oct 2022].

HM Government, 2022. Building the Right Support for People with a Learning Disability and Autistic People: Action Plan. https://assets.publishing.service.gov.uk/government/uploads/system/uploads/attachment_data/file/1092537/Building-the-Right-Support-for-People-with-a-Learning-Disability-and-Autistic-People-Action-Plan-accessible.pdf [Accessed 31 Oct 2022].

Hogarth, R. M., 2001. *Educating Intuition*. Chicago: University of Chicago Press.

Holland, M. and Prost, S., 2021. The end of life within social work literature: A conceptual review. *Journal of Death and Dying*, 82(4), 668–691.

Holsapple, C. W., 2008. Decisions and knowledge. *In*: Burstein, F. and Holsapple, C. W., eds. *Handbook on Decision Support Systems 1. Basic Themes*. Berlin: Springer, 21–54.

Holt, A., 2016. *Working with Adolescent Violence and Abuse Towards Parents: Approaches and Contexts for Intervention*. London and New York: Routledge Taylor & Francis Group.

Holt, A. and Lewis, S., 2021. Constituting child-to-parent violence: Lessons from England and wales. *The British Journal of Criminology*, 61, 3792–811.

Home Office, 2015. *Information Guide: Adolescent to Parent Violence and Abuse (APVA)* [online]. Available from: https://www.gov.uk/.

Horner, N., 2019. *What Is Social Work? Context & Perspectives* (5th ed). Exeter: Learning Matters.

House of Commons, Home Affairs Committee, 2020. Available from: https://publications.parliament.uk/pa/cm5801/cmselect/cmhaff/321/321.pdf [Accessed 21 Mar 2022].

House of Lords, 2022. *Adult Social Care Committee. Report of Session 2022-23: A "Gloriously Ordinary Life": Spotlight on Adult Social Care*. Available from: https://microsites.bournemouth.ac.uk/hss/files/2022/12/House-of-Lords-Adult-Social-Care-Committee-report-A-gloriously-ordinary-life.pdf.

House of Lords, 2014. *Select Committee on the Mental Capacity Act 2005 Post Legislative Scrutiny Report*. London: TSO.

Howarth, G., 2007. *Death and Dying: A Sociological Introduction*. Cambridge: Polity Press.

Howe, D., 2008. *The Emotionally Intelligent Social Worker*. London: Palgrave MacMillan.

Hughes, D., 2016. *Parenting a Child Who Has Experienced Trauma (Parenting Matters)*. London: CoramBAAF.

Hughes, K., Bellis, M. A., Sethi, D., Andrew, R., Yon, Y., Wood, S., Ford, K., Baban, A., Boderscova, L., Kachaeva, M., Makaruk, K., Markovic, M., Povilaitis, R., Raleva, M., Terzic, N., Veleminsky, M., Włodarczyk, J. and Zakhozha, V., 2019. Adverse childhood experiences, childhood relationships and associated substance use and mental health in young Europeans. *European Journal of Public Health*, 29(4), 741–747.

Hughes, M., 2019. *A Guide to Statutory Social Work Interventions: The Lived Experience*. London: Palgrave.

Human Rights Act 1998.

Ibabe, I., Arnoso, A. and Elgorriaga, E., 2014a. Behavioural problems and depressive symptomatology as predictors of child-to-parent violence. *I The European Journal of Psychology Applied to Legal Context*, 6, 53–61.

Ibabe, I., Arnoso, A. and Elgorriaga, E., 2014b. The clinical profile of adolescent offenders of child-to-parent violence. *Procedia – Social and Behavioral Sciences*, 131, 377–381.

In the matter of D (A Child) [2019] UKSC 42.

International Federation of Social Workers (IFSW) and International Association of Schools of Social Work (IASSW), 2018. *Global Social Work Statement of Ethical Principles*. Rheinfelden: International Federation of Social Workers (IFSW).

International Federation of Social Workers, 2014. *Global Definition of Social Work*. Available from: https://www.ifsw.org/what-is-social-work/global-definition-of-social-work/.

James, G., 2016a. Family-friendly employment laws (Re)assessed: The potential of care ethics. *Industrial Law Journal*, 45(4), 477–502. doi:10.1093/indlaw/dww029.

James, S., 2016b. *Addicted to the Life*. Create Space Independent Publishing Platform.

Janis, I. L. and Mann, L., 1977. *Decision Making: A Psychological Analysis of Conflict, Choice, and Commitment*. Free Press.

Janis, I. L., 1983. *Groupthink*. Houghton Mifflin Boston.

Jesper, E., Griffiths, F. and Smith, L., 2008. A qualitative study of the health experience of Gypsy Travellers in the UK with a focus on terminal illness. *Primary Health Care Research & Development*, 9(2), 157–165.

John, E., Thomas, G. and Touchet Scope, A., 2019. *The Disability Price Tag*. Available from: https://www.scope.org.uk/campaigns/extra-costs/disability-price-tag/.

Johns, R., 2017. *Using the Law in Social Work* (7th ed). Exeter: Learning Matters.

Jones, R., 2020. 1970–2020: A fifty year history of the personal social services and social work in England and across the UK. *Social Work and Social Sciences Review*, 21(3), 8–44.

Jones, R. and Piffaretti, E., 2018. *Mental Capacity Act Manual* (8th ed). London: Sweet and Maxwell.

Joshua, P. M., Topitzes, J. and Britz, L., 2019. Promoting evidence based, trauma-informed social work practice. *Journal of Social Work Education*, 55(4), 645–657.

Kahneman, D. and Tversky, A., 1979. Prospect theory: An analysis of decision under risk Daniel Kahneman; Amos Tversky. *Econometrica*, 47(2), 263–292.

Kahneman, D., 2013. *Thinking, Fast and Slow*. [online]. New York: Farrar, Straus and Giroux.

Kelly, A., 2008. Living loss: An exploration of the internal space of liminality. *Mortality*, 13(4), 335–350.

Kemshall, H., Wilknson, B. and Baker, K., 2013. *Working with Risk* [online]. Cambridge: Polity Press.

Kinderman, P., 2019. *A Manifesto for Mental Health; Why We Need a Revolution in Mental Health Care*. Switzerland: Palgrave Macmillan (Springer Nature Switzerland AG).

Kings Fund, 2018. *2018 GSK IMPACT Awards: Leeds Gypsy and Traveller Exchange (Leeds GATE)*. Available from: https://www.kingsfund.org.uk/audio-video/2018-gsk-impact-awards-leeds-gypsy-and-traveller-exchange [Accessed 29 Jan 2021].

Kingstone, T., Campbell, P., Andras, A., Nixon, K., Mallen, C., Dikomitis, L. and the Q-COVID-19 Group, 2022. Exploring the impact of the first wave of COVID-19 on social work practice: A qualitative study in England, UK. *The British Journal of Social Work*, 52(4), 2043–2062. doi: 10.1093/bjsw/bcab166.

Kirkman, E. and Melrose, K., 2014. *Clinical Judgement and Decision-Making in Children's Social Work: An Analysis of the 'Front Door' System*. Department for Education Research Report.

Kitwood, T., 1997. *Dementia Reconsidered*. Buckingham: Oxford University Press.

Klein, A., 2011. Khat deaths or the social construction of a non-existent problem? A response to corkery et al. "Bundle of fun" or "bunch of problems"? Case series of khat-related deaths in the UK. *Drugs: Education, Prevention and Policy*, 18(6), 426–427. doi:10.3109/09687637.2011.594115.

Klein, G., 2000. Using cognitive task analysis to build a cognitive model. *Proceedings of the Human Factors and Ergonomics Society Annual Meeting*, 44, 596–599.

Klein, G., 2008. Naturalistic decision making. *Human factors*, 50(3), 456–460.

Klein, G., 2015. A naturalistic decision making perspective on studying intuitive decision making. *Journal of Applied Research in Memory and Cognition* [online], 4(3), 164–168.

Kong, C. and Ruck Keene, A., 2019. *Overcoming the Challenges of the Mental Capacity Act 2005 – Practical Guidance for Working with Complex Issues*. London: Jessica Kingsley.

Koprowska, J., 2020. Communication and interpersonal skills. *In*: Parker, J., ed. *Introducing Social Work*. London: Learning Matters.

Kubler-Ross, E., 1969. *On Death and Dying*. New York: Macmillan.

Lansley, M. and Mack, J., 2015. *Breadline Britain – the Rise of Mass Poverty*. London: Oneworld.

Ledwith, M., 2016. *Community Development in Action: Putting Freire into Practice*. Bristol: Policy Press.

Lee, J. Y., et al., 2020. Adolescent risk and protective factors predicting triple trajectories of substance use from adolescence into adulthood. *Journal of Child and Family Studies*, 29(2), 403–412. doi:10.1007/s10826-019-01629-9.

Lee, S., 2021. Disability and social work: Partnerships to promote sexual wellbeing. *In*: Shuttleworth, R. and Mona, L., eds. *The Routledge Handbook of Disability and Sexuality*. Abingdon: Routledge, 474–487.

Lee, S., 2022. Social inclusion and the role of social workers. *In*: Liamputtong, P., ed. *Handbook of Social Inclusion: Research and Practices in Health and Social Sciences*. Springer, 2107–2122.

Legal Action Group, 2021. Available from: https://www.lag.org.uk/article/211090/domestic-abuse-act–a-missed-opportunity- [Accessed 16 Dec 2021].

Lemon, B. W., Bengtson, V. L. and Peterson, J. A., 1972. An exploration of the activity theory of ageing. *Journal of Gerontology, 27*(4), 511–523.

Levenson, J., 2017. Trauma-informed social work practice. *Social Work, 62,* (2), 105–113.

Levenson, J., 2020. Translating trauma-informed principles into social work practice. *Social Work, 65*(3), 288–298.

Levitas, R., 2005. *The Inclusive Society? Social Exclusion and New Labour* (2nd ed). Basingstoke: Palgrave Macmillan.

Lewis, G. and Fox, S., 2019. Between theory and therapy: Grief and loss skills-based training for hospital social workers. *Advances in Social Work & Welfare Education, 21*(1), 110–114.

LGA and ADASS, 2017. *Making Safeguarding Personal: Supporting Increased Involvement of Service Users*. Available from: https://www.local.gov.uk/making-safeguarding-personal-supporting-increased-involvementservices-users.

Liabo, K., Boddy, K., Burchmore, H., Cockcroft, E. and Britten, N., 2018. Clarifying the roles of patients in research. *BMJ, 361*, k1463.

Liddiard, K., 2021. Theorising disabled people's sexual, intimate, and erotic lives: Current theories for disability and sexuality. *In*: Shuttleworth, R. and Mona, L., eds. *The Routledge Handbook of Disability and Sexuality*. Abingdon: Routledge, 39–52.

Liegeois, J.-P., 2005. *Gypsies an Illustrated History*. London: Saqi Books.

Lindert, J., et al., 2014. Sexual and physical abuse in childhood is associated with depression and anxiety over the life course: Systematic review and meta-analysis. *International Journal of Public Health, 59*(2), 359.

Lishman, J., Yuill, C., Brannan, J. and Gibson, A., 2018. *Social Work an Introduction* (2nd ed). London: SAGE.

Lloyd, C., 1998. Risk factors for problem drug use: Identifying vulnerable groups. *Drugs: Education, Prevention and Policy, 5*(3), 217–232. doi:10.3109/09687639809034084.

Lloyd, C. and Godfrey, C., 2010. Commentary on Pinkerton (2010): Drug consumption rooms – time to accept their worth. *Addiction, 105*(8), 1437–1438. doi:10.1111/j.1360-0443.2 010.03027.x.

Local Government Association, 2021. *People with a Learning Disability and Autism in the Criminal Justice System*. Available from: www.local.gov.uk/publications/people-learning-disability-and-autism-criminal-justice-system [Accessed 04 Dec 2022].

Local Government Association, Association Directors of Adult Services, 2015. *Adult Safeguarding and Domestic Abuse – A Guide to Support Practitioners and Managers Adult-safeguarding-and-do-cfe.Pdf* (2nd ed) (local.gov.uk).

Lyne, M. and Lee, S. 2020. The history and current context of mental capacity legislation and policy. *In*: Lee, S., Fenge, L., Brown, K. and Lyne, M., eds. Demystifying Mental Capacity A Guide for Health and Social Care Professionals. London: SAGE.

Lyons, J., Bell, T., Fréchette, S. and Romano, E., 2015. Child-to-Parent violence: Frequency and family correlates. *Journal of Family Violence, 30*, 729–742.

MacInnes, J., Wilson, P., Sharp, R., Gage, H., Jones, B., Frere-Smith, K., Abrahamson, V., Eida, T. and Jaswal, S., 2021. *Community-Based Volunteering in Response to COVID-19* [online]. The NIHR Applied Research Collaboration (ARC), Kent, Surrey and Sussex. Available from: https://arc-kss.nihr.ac.uk/news/voluntary-sector-plays-key-role-in-delivering-community-services-during-lockdown [Accessed 12 Jun 2022].

Maclean, S. and Harrison, R., 2015. *Theory and Practice: A Straightforward Guide to Practice* (3rd ed). Kirwin Maclean Associates Ltd.

Mactier, H., 2011. The management of heroin misuse in pregnancy: Time for a rethink?. *Archives of Disease in Childhood – Fetal & Neonatal Edition, 96*(6), 457–601.

Mandelstam, M., 2017. *Care Act 2014. An A–Z of Law and Practice.* London: Jessica Kingsley.

Manthorpe, J., Morriarty, J., Brimblecombe, Knapp, M., Ferandez, J. and Snell, T., 2020. Carers and the care Act: Promise and potential. *In:* Braye, S. and Preston-Shoot, M., eds. *The Care Act 2014. Wellbeing in Practice.* London: SAGE, 52–66.

Marmot, M., 2010. *Fair Society, Healthy Lives: The Marmot Review: Strategic Review of Health Inequalities in England Post-2010.* https://www.instituteofhealthequity.org/resources-reports/fair-society-healthy-lives-the-marmot-review/fair-society-healthy-lives-full-report-pdf.pdf.

Marmot, M., 2020. *Health Equity in England: The Marmot Review 10 Years on.* Available from: https://www.health.org.uk/publications/reports/the-marmot-review-10-years-on.

Marson, S. M. and Powell, R. M., 2014. Goffman and the infantalization of elderly persons: A Theory in development. *Journal of Sociology & Social Welfare, XLI*(4).

Martínez-Ferrer, B., Romero-Abrio, A., León-Moreno, C., Villarreal-González, M. E. and Musitu-Ferrer, D., 2020. Suicidal ideation, psychological distress and child-to-parent violence: A gender analysis. *Frontiers in Psychology, 11,* 3273–3282.

Mayall, D., 2004. *Gypsy Identities 1500–2000: From Egipcyans and Moon-Men to the Ethnic Romany.* Abingdon: Routledge.

McAuley, A., et al., 2012. From evidence to policy: The Scottish national naloxone programme. *Drugs: Education, Prevention and Policy, 19*(4), 309–319. doi:10.3109/09687637.2012.682232.

McCarthy, M., 2017. What kind of abuse is him spitting in my food?: Reflections on the similarities between disability hate crime, so called mate crime and domestic violence against women with intellectual disabilities, *Disability & Society, 32*(4), 595–600.

McFadden, A., Siebelt, L., Gavine, A., Atkin, K., Bell, K., Innes, N., Jones, H., Jackson, C., Haggi, H. and MacGillivray, S., 2018. Gypsy, Roma and traveller access to and engagement with health services: A systematic review. *European Journal of Public Health, 28*(1), 74–81.

McKay, M. T., Cannon, M., Chambers, D., Conroy, R. M., Coughlan, H., Dodd, P., Healy, C., O'Donnell, L. and Clarke, M. C., 2021. Childhood trauma and adult mental disorder: A systematic review and meta-analysis of longitudinal cohort studies. *Acta Psychiatrica Scandinavica, 143*(3), 189–205.

McLaughlin, H., Robbins, R., Bellamy, C., Banks, C. and Thackery, D., 2018. Adult social work and high risk domestic abuse cases. *Journal of Social Work, 18*(3), 288–306.

McNamara, R. and Morgan, S., 2016. *Risk Enablement: Frontline Briefing.* Darington: Research in Practice for Adults.

Mencap, 2022a. *Communicating with People with a Learning Disability.* Available from: www.mencap.org.uk/learning-disability-explained/communicating-people-learning-disability [Accessed 04 Dec 2022].

Mencap, 2022b. *How Common Is Learning Disability?.* Available from: www.mencap.org.uk/learning-disability-explained/research-and-statistics/how-common-learning-disability[Accessed 04 Dec 2022].

Mental Capacity Act 2005.

Mental Health Act 1983.

Mental Health Act 1983 (Amended 2007).

Mental Health Act 1983/2007.

Middleton, J. S., Bloom, S. L., Strolin-Goltzman, J. and Caringi, J., 2019. Trauma-informed care and the public child welfare system: The challenges of shifting paradigms: Introduction to the special issue on trauma-informed care. *Journal of Public Child Welfare, 13*(3), 235–244.

Miles, C. and Condry, R., 2016. Adolescent to parent violence: The police response to parents reporting violence from their children. *Policing and Society, 26*(7), 804–823.

Milne, A., 2020. *Mental Health in Later Life: Taking a Life Course Approach.* Bristol: Policy Press.

Milne, A., Sullivan, M. P., Tanner, D., Richards, S., Ray, M., Lloyd, L., Beech, C. and Phillips, J., 2014. *Social Work with Older People: A Vision for the Future*. BASW.

Mitchell, W. and Glendinning, C., 2017. Allocating personal budgets/grants to carers. *Journal of Social Work*, 17(6), 695–714. doi:10.1177/1468017316651994.

Mitra, S. and Shakespeare, T., 2019. Remodelling the ICF. *Disability and Health Journal*, 12, 337–339.

Monkton- Smith, J., 2019. Available from: https://www.youtube.com/watch?v=lPF_p3ZwLh8 [Accessed 18 Apr 2022].

Morgan, S. and Williamson, T., 2014. *How Can 'Positive Risk-Taking' Help Build Dementia-Friendly Communities?* [online]. Jrf.org.uk. Available from: https://www.jrf.org.uk/sites/default/files/jrf/migrated/files/Positive-risk-taking-dementia-summary.pdf [Accessed 11 Jun 2022].

Morrison, J., 2019. *Scroungers: Moral Panics and Media Myths*. London: Zed Books.

Moulds, L., Day, A., Mildred, H., Miller, P. and Casey, S., 2016. Adolescent violence towards parents – the known and unknowns. *Journal of Theoretical Psychology*, 37(4), 547–557.

Munro, E., 1996. Avoidable and unavoidable mistakes in child protection work. *British Journal of Social Work* [online], 26(6), 793–808.

Munro, E., 1999. Common errors of reasoning in child protection work. *Child Abuse and Neglect*, 23(8), 745–758.

Murty, S., Sanders, S., and Stensland, M., 2015. End-of-Life care as a field of practice in the social work curriculum. *Journal of Social Work in End-of-Life & Palliative Care*, 11, 11–26. doi: 10.1080/15524256.2015.1021071.

My Life My Choice, 2019. *Panorama and the Abuse at Whorlton Hall: A Response from MLMC*. Available from: https://www.mylifemychoice.org.uk/articles/124-panorama-and-the-abuse-at-whorlton-hall-a-response-from-mlmc [Accessed 31 Oct 2022].

National Health Services, 2015. *End of Life Care*. Available from: http://www.nhs.uk/Planners/end-oflife-care/Pages/what-it-involves-and-when-it-starts.aspx.

National Institute for Health and Care Excellence, 2022. *Hospital Care* [online]. NICE. Available from: https://www.nice.org.uk/about/what-we-do/into-practice/measuring-the-use-of-nice-guidance/impact-of-our-guidance/niceimpact-dementia/ch3-hospital-care [Accessed 11 Jun 2022].

National Institute for Health Research, 2018. *Help at Home – Use of Assistive Technology for Older* [online]. Research.amanote.com. Available from: https://research.amanote.com/publication/dY921HMBKQvf0Bhi8q1U/help-at-home--use-of-assistive-technology-for-older-people [Accessed 10 Jun 2022].

Newell, B., 2015. *Straight Choices: The Psychology of Decision Making* (2nd ed). New York: Psychology Press.

NHS, 2022b. *Carer's Assessments*. Available from: https://www.nhs.uk/conditions/social-care-and-support-guide/support-and-benefits-for-carers/carer-assessments/. Accessed on 22nd March 2023.

NHS Digital, 2022a. *Learning Disability Services Monthly Statistics, AT*. Available from: https://digital.nhs.uk/data-and-information/publications/statistical/learning-disability-services-statistics/at-february-2022-mhsds-december-2021-final/summary-report--at [Accessed 31 Oct 2022].

NHS Digital, 2022b. *Measures from the Adult Social Care Outcomes Framework*. Available from: https://digital.nhs.uk/data-and-information/publications/statistical/adult-social-care-outcomes-framework-ascof [Accessed 11 Feb 2022].

NHS England, 2015. *Building the Right Support. A National Plan to Develop Community Services and Close Inpatient Facilities for People with a Learning Disability And/or Autism Who Display Behaviour that Challenges, Including Those with a Mental Health Condition*. Available from: https://www.england.nhs.uk/wp-content/uploads/2015/10/ld-nat-imp-plan-oct15.pdf [Accessed 11 Feb 2022].

NHS England, 2016. https://www.england.nhs.uk/about/equality/equality-hub/patient-equalities-programme/equality-frameworks-and-information-standards/accessibleinfo/ [Accessed 31 Oct 2022].

NHS England, 2019. *Beyond the High Fence: From the Unheard Voices of People with a Learning Disability, Autism or Both.* Available from: www.england.nhs.uk/wp-content/uploads/2019/02/beyond-the-high-fence.pdf [Accessed 4 Oct 2022].

NHS England, 2022a. Available from: https://www.england.nhs.uk/about/equality/equality-hub/patient-equalities-programme/equality-frameworks-and-information-standards/accessibleinfo/ [Accessed 31 Oct 2022].

NHS England, 2022b. Available from: https://www.nhs.uk/conditions/social-care-and-support-guide/support-and-benefits-for-carers/carer-assessments/.

NHS. 2022. What End of Life Care Involves. Available from: https://www.nhs.uk/conditions/end-of-life-care/what-it-involves-and-when-it-starts/.

NICE, 2015. *Caring for Adults in Their Last Days of Life Information for the Public.* Available from: https://www.nice.org.uk/guidance/ng31/ifp/chapter/About-this-information.

Nowakowski-Sims, E., 2019. An exploratory study of childhood adversity and delinquency among youth in the context of child-to-parent and sibling-to-sibling violence. *Journal of Family Social Work, 22*(2), 126–145.

Nutt, D., 2012. *Drugs – Without the Hot Air: Minimizing the Harms of Legal and Illegal Drugs.* Cambridge: UIT Cambridge.

Office of National Statistics, 2022a. Available from: https://www.ons.gov.uk/peoplepopulationandcommunity/crimeandjustice/bulletins/domesticabuseinenglandandwalesoverview/november2021#police-recorded-crime [Accessed 02 Dec 2022].

Office of National Statistics, 2022b. Available from: https://www.ons.gov.uk/peoplepopulationandcommunity/crimeandjustice/articles/domesticabuseprevalenceandtrendsenglandandwales/yearendingmarch2021 [Accessed 02 Dec 2022].

Office of the Public Guardian, 2022. *About Us.* Available from: https://www.gov.uk/government/organisations/office-of-the-public-guardian/about [Accessed 20 May 2022].

Okely, J., 1983. *The Traveller-Gypsies.* Cambridge: Cambridge University Press.

Oliver, L. and Lee, S., 2020. Working with disabled children and young people. *In*: Parker, J. and Ashencaen Crabtree, S., eds. *Human Growth and Development in Children and Young People.* Bristol: Policy Press.

Oliver, M., 2013. The social model of disability: Thirty years on. *Disability & Society, 28*(7), 1024–1026.

Oliver, M., Sapey, B. and Thomas, P., 2012. *Social Work with Disabled People* (4th ed). Basingstoke: Palgrave Macmillan.

The Omen., 1976. [Film, Video]. Directed by Donner, R. UK: BBC1.

Onega, L. L. and Tripp-Reimer, T., 1997. Expanding the scope of continuity theory. Application to gerontological nursing. *Journal of Gerontological Nursing, 23*(6), 29–35.

Orr, D., 1992. *Ecological Literacy: Education for a post-modern World.* Albany, NY: State University of New York.

Ortiz, R., Gilgoff, R. and Burke Harris, N., 2022. Adverse childhood experiences, toxic stress, and trauma-informed neurology. *JAMA Neurology, 79*(6), 539–540.

Owens, T. and de Than, C., 2014. Supporting Disabled People with Their Sexual Lives: A Clear Guide for Health and Social Care Professionals. London: Jessica Kingsley Publishers.

Papamichail, A. and Bates, E. A., 2020. "I want my mum to know that I Am a good guy…": A thematic analysis of the accounts of adolescents who exhibit child-to-parent violence in the United Kingdom. *Journal of Interpersonal Violence*, 1–24.

Parker, J. and Aschencaen Crabtree, S., 2018. *Social Work with Disadvantaged and Marginalised People.* London: SAGE.

Parker, G. and McVeigh, C., 2013. Do not cut the grass: Expressions of British gypsy-traveller identity on cemetery memorials. *Mortality*, 18(3), 290–312.

Parker, J., 2012. Landscapes and portraits: Using multiple lenses to inform social work theories of old age. *In*: Davies, M., ed. *Social Work with Adults: From Policy to Practice*. London: Palgrave Macmillan, 285–299.

Parker, J., 2021a. *Social Work Practice Assessment, Planning, Intervention and Review*. London: Learning Matters.

Parker, J., 2021b. *Social Work Practice* (6th ed). Exeter: Learning Matters.

Parker, J., 2023. *Analysing British Social Welfare*. Bristol: Policy Press.

Parker, J. and Ashencaen Crabtree, S., 2020a. Introduction and history: Approaches to human growth and development with adults. *In*: Parker, J. and Ashencaen Crabtree, S., eds. *Human Growth and Development in Adults Theoretical and Practice Perspectives*. Bristol: Policy Press, *Vol. 2*, 11–26.

Parker, J. and Ashencaen Crabtree, S., 2020b. Critical perspectives on human growth and development in adults. *In*: Parker, J. and Ashencaen Crabtree, S., eds. *Human Growth and Development in Adults Theoretical and Practice Perspectives*. Bristol: Policy Press, *Vol. 2*, 81–99.

Parsons, A. L., Reichl, A. J. and Pedersen, C. L., 2017. Gendered ableism: Media representations and gender role beliefs' effect on perceptions of disability and sexuality. *Sexuality and Disability*, 35(2), 207–225.

PC & NC v City of York Council [2013] EWCA Civ 478.

Penna, S., 2020. *Guide to Adverse Childhood Experiences (ACEs). Practice Guidance* [online]. Community Care Inform. https://www.ccinform.co.uk/practice-guidance/guide-to-adverse-childhood-experiences-aces/ [Accessed 7 Feb 2023].

Petrillo, M., Bennett, M. R. and Pryce, G., 2022. *Cycles of Caring: Transitions in and Out of Unpaid Care*. London: Carers UK.

Phillips, J., Ray, M. and Marshall, M., 2006. *Social Work with Older People* (4th ed). Basingstoke: Palgrave Macmillan.

Pickard, L., Brimblecombe, N., King, D., and Knapp, M., 2018. *"Replacement Care" for Working Carers?*. A Longitudinal Study in England, 2013–15: Social Policy & Administration, 52: 690–709. doi: 10.1111/spol.12345.

Pickett, K. and Wilkinson, D., 2010. *The Spirit Level: Why Greater Equality Makes Societies Stronger*. New York: Bloomsbury.

Pitt, M. A., Myung, I. J. and Zhang, S., 2002. Toward a method of selecting among computational models of cognition. *Psychological Review*, 109(3), 472–491.

Police and Criminal Evidence Act 1984.

Public Health England, 2020. *People with Learning Disabilities in England. Research and Analysis*. Chapter 3: Safeguarding. Available from: www.gov.uk/government/publications/people-with-learning-disabilities-in-england/chapter-3-safeguarding#people-with-learning-disabilities-in-england [Accessed 04 Oct 2022].

Purcell, R., Baksheev, G. N. and Mullen, P. E., 2014. A descriptive study of juvenile family violence: Data from intervention order applications in a Childrens Court. *International Journal of Law and Psychiatry*, 37(6), 558–563.

Radcliffe, P. and Stevens, A., 2008. Are drug treatment services only for "thieving junkie scumbags"? Drug users and the management of stigmatised identities. *Social Science & Medicine*, 67(7), 1065–1073.

Reamer, F., 2018. *Social Work Values and Ethics* (5th ed). New York: Columbia University Press.

Reith, M. and Payne, M., 2009. *Social Work in End-of-Life and Palliative Care*. Bristol: The Policy Press.

Research in Practice for Adults (RiPfA). Available from: https://www.ripfa.org.uk/.

Retief, M. and Letšosa, R. 2018. Models of disability: A brief overview. *HTS Teologiese Studies/ Theological Studies*, 74(1), 1–8.

Revenga, A., Ringold, D. and Tracy, W. M., 2002. *Poverty and Ethnicity: A Cross-Country Study of Roma Poverty in Central Europe*. Washington, DC: The World Bank. World Bank Technical Paper No. 531.

Rine, C. M., 2018. Is social work prepared for diversity in hospice and palliative care? *Health Social Work*, 43(1), 41–50. doi:10.1093/hsw/hlx048. PMID: 29244119.

Robbins, R., Banks, C., McLaughlin, H., Bellamy, C. and Thackery, D., 2016. Is domestic abuse an adult social work issue?. *Social Work Education*, 35(2), 131–143.

Rock Poole Life C.I.C Training Consultant Available from: https://rockpool.life/.

Rogers, C., 2016. *Beyond Bereavement: Is Close Kinship Enough? An Exploration of the Bereavement Experiences and Support in Gypsy and Traveller Families* Thesis (PhD). Coventry University and Buckinghamshire New University.

Rosati, A. G., 2017. Decision making under uncertainty: Preferences, biases, and choice. *In*: Call, J., Burghardt, G. M., Pepperberg, I. M., Snowdon, C. T. and Zentall, T., eds. *APA Handbook of Comparative Psychology: Perception, Learning, and Cognition*. [online]. Washington, DC: American Psychological Association, 329–357.

Routt, G. and Anderson, L., 2011. Adolescent violence towards parents. *Journal of Aggression, Maltreatment & Trauma*, 20(1), 1–18.

Royal College of Psychiatrists, 2019. *National Audit of Dementia Care in General Hospitals 2018–2019* [online]. London: Royal College of Psychiatrists. Available from: https://www.hqip.org.uk/wp-content/uploads/2019/07/ref-113-national-audit-of-dementia-round-4-report-final-online-v4.pdf [Accessed 16 Jun 2022].

Ruck Keene, A., 2015. *Capacity Is Not an off Switch*. Mental Capacity Law and Policy. Available from: https://www.mentalcapacitylawandpolicy.org.uk/capacity-is-not-an-off-switch/ [Accessed 15 Mar 2022].

Ruck Keene, A., Butler-Cole, V., Allen, N., Lee, A., Kohn, N., Scott, K., Barnes, K. and Edwards, S., 2021. Guidance note: Relevant information for different categories of decisions. *39 Essex.com*. Available from: https://1f2ca7mxjow42e65q49871m1-wpengine.netdna-ssl.com/wp-content/uploads/2021/05/Mental-Capacity-Guidance-Note-Relevant-Information-for-Different-Categories-of-Decision-1.pdf [Accessed 13 Mar 2022].

Ruck Keene, A., Butler-Cole, V., Allen, N., Lee, A., Kohn, N., Scott, K., Barnes, K. and Edwards, S., 2022. Carrying out and recording capacity assessments. *39 Essex.com*. Available from: https://www.39essex.com/mental-capacity-guidance-note-assessment/ [Accessed 1 May 2022].

Ryan-Morgan, T., 2019. *Mental Capacity Casebook: Clinical Assessment and Legal Commentary*. London: Routledge.

Ryde, J., 2019. *White Privilege Unmasked: How to Be Part of the Solution*. London: Jessica Kingsley Publishers.

Ryder, A., Cemlyn, S. and Acton, T., eds. 2014. *Hearing the Voices of Gypsy, Roma and Traveller Communities: Inclusive Community Development*. Bristol: Policy Press.

Safelives, 2016. Available from: https://safelives.org.uk/sites/default/files/resources/Safe%20Later%20Lives%20-%20Older%20people%20and%20domestic%20abuse.pdf [Accessed 3 Dec 2021].

Saleebey, D., ed. 2013. *The Strengths Perspective in Social Work Practice*. London: Pearson.

Saltiel, D. and Lakey, R., 2020. Analysing invisibility: The decision-making ecology and home visits. *CFS Child & Family Social Work*, 25(1), 37–44.

Samson, P. L., 2015. Practice wisdom: The art and science of social work. *Journal of Social Work Practice*, 29(2), 119–131.

Samuel, M., 2021. More demand, less supply and less personalisation, finds five-year analysis of adult social care. *Community Care online*. Available from: https://www.communitycare.co.uk/

2021/05/07/more-demand-less-supply-and-less-personalisation-finds-five-year-analysis-of-adult-social-care/.

Sauvain-Dugerdil, C., Leridon, H. and Mascie-Taylor, N., eds. 2006. *Human Clocks: The Bio-Cultural Meanings of Age.* Bern: Peter Lang AG.

Scope, 2022. *Attitudes Towards Disabled People.* Available from: https://www.scope.org.uk/campaigns/research-policy/attitudes-towards-disabled-people/.

Seligman, M. E. P. and Kahana, M., 2013. Perspectives on psychological science A conjecture. *Perspectives on Psychological Science.*

Shakespeare, T. and Richardson, S., 2018. The sexual politics of disability, twenty years on. *Scandinavian Journal of Disability Research, 20*(1), 82–91. http://doi.org/10.16993/sjdr.25.

Sheldon, F. M., 2000. Dimensions of the role of the social worker in palliative care. *Palliative Medicine, 14*(6), 491–498.

Shildrick, T. and Rucell, J., 2015. *Sociological Perspective on Poverty* Report for Joseph Rowntree Foundation. Available from: ///F:/Social%20exclusion%20and%20discrimination%20unit/Week%205%20Poverty/sociological-perspectives-poverty-full.pdf.

Shonkoff, J. P. and Garner, A. S., 2012. The lifelong effects of early childhood adversity and toxic stress. Committee on Psychosocial Aspects of Child and Family Health; Committee on Early Childhood, Adoption, and Dependent Care; Section on Developmental and Behavioral Pediatrics. *Pediatrics,* Jan, *129*(1), e232–46. doi:10.1542/peds.2011-2663. Epub 2011 Dec 26. PMID: 22201156.

Simcock, P. and Castle, R., 2016. *Social Work and Disability.* Cambridge: Polity Press.

Simon, H. A., 1955. A behavioral model of rational choice. *The Quarterly Journal of Economics* [online], *69*(1), 99.

Simon, H. A., 1960. *The New Science of Management Decision.* New York: Harper.

Smale, G., Tuson, G., Biehal, N. and Marsh, P., 1993. *Empowerment, Assessment, Care Management and the Skilled Worker.* London: HMSO.

Smale, G., Tuson, G., Biehal, N. and Marsh, P., 1993. *Empowerment, Assessment, Care Management and the Skilled Worker.* London: National Institute for Social work.

Small, N., 2001. Social work and palliative care. *British Journal of Social Work, 31,* 961–971.

Smith, D. M. and Greenfields, M., 2015. Resisting assimilation: Survival and adaptation to 'alien' accommodation forms. The case of British gypsies/travellers in housing. *Today's Children Tomorrow's Parents: An Interdisciplinary Journal, 40–41,* 68–81.

Social Care Institute for Excellence, 2020. *What Other People Can Due to Help Me Live Well – Dementia.* SCIE [online]. Scie.org.uk. Available from: https://www.scie.org.uk/dementia/after-diagnosis/knowing-the-person/help-me-live-well.asp [Accessed 15 Jun 2022].

Social Care Institute for Excellence, 2022a. *Dementia: At a Glance* – SCIE [online]. Scie.org.uk. Available from: https://www.scie.org.uk/dementia/about/ [Accessed 15 Jun 2022].

Social Care Institute for Excellence, 2022b. *Care Act Guidance on Strengths-Based Approaches* [online]. Social Care Institute for Excellence (SCIE). Available from: https://www.scie.org.uk/strengths-based-approaches/guidance#whatis [Accessed 13 Jun 2022].

Social Services and Well-Being (Wales) Act, 2014. Available at: https://www.legislation.gov.uk/anaw/2014/4/pdfs/anaw_20140004_en.pdf.

Social Work England, 2019a. *Professional Standards Guidance.* [online] Available from: https://www.socialworkengland.org.uk/standards/professional-standards-guidance/#top.

Social Work England, 2019b. *Professional Standards.* Available from: https://www.socialworkengland.org.uk/standards/professional-standards/.

Social Work England, 2021. *Professional Standards.* Available from: www.socialworkengland.org.uk/standards/professional-standards/ [Accessed 04 Oct 2022].

Social Work England, 2023. *Professional Standards.* www.socialworkengland.org.uk/standards/professional-standards/ [Accessed 07 Feb 2023].

Solas, J., 2018. Deserving to deserve: Challenging discrimination between the deserving and undeserving in social work. *Journal of Social Work Values and Ethics*, 15(2), 62–68.

Stalker, K., 2003. Managing risk and uncertainty in social work. *Journal of Social Work*, 3(2), 211–233.

Stan, Social Care Institute for Excellence, 2020. *What Other People Can Due to Help Me Live Well – Dementia* [online]. SCIE. Scie.org.uk. Available from: https://www.scie.org.uk/dementia/after-diagnosis/knowing-the-person/help-me-live-well.asp [Accessed 15 Jun 2022].

Star Wars: Episode VI – Return of the Jedi., 1983. [Film, Video]. Directed by Marquand, R. USA: Lucasfilm Ltd.

Story, K., Shute, T. and Thompson, A., 2008. Building a culture of recovery: A comprehensive recovery education strategy. *Journal of Ethics in Mental Health*, 3(April).

Stuart, G. L., et al., 2009. Examining the interface between substance misuse and intimate partner violence. *Substance Abuse: Research & Treatment*, 3, 25–29.

Sue and Spicer, E., 2019. I had a carer's assessment. *In*: Hughes, M., ed. *A Guide to Statutory Social Work Interventions: The Lived Experience*. London: Red Globe.

Swain, J., French, S., Barnes, C. and Thomas, C., 2013. *Disabling Barriers: Enabling Environments* (3rd ed). London: SAGE.

Szto, P., 2020. Moral, spiritual and existential development. *In*: Parker, J. and Ashencaen Crabtree, S., eds. *Human Growth and Development in Adults: Theoretical and Practice Perspectives*. Bristol: Policy Press, 45–61.

Taels, B., Hermans, K., Van Audenhove, C., Boesten, N., Cohen, J., Hermans, K. and Declercq, A., 2021. How can social workers be meaningfully involved in palliative care? A scoping review on the prerequisites and how they can be realised in practice. *Palliative Care & Social Practice*, 15, 1–16. doi:10.1177/26323524211058895.

Taylor, B. J., 2013. DARE 2012 symposium, belfast, northern Ireland. *Research on Social Work Practice*, 23(2), 241–242.

Taylor, B., 2014. *Another Darkness, Another Dawn: A History of Gypsies, Roma and Travellers*. London: Reaktion Books.

Tew, J., 2011. *Social Approaches to Mental Distress*. Basingstoke: Palgrave Macmillan.

Thaler, R. H., 2015. *Misbehaving: The Making of Behavioral Economics* [online]. New York: W W Norton & Co.

T*The Boy Who Cried Bitch* (1992) [film, Video]. Directed by Campanella J., J. USA Pilgrims 3 Cooperation.

The British Medical Association and The Law Society, 2015. *Assessment of Mental Capacity: A Practical Guide for Doctors and Lawyers* (4th ed). London: The Law Society.

The Good Son, 1993. [Film Video]. Directed by Rubin 1993. USA: 20th Century Fox.

The Health Foundation, 2014. *Person-centred Care Made Simple What Everyone Should Know about Person-Centred Care (Quick Guide)*. [on-line]. Available from: https://www.basw.co.uk/system/files/resources/basw_25220-6_0.pdf.

The Justice Gap, 2019. *Cases the Changed Us: Maxwell Confait*. Available from: www.thejusticegap.com/cases-the-changed-us-maxwell-confait/ [Accessed 04 Oct 2022].

The Makaton Charity: What Is Makaton?, 2022. Available from: makaton.org/TMC/About_Makaton/What_is_Makaton.aspx [Accessed 10 Apr 2022].

The Policy, Ethics and Human Rights Committee, 2015. *BASW Human Rights Policy* [online]. Birmingham: British Association of Social Workers. Available from: https://www.basw.co.uk/system/files/resources/basw_30635-1_0.pdf [Accessed 11 Jun 2022].

Thevenot, A., 2019. Women subjected to domestic violence: The impossibility of separation. *Psychoanalytic Psychology*, 36(1), 36–43.

Thompson, N., 2018. *The Social Workers Practice Manual*. Avenue Media Solutions.

Thompson, N., 2020. *Anti Discriminatory Practice: Equality, Diversity and Social Justice* (7th ed). Basingstoke: Palgrave Macmillan.

Thompson, N., 2021. *Anti-Discriminatory Practice* (7th ed). London: Red Globe Press.

Thorley, W. and Coates, A., 2018. *Let's Talk About: Child-Parent Violence and Aggression (COVA) 2018 Survey Extended SumGael.* [online] CEL&T.

Thorley, W. and Coates, A., 2019. *Let's Talk About: Childhood Challenging, Violent or Aggressive Behaviour (CCVAB) in the Home* (2nd ed). KDP-Amazon Publishers.

Thornton, R., Nicholson, P. and Harms, L., 2020. Creating evidence: Findings from a grounded theory of memory-making in neonatal bereavement care in Australia. *Journal of Paediatric Nursing, 53,* 29–35.

Tiger, R., 2015. Celebrity gossip blogs and the interactive construction of addiction. *New Media and Society, 17*(3), 340–355. doi:10.1177/1461444813504272.

Turner, M. G., et al., 2013. Bullying victimization and adolescent mental health: General and typological effects across sex. *Journal of Criminal Justice, 41*(1), 53–59. doi:10.1016/j.jcrimjus.2012.12.005.

Tversky, A. and Kahneman, D., 1974. Judgment under uncertainty: Heuristics and biases. *Science, 185,* 1124–1131.

Tversky, A. and Kahneman, D., 1981. The framing of decisions and the psychology of choice. *Science, 211,* 453–458.

Tversky, A. and Kahneman, D., 1986. Rational choice and the framing of decisions. *The Journal of Business, 59*(S4), S251.

Tyler, I., 2013. *Revolting Subjects: Social Abjection and Resistance in Neoliberal Britain.* London: Zed Books Ltd.

United Nations, 2006, Dec. Convention on the rights of persons with disabilities. *Treaty Series, 2515.*

United Nations Convention on the Rights of Persons with Disabilities (CRPD), 2017. *Committee on the Rights of Persons with Disabilities. Concluding Observations on the Initial Report of the United Kingdom of Great Britain and Northern Ireland.* Available from: http://docstore.ohchr.org/SelfServices/FilesHandler.ashx?enc=6QkG1d%2fPPRiCAqhKb7yhspCUnZhK1jU66fLQJyHIkqMIT3RDaLiqzhH8tVNxhro6S657eVNwuqlzu0xvsQUehREyYEQD%2bldQaLP31QDpRcmG35KYFtgGyAN%2baB7cyky7.

Van Cleemput, P., 2010. Social exclusion of gypsies and travellers: Health impact. *Journal of Research in Nursing, 15,* 315–327.

Van Der Kolk, B., 2014. *The Body Keeps the Score: Mind, Brain and Body in the Transformation of Trauma.* New York & London: Penguin Books.

von Neumann, J. and Morgenstern, O., 2007. *Theory of Games and Economic Behavior: 60th Anniversary Commemorative Edition* [online]. Princeton: Princeton University Press.

Villanueva, L. and Gomis-Pomares, A., 2021. The cumulative and differential relation of adverse childhood experiences and substance use during emerging adulthood. *Child Psychiatry and Human Development, 52*(3), 420–429. doi:10.1007/s10578-020-01029-x.

Waite, R. and Ryan, R., 2019. *Adverse Childhood Experiences: What Students and Health Practitioner Need to Know.* Abingdon: Taylor & Francis.

Walker-Rodriguez, A. and Hill, R., 2011. Human sex trafficking. *FBI Law Enforcement Bulletin, 80*(3), 1–9.

White, E., 2017. Assessing and responding to risk. In: Cooper, A. and White, E., eds. *Safeguarding Adults under the Care Act 2014: Understanding Good Practice.* London & Philadelphia: Jessica Kingsley, 110–127.

WHO, 2002. *National Cancer Control Programmes. Policies and Managerial Guidelines.* World Health Organization. Available from: https://www.who.int/.

Williams, L., Ralphs, R. and Gray, P., 2017. The normalization of cannabis use among Bangladeshi and Pakistani youth: A New frontier for the normalization thesis?. *Substance Use and Misuse*, *52*(4), 413–421. doi:10.1080/10826084.2016.1233565.

Wills, R., 2020. *The Gypsy Camp*. Dorset: Lulu.

Wilson, T. D. and Schooler, J. W., 2008. Thinking too much: Introspection can reduce the quality of preferences and decisions. *In*: Fazio, R. H. and Petty, R. E., eds. *Attitudes: Their Structure, Function, and Consequences*. [online]. New York: Psychology Press, 299–317.

Wiltshire Council, 2019. *Health Needs Assessment for Gypsy, Traveller and Boater Populations Living in Wiltshire*. Trowbridge: Wiltshire Council. Available from: https://www.wiltshireintelligence. org.uk/library_/gypsy-traveller-and-boater-populations-health-needs-assessment/ [Accessed 28 Jan 2021].

Wolfelt, A. D., 2009. *The Handbook for Companioning the Mourner: Eleven Essential Principles*. Canada: Companion Press.

Woolham, J., et al., 2018. The impact of personal budgets on unpaid carers of older people. *Journal of Social Work*, *18*(2), 119–141. doi:10.1177/1468017316654343.

World Health Organisation (WHO), 1990. *The ICD-10 Classification of Mental and Behavioural Disorders Clinical Descriptions and Diagnostic Guidelines*.

World Health Organisation (WHO), 2019. *The ICD-11 International Classification of Diseases 11th Revision*. (online). Available from ICD-11 (who.int).

Wydall, S. and Zerk, R., 2017. Domestic abuse and older people: Factors influencing help seeking. *The Journal of Adult Protection*, *19*(5), 247–260.

Young, I., 1990. *Justice and the Politics of Difference*. Princeton, NJ: Princeton University Press.

Young-Bruehl, E., 2013. *Childism: Confronting Prejudice against Children*. Yale: Yale University Press.

Index

A

Abuse, 33, 112
  childhood, 30
  domestic, 28, 74, 96–105
  physical, 74
  psychological impact of, 98
  safeguarding, 137
  sexual, 74
  substance, 74
Accessible Information Standard, 135
Accountability, 10, 188, 199
ACEs. *See* Adverse childhood experiences (ACEs)
Ackoff, R. L., 38
Acquired brain injuries, 65, 67
Acute trauma, 28
ADRT. *See* Advance Decision to Refuse Treatment (ADRT)
Advance Decision to Refuse Treatment (ADRT), 65, 69
Adverse childhood experiences (ACEs)
  impacts, 30
  score, 30, 31
  stress, 31
  substance use, 75
  wellbeing and, 30
Adversity, 28, 30
  coping with, 31
  trauma and, 33
Advocacy, 135–136
  legislation, 136–138
Affirmative model, 122
Ageism, 143–144
  activity theory, 145
  biographical approaches, 146
  continuity theory, 145
  critical theories of, 146
  functional theory, 145
  psychological and functionalist sociological approaches, 145
Alcohol, 75
Alzheimer's Society (2022a), 155
Anderson, L., 115
Animal, 122
Anti-discriminatory practice, 8, 11, 14, 22, 120, 123, 125–126, 133, 188
Anti-oppressive practice, 8, 11, 17, 21, 22, 120, 123, 125–126, 132, 133, 188

Anxiety, 17, 32, 51, 115
Assessments, 17
  capacity, 65
  carers, 183
  communication, prioritise, 19–21, 88–89
  consent and, 23–24
  COVID-19 pandemic, 20
  exchange model of, 25
  expectations, 21–22
  online/phone, 20
  outcomes and wellbeing, 24–25
  power and promote empowerment, 18–19
  product of, 26
  in social work practice, 22–23
Auditory hallucinations, 52
Autism, 115
Autonomy, 12–13, 69, 158

B

Bancroft, L., 99
BASW. *See* British Association of Social Workers (BASW)
Bates, E. A., 115
Beliefs, 45, 76, 86
  cultural, 170
  death rituals and, 92
Bereavement, 92–93, 162, 165
Biases, 9, 45, 99, 101
Biological reductionism, 145
The Boy Who Cried Bitch (1992), 107
Bradfield, J., 122
Brain development, 11, 36
  stress, 31
  toxic stress, 32–33
Brain impairment, 154
Brandt, S., 99
British Association of Social Workers (BASW), 6, 7, 10, 131
Bronfenbrenner's ecological approach (1979), 13
Bulgaria, 87
Bullying, 74

C

Calvete, E., 114
CAMHS. *See* Child and Adolescent Mental Health Service (CAMHS)

Cannabis, 75
Capacity, 63. *See also* Mental Capacity Act 2005 (MCA)
    assessment, 65, 67
    fluctuating, 66–67
    presumption of, 64, 67, 68
Care Act (2014), 9, 13, 19, 22, 53, 124, 126, 187
    advocacy, 136
    carer's assessment, 178
    dementia, 157, 158
    domestic abuse, 101–103, 102 (figure)
    outcomes, 24
    Section 9 (1), 23
    Section 10 (1), 23
    Section 18 (1) (a), 88
    Section (67), 135
    vulnerable, 138
    wellbeing, 25
Care and Support Statutory Guidance (2022), 23
Care concept, 174–175
Care crisis, 158
Care giving, 175
Care, power dynamics of, 175–176
Carers, 8, 53, 175
    assessment practice, 17–18
    Care Act (2014), 178
    definition of, 179
    experience of, 182–183
    Gypsy, Traveller and Roma (GTR) communities,
        89, 90
    palliative care, 164, 167–170
    service users and, 194–195
    unpaid, 158 (*See also* Unpaid carers)
Carney, G. M., 144
Carrie (2013), 107
Causative nexus, 64
Charity Organisation Society (COS), 7
Child and Adolescent Mental Health Service
    (CAMHS), 28
Children, 18. *See also* Child-to-parent violence and
    abuse (CPVA)
    brain, 33
    stress, 31
    substance use, 74, 75
    toxic stress, 32
    trauma in, 32
Child-to-parent violence and abuse (CPVA), 107
    bi-directional relationship, 113
    definitions of, 108, 109 (table)
    detrimental impact of, 115
    financial instability, 113
    mental health problems, 112
    parental experience of, 111
    perpetrating abuse, 113–114
    power and control, 114, 115
    risk factor, 110

    support services for, 112
    TED questions, 111
Chronic illness, 118
Chronic stress, 33
Chronic trauma, 28
CH v A Metropolitan Council (2017), 133
Clark, C. S., 34, 87
Clarke, K., 112
Classen, C. C., 34
Coates, A., 115
Coercive control, 101
Cognitive engagement, 22
Collective disability consciousness, 122
Colwell, M., 8
Commission on Race and Ethnic Disparities, 87
Communication, 19–21, 52, 123–124, 188
    dementia, 155–156
    learning disabilities, 133–135
    skills, 198
Community engagement, 93
Complexity, 13–15, 38
    of mental capacity work, 63, 66–68
Complex trauma, 28
Consent, 23–24
Cook, L. L., 40
CoP. *See* Court of Protection (CoP)
Coping, 31
COS. *See* Charity Organisation Society (COS)
Court of Protection (CoP), 24, 42, 63–65, 71–72
COVID-19 pandemic, 20, 125
CPVA. *See* Child-to-parent violence and abuse (CPVA)
Criminal justice system, 138
Critical reflection, 45
Cultural belief systems, 10, 170
Cultural competence, 170
Cultural discrimination, 127
Cultural heritage, 92
Cultural literacy, in palliative care, 170–171
Culture, 53, 86, 122
Cumming, E., 145

D
Data Protection Act, 24
Death, 92–93, 162, 165
    medicalisation of, 163
    palliative care, 164
    rituals and beliefs, 92
Decision-making, 13, 18, 38, 65, 68
    assessment, 26
    heuristic, 43–45
    intuitive, 40–41
    Mental Capacity Act 2005 (MCA), 69, 70 (figure)
    one-reason, 44
    rational, 41–43
    recognition-based, 44

Deliberation, 45
Dementia, 65, 145
    care planning, approaches to, 157–158
    communication, 155–156
    creative and resourceful, 158–159
    definition of, 152
    hospital discharge, 153
    information gathering, 153–155
    person-centred approach, 153–155
Department of Health (2011), 138
Dependency, 74, 78, 79, 198
Depression, 51, 113, 177
Deprivation
    liberty, 65, 72
    negative impacts of, 10
Desexualisation, of disabled people, 127
Digital period, 9
Disability. *See also* Learning disabilities
    affirmative model, 122
    anti-discrimination, 125–126
    anti-oppression, 125–126
    bio-psycho-social model of, 122–123
    choice and control, 124–125
    communication, 123–124
    contemporary practice, 126
    definition of, 118
    dignity, 124–125
    direct payments, 124
    discrimination, 120
    environment in, 118–120
    forces within society, 126–128
    impairments, 118, 119, 122
    medical model of, 120–121
    oppression, 120
    social model of, 121–123
    social work practice with, 123–128
Disablism, 126, 127
Discrimination, 11, 12, 22, 120, 126. *See also* Social
    justice
    ageism, 143
    cultural, 127
    disability, 126, 127
    intersectionality of, 14
Diversity, 4, 11, 12, 33, 52, 191
    awareness of, 14
Domestic abuse, 28, 74, 96. *See also* Child-to-parent
    violence and abuse (CPVA)
    Care Act (2014), 101–103, 102 (figure)
    Domestic Abuse Act (2021), 103–104
    relationship-based approach, 101
    stereotypes, 97–98
    trauma-informed approach to, 98–100
Domestic Abuse Act (2021), 103–104, 110
Domestic violence, 97, 102, 103
Donnelly, S., 154

Down's syndrome, 133
Drug use, 75, 78, 79
    social constructions, 81
    social media, 80
Dying, 162, 163

E
Ecomap exercise, 25
Economic wellbeing, 5
Emotional intelligence, 167
Emotionally Unstable Personality Disorder (EUPD),
    56
Empathy, 59, 149
    substance use, 78
Employment, 5
Empowerment, 18–19
End-of-life care, 90–92, 164
ENGAGE model, 59, 60 (figure)
England, 9, 13, 53, 141
    Care Act (2014) in, 146
    legislation, 50
    working with older people, 149 (figure)
Equality, 191
Equality Act (2010), 11, 89, 126, 133
    age, 143
    Section (6), 118
Ethics, 7–9, 191, 194
Ethnicity, 53
EUPD. *See* Emotionally Unstable Personality
    Disorder (EUPD)
Evans, E., 136
Evidence-based practice, 40
Exchange model of assessment, 25
Executive dysfunction, 67
Expected Utility Theory, 42, 43
    heuristic decision-making, 44
Exploitation, 96

F
Face-to-face assessment, 21
Fairground Travellers, 87
Fairness, 10
Fear, 100
Fluctuating capacity, 66–67
Frontal lobe paradox, 67
Frontal lobe syndrome, 67
Frustration, 11, 56

G
Gallagher, E., 108, 115
Gassmaier, W., 44
George, M., 67
Gigerenzer, B., 44
Gilbert, S., 67
Gilleard, C., 146

The Good Son (1993), 107
Grenier, A., 146
Grieving process, 170
Gut decisions, 40
Gypsies, Roma, Travellers (GRT) communities, 87
Gypsy, Traveller and Roma (GTR) communities,
    86
    assessment of needs, 88–89
    bereavement, 92–93
    care and support planning, 89
    cleanliness, 90
    community engagement, 93
    culturally appropriate care and support, 89–90
    death, 92–93
    definition of, 86–87
    end-of-life care, 90–92
    hygiene, 90
    Lady-Jacqueline Aster, 88
    social work and, 87–88

H
Hale, B., 70
Head, hand and heart model, 5, 6, 166
The Health Foundation (2014), 188
Henry, W., 145
Heuristic decision-making, 43–45
    categories of, 44
Higgs, P., 146
Hogarth, R. M., 40
Holsapple, C. W., 38
Holt, A., 109
Homicide, 104
Hormones, 31
Hughes, M., 30
Human distress, 4, 9–10
Humanity, 59
Human rights, 11, 12
Human Rights Act (1998), 11, 53, 126, 133, 137
Human wellbeing, 4, 9–10
Hypothalamus, 31

I
IFSW. *See* International Federation of Social Work
    (IFSW)
IMCA. *See* Independent Mental Capacity Advocate
    (IMCA)
Independent Mental Capacity Advocate (IMCA), 65
Inequality, 10, 14
    negative impacts of, 10
Informed consent, 57
Integrity, 8
International Classification of Diseases (ICD) 11th
    Edition, 56
International Classification of Functioning,
    Disability and Health (ICF), 122, 123

International Federation of Social Work (IFSW), 5,
    9, 10
Interpersonal neurobiology, 14
Intersectionality, 126
Intuitive decision-making, 40–41

J
John, E., 126

K
Kahneman, D., 41, 43, 44
Kitwood, T., 154
Klein, G., 80
Knowledge, 5, 22, 35, 75, 191
    executive dysfunction, 67
    guidance, 171
    mental capacity legislation, 171
    palliative care, 166
    trauma, 100

L
LAG. *See* Legal Action Group (LAG)
Language, 120
    domestic abuse, 103
    domestic violence, 103
    intuitive decision-making, 40
    mental health, 50
    parent non-blaming, 111
    safeguarding, 103
    victim-blaming, 110
Lasting Power of Attorney (LPA), 59, 64
Learning disabilities, 63, 65
    advocacy, 135–136
    background information, 131
    case reviews, 138
    communication, 133–135
    definition of, 130–131
    legislation supports advocacy, 136–138
    social work role, 131–133
    statistics, 131
Lee, S., 136
Legal Action Group (LAG), 104
Legislation, 22, 50, 63, 126, 135
    supports advocacy, 136–138
Lewis, S., 109
LHPA. *See* Limbic-hypothalamic-pituitary-adrenal-
    axis (LHPA)
Limbic-hypothalamic-pituitary-adrenal-axis
    (LHPA), 31, 32
Local Government Association (2021),
    138
LPA. *See* Lasting Power of Attorney (LPA)

M
Maclean, R., 131
Maclean, S., 131

Making Safeguarding Personal (MSP), 102
Marginalisation, 12
Marson, S. M., 97
McLaughlin, H., 102
McNamara, R., 158
Media, 79
Medical model of disability, 120–121
Meltdown, 50, 51, 54
Memory loss, 153
Memory-making, 92
Mental Capacity Act 2005 (MCA), 23, 53, 100, 137
  Advance Decision to Refuse Treatment (ADRT), 65, 69
  autonomy, 69
  causative nexus, 64
  Code of Practice, 63, 72
  complexity of, 66–68
  Court of Protection (CoP), 64, 71–72
  decision making, 69, 70 (figure)
  definition of, 63
  dementia, 154
  executive dysfunction, 67
  fluctuating capacity, 66–67
  House of Lords, 67, 69
  misunderstanding principles, 67–68
  Office of the Public Guardian (OPG), 71–72
  person centred, 68–71
  principles, 64
  Section 1, 64, 68
  Section 1 (2), 69
  Section 1 (5), 69
Mental distress, 53
Mental health
  avoid fuelling barriers, 58
  calm, kind environment, 58–59
  challenges, 54–57
  child-to-parent violence and abuse (CPVA), 112
  diagnosis, 64
  empathy, 59
  ENGAGE model, 59, 60 (figure)
  experience of services, 53–54, 55 (figure)
  Hazel and Sarah's experience, 50–52, 57–59
  humanity, 59
  legal framework, 53
  levels of, 54, 55 (figure)
  meet with the person, 57–58
  people perspective, 58
  social work and, 52
  wellbeing and, 50, 52
  word cloud, 57, 57 (figure)
Mental Health Act (1983), 23
Mental illness, 50, 58
Milne, A., 146
Mitra, S., 122, 123
Morality, 8

Morgan, S., 158
Morgenstern, O., 42, 43
Motor impairments, 118
Moulds, L., 113, 114
Multi-disciplinary team (MDT), 157, 158
My Life My Choice (2019), 138

N
Nash, P., 144
Neglect, 30, 74, 103
  safeguarding, 137
Neuro-divergency, 51
Neurological impairments, 118
Neuroscience, 14, 32
Newell, B., 42
No Recourse to Public Funds (NRPC), 104
Normalisation, 79
Northern Ireland Social Care Council, 6
No Secrets (2000), 13
Nowakowski-Sims, E., 115
Nutt, D., 80

O
Office of the Public Guardian (OPG), 71–72
Okely, J., 92, 93
Older people, 18, 82
  ageism, 143–146
  learning disability, 97
  mental health condition, 97
  physical impairment, 97
  social work and, 142–143, 146–147
  social worker with, 147–149, 149 (figure)
The Omen (1976), 107
One-reason decision-making, 44
Oppression, 11, 12, 15. See also Social justice
Outcomes, 24–25
Overconfidence, 45

P
Palliative care, 90
  cultural literacy in, 170–171
  definition of, 163
  emotional intelligence, 167
  families and carers, 167–170
  principles of, 163–164
  social work, 165–167
  strengths-based practice, 166
  where and to whom, 164
Papamichail, A., 115
Paranoid delusions, 52
Parental mental ill health, 30
Parental separation, 30
Parker, J., 25
PCF. See Professional capabilities framework (PCF)
Peer drug use, 75

Personal attitudes, 127
Personal, cultural and structural (PCS) model, 127
Personal Independence Payment (PIP), 144
Personality disorder, 56
Person-centred approaches, 83, 188
    in dementia, 153–155
Petrillo, M., 176
Physical abuse, 74
Physical health, 33, 56, 74
Physical impairment, 97
Picture Exchange Communication system, 133
Police and Criminal Evidence Act 1984 (PACE),
    137
Poverty, 126
    negative impacts of, 10
    social exclusion, 11
Powell, R. M., 97
Power, 18–19
    control and, 114
Practitioners, 5–7, 9, 13, 34, 52, 53, 69
    assessment, 17, 20, 22
    child-to-parent violence and abuse (CPVA), 110
    communication, 19
    complexity, 14
    death and bereavement, 165
    domestic violence, 102
    safeguarding, 102
    trauma-informed, 28, 35
Pregnancy, 74, 92
    stress during, 32
Problem-solving skills, 197–198
Professional capabilities framework (PCF), 4, 6, 29,
    191–192
Professionalism, 191
Professional leadership, 192
Professional values, 7–9, 19, 91
Prospect Theory, 43
    heuristic decision-making, 44
Psychological health, 74
Psychopathology, 14
Psychosis, 52
Public Health England (2020), 137

Q
Quality of life, 21

R
Rational decision-making, 41–43
Reamer, F., 8
Reassessment, 18
Recognition-based decision-making, 44
Relationship-based approach, 76, 101
Research in Practice for Adults (RIPFA), 25
RIPFA. See Research in Practice for Adults (RIPFA)
Risk management, 8, 12–13, 21

    abuse, 96
    exploitation, 96
    harm, 96, 119
    homicide, 104
    substance use, 82–83
    using cannabis and alcohol, 75
Risk perception, 45
Risk, substance use, 74
Romany Gypsies, 86
Routt, G., 115
Ruck Keene, A., 65, 67, 100
Rudden, M., 99
Ryan-Morgan, T., 67

S
Safeguarding, 12–13, 141
    abuse/neglect, 137
    advocacy, 136
    coercive control, 101
    domestic abuse and, 101
    neglect and omission, 103
    perspectives, 103
    principles, 102, 102 (figure)
S1 Care Act (2014), 53
Schooler, J. W., 40
Scotland, 146
Second World War, 12
Self-care, 29
Self-control, 75
Self-harm, 51
Self-neglect, 74, 100
Sense of safety, 34
Sensory impairments, 118
Sensory overload, 50
Severe disfigurement, 118
Sex trafficking, 74
Sexual abuse, 74
Sexual disenfranchisement, 127
Sexual wellbeing, 127
Shakespeare, T., 122, 123
Sheldon, F. M., 90
Shonkoff, J. P., 31
Sign language, 133
Skunk cannabis, 79
Social action, 7
Social care, 21, 52
    older people, 144
Social Care Institute for Excellence (SCIE), 152
Social change, 4
Social constructions, 81
Social exclusion, 11. See also Social justice
Social injustice, 11
Social justice, 10–11
Social media, 80
Social model of disability, 121–123

Social norms, 10
Social policy, 6, 7, 9, 22, 88–89
  expectations, 21
Social risks, 74
Social work, 141
  with adults, 4–6, 13
  assessments. *See* Assessments
  definition of, 5
  disability, 118, 125
  diversity of, 4
  gut decisions, 40
  Gypsy, Traveller and Roma (GTR) communities
    and, 87–88
  learning disabilities, 131–133
  mental health and, 52
  nautical star for, 4, 5 (figure)
  older people and, 142–143, 146–147
  palliative care, 165–167
  political, 6–7
  professional values and ethics, 7–9
  subject benchmark for, 193–199
  in United Kingdom, 6
Social Work Action Network, 7
Social Work England (2023), 6, 131, 133, 165
Social workers, 7, 11
  adverse childhood experiences (ACEs), 30
  anti-oppressive practice, 21
  assessment, 17, 22
  decision-making, 13
  learning disabilities, 131, 132
  mental health, 50
  nautical star for, 4, 5 (figure)
  nuance and complexity, 13
  with older people, 147–149, 149 (figure)
  palliative care, 90, 165
  personal skills, 6
  person-centred approach, 83
  poverty, 11
  social justice, 10, 11
  stereotypes, 18
  substance use, 74, 75
  trauma, 29
Social work practice, 162, 195
  assessments in, 22–23
  critical reflection, 45
  decision-making, 38
  with disability, 123–128
  product of assessment in, 26
  supervision, 45
  trauma, 33–34
Scottish Social Services Council, 6
Social Care Wales, 6
Societal discrimination, 127
Societal expectations, 51
Sowing the seeds, 101

Star Wars: Episode VI – Return of the Jedi (1983),
    107
Statistics
  dementia, 153
  learning disabilities, 131
  unpaid care, 176
Stereotypes, 18, 57, 122
  domestic abuse, 97–98
  of drug users, 79
  Gypsy, Traveller and Roma (GTR) communities,
    86
Stigma, 80
Strengths-based assessment, 19, 166
Stress
  chronic, 33
  maternal, 32
  toxic, 31
Structured decisions, 38
Substance abuse, 74
Substance misuse, 30
Substance use, 74
  barriers to support, 79–82
  lived experience, 78–79
  mind map, 76, 77 (figure)
  motivations for, 74–78
  risk management, 82–83
Suicidal thoughts, 51
Supervision, 45

T
Tallying, 44
Thompson, N., 15, 127
Thorley, W., 115
Toxic stress, 30, 31
  effect of, 32–33
Trade-off, 44
Traditions, 92–93
Trauma, 20, 65
  acute, 28
  adversity and, 28, 33
  chronic, 28
  complex, 28
  definition of, 28
  domestic abuse, 98–100
  event(s), 28, 29
  secondary/vicarious, 29
Trauma-informed meeting, 34–36
Trauma-informed practice
  adverse childhood experiences (ACEs), 30–31
  Josie's story, 33
  planning, 34–36
  principles, 29, 34
  social work practice, 33–34
  toxic stress on, 32–33
Travelling Showmen, 87

Trust, 34, 101
    community engagement, 93
Trustworthiness, 8
Tversky, A., 43, 44

U
United Kingdom, 6, 7, 86, 195
    child-to-parent violence and abuse (CPVA), 108,
        110
    dementia, 152
    disablism in, 127
    Equality Act (2010), 11
    health inequalities in, 126
    human rights, 11
    learning disabilities, 131
    older people, 144
    palliative care, 164
    social justice, 10
    social model of disability, 122
    unpaid carers, 174, 176, 177
Unpaid carers, 174
    breaks down, 183–184
    carers support, 180–182
    engaging successfully with, 180
    social context of, 176–178
    social work law, 178–180
    undervaluing, 183

V
Values, 191, 194
    period, 8
    substance use, 76
Valuing People (2001), 131
Valuing People Now (2009), 131
Victim-blaming language, 110
Violence, 12, 30
von Neumann, J., 42, 43

W
Wales, 13
Wellbeing, 6, 7, 9, 50, 182. *See also specific types*
    adverse childhood experiences (ACEs) and, 30
    culture and ethnicity on, 53
    domains of, 9–10, 12
    mental health and, 52, 53
    outcomes and, 24–25
    risk, 12
    subjectivity of, 10
Welsh Gypsie, 86
We need to talk about Kevin (Shriver 2003), 107
Wilson, T. D., 40
World Health Organisation (WHO), 122, 163

Y
Young, I., 15